"Anthropologist Brian Howell brings rich research skills in participant observation and expertise in social theory to this fascinating project. His book is at the cutting edge of emerging scholarship on the topic of short-term missions. Scholars, students and participants in short-term mission trips will all find this book educational, insightful and provocative."

ROBERT J. PRIEST, professor of mission and anthropology,
G. W. Aldeen Professor of International Studies, Trinity Evangelical Divinity School

"A fascinating study on how language inadvertently undermines the best-laid plans. Howell's insights and practical suggestions provide great recommendations for thoughtful mission leaders. Whether your sphere is a church mission program, young adults, high schoolers, a mission agency or in missions mobilizing, *Short-Term Mission* can help cultivate lasting impact. Giving voice to our Majority World partners, revealing invisible aspects like structure and power, this book is surprising in its scope."

NIKKI TOYAMA-SZETO, program director, Urbana Student Missions Conference,
coeditor, *More Than Serving Tea*

"Brian Howell's insight into the overarching narrative of short-term trips is thought-provoking and practical. I hope many pastors and trip leaders read this book. Everyone involved in these trips—those going and those being visited—deserves a more thoughtful, eyes-wide-open approach like Howell advocates for here."

KENT ANNAN, codirector, Haiti Partners,
author, *Following Jesus Through the Eye of the Needle* and *After Shock*

"Christian colonialism, sanctified vacations, or life-transforming service—short-term missions (STM) has evoked positive and negative comments from supporters and naysayers alike. Getting behind the photos, theologies and histories of the STM movement, Howell offers engaging anthropological insight into the narratives that shape and sustain the experience of STM. Bringing a keen ethnographic eye to his subject of STM narratives, Howell's book is lucid and accessible, striking a helpful balance between constructive criticism and affirmation. If you are at all interested in short-term missions, this book is for you."

CHARLES E. FARHADIAN, associate professor of world religions
and Christian mission, Westmont College

"*Short-Term Mission* is a fascinating look at the effects of short-term missions trips. Why is it that when students or adults return from a missions experiences they all seem to share the same story? Have we romanticized the experiences so much that we can't learn what God wants to teach us? Brian Howell explores how the pretrip narrative is driving the experience. Brian also exams how the culture of short-term missions gets in the way of experiencing and learning from the culture we are going to serve. If you are leading short-term mission trips, you need to read this book. The research that Brian has done clearly points to the need for rethinking and adjusting our short-term missions experiences."

DOUG FRANKLIN, president, LeaderTreks

"With scholarly sophistication and insider humor, Brian Howell offers invaluable critique of the popular international short-term mission trip. He tracks the history and treks along with church groups. Most importantly, Howell scrutinizes the unhelpful narratives evangelicals tell themselves about what they are doing—and calls us all to greater self-awareness, crosscultural respectfulness and justice-informed engagement. A must-read for leaders of our global generation."

KERSTEN BAYT PRIEST, assistant professor of sociology, Indiana Wesleyan University

"Howell's intercultural anthropological study of the dynamics and impact of Christian travel narrative on short-term mission (STM) is fascinating. This inter-disciplinary study served as a warning for me that the lore of STM needs scrutiny. On the other hand, the narratives of God's mission have intrinsic value in and of themselves. A surprisingly intriguing yet academic read!"

MIKE BARNETT, dean of the College of Intercultural Studies, Columbia International University

"*Short-Term Mission* is an essential resource for short-term missionaries, leaders and supporters. Brian Howell is an expert guide, offering the wisdom of a devout Christian, the education of an anthropologist and the experience of a short-term missionary. This book shows as well as tells; the reader accompanies Brian on his own short-term mission, from preparation and the trip itself to post-trip reflection. He is both participant and observer, using his anthropological skills to interpret the strengths and weaknesses of contemporary approaches to short-term mission. He breaks down any simple notion of 'helping,' 'rescuing,' 'befriending' and even 'evangelizing,' and offers both critical and spiritual wisdom that can help short-term missionaries plan and conduct their projects in the best way possible. This book will help churches and groups do short-term mission with strong preparation, realistic and respectful crosscultural relationships, spiritual reflection and follow-up, and most importantly, faithfulness to the Great Commission. Every short-term missionary comes back with a story to tell. Listen to Brian's narrative, and let it shape how you plan, experience and tell your own story of short-term mission."

JENELL WILLIAMS PARIS, professor of anthropology, Messiah College

SHORT-TERM
MISSION

An Ethnography of Christian Travel
Narrative and Experience

◆ ◆ ◆

BRIAN M. HOWELL

IVP Academic

An imprint of InterVarsity Press
Downers Grove, Illinois

InterVarsity Press
P.O. Box 1400, Downers Grove, IL 60515-1426
World Wide Web: www.ivpress.com
E-mail: email@ivpress.com

InterVarsity Press® is the book-publishing division of InterVarsity Christian Fellowship/USA®, a movement of
students and faculty active on campus at hundreds of universities, colleges and schools of nursing in the United States
of America, and a member movement of the International Fellowship of Evangelical Students. For information
about local and regional activities, write Public Relations Dept., InterVarsity Christian Fellowship/USA, 6400
Schroeder Rd., P.O. Box 7895, Madison, WI 53707-7895, or visit the IVCF website at <www.intervarsity.org>.

Scripture quotations, unless otherwise noted, are from the New Revised Standard Version of the Bible, copyright
1989 by the Division of Christian Education of the National Council of the Churches of Christ in the USA. Used by
permission. All rights reserved.

While all stories in this book are true, some names and identifying information in this book have been changed to
protect the privacy of the individuals involved.

Cover design: Cindy Kiple
Images: © MShep2/iStockphoto
Interior design: Beth Hagenberg

ISBN 978-0-8308-3973-5

Printed in the United States of America ∞

 InterVarsity Press is committed to protecting the environment and to the responsible use of natural
resources. As a member of Green Press Initiative we use recycled paper whenever possible. To learn
more about the Green Press Initiative, visit <www.greenpressinitiative.org>.

Library of Congress Cataloging-in-Publication Data has been requested.

P	15	14	13	12	11	10	9	8	7	6	5	4	3	2	1
Y	24	23	22	21	20	19	18	17	16	15	14	13	12		

Contents

PART FOUR: The Future of the Narrative

Preface and Acknowledgments

♦ ♦ ♦

W<small>HEN</small> I <small>FIRST BEGAN TEACHING ANTHROPOLOGY</small> as an adjunct professor in St. Louis in 1997, I would often ask students to describe their previous crosscultural experiences. I encouraged them to interpret this broadly, including encounters with ethnic minority neighborhoods in the United States, family or friends who may come from a different cultural background. For those students not in the majority, just being at the university was a new cultural environment. In a few courses at the small private schools where I taught (Christian and secular), some students could not come up with anything. Some had never left St. Louis, ventured beyond their community or befriended someone culturally distinct. One young woman could not even think of a time she had been to a ethnic restaurant.

In 2001, I began teaching at Wheaton College, a nondenominational Christian liberal arts school thirty miles west of Chicago. Asking the same question to my students here, I received very different responses. Admittedly, this relatively selective, academically demanding private school draws from a different demographic than the St. Louis schools, but the responses I received were not connected simply to exotic vacations or elite jet-setting. When I asked the students to share crosscultural experiences, I heard about trips to Northern Ghana, two weeks spent at an orphanage in rural China, a month in the Mexican state of Oaxaca teaching summer school, and experiences in Romania working at an English-language summer camp.

Despite the seeming randomness of the destinations and even the diversity of activities, it was clear that these were not disconnected events. Few of these students had undertaken these trips alone or with family, but they were linked to churches, parachurch groups, Christian schools and mission organizations. The students recognized the disparate accounts of travel as having a common motivation or purpose. Most significantly, virtually all these trips could be subsumed under one label: short-term missions (STM).

One does not have to be Christian to have knowledge of STM. Secular scholars and members of other faith communities study and participate in these trips. Although this book will focus on an evangelical group, the research summarized in chapters one and two will make clear that STM is a phenomenon widespread throughout religious communities globally. As I encountered the practice among my students and fellow evangelicals, the ubiquity of the term and apparently well-established understanding of how to do a short-term mission made it a fascinating subject with obvious relevance to my own religious community. But I have learned that it is far from limited to this sphere. It is my hope that this book will find interested readers among members of every religious community, as well as the scholars who study them.

In particular, my desire with this research is to perform a classically anthropological intervention to "[gain] access to the conceptual world in which our subjects live so that we can, in some extended sense of the term, converse with them" (Geertz 1973, p. 24). That is, like other cultural phenomena, short-term mission trips possess a history and social context that make them a "thing" apprehended by both those closest to them and those observing from a distance. This research is meant to close the distance of those observing while helping those close to it gain insight into their own actions and understandings. As I discuss later, there are many ways such research could be conducted or framed. My interest, coming from the language of my students, has been on the ways participants enter into a cultural construction they did not create, even as they recreate, employ, resist and recast the cultural context in which they experience these travels.

The central argument of this book is that we produce narratives—framing discourses—that profoundly shape the experiences of these travels. These narratives have a history and social context that we should understand if we are to understand how individuals encounter themselves and others through STM. I do not present this particular ethnographic study as definitive or even necessarily representative of this wide and diffuse movement. Rather, I argue that to understand how people think about these experiences, we must understand the creation and maintenance of narratives being generated in specific places at specific times.

Although STM has become an enormous movement involving millions of participants every year, the research on this phenomenon is still relatively thin. Robert Priest, an anthropologist at Trinity Evangelical Divinity School and a frequent interlocutor of mine, has made a concerted effort to draw researchers into this area and has produced more research-based publications on this phenomenon than any other scholar. Several of his students have produced high-quality theses and dissertations on the topic along with his own articles and edited books. Most of his research is cited somewhere in this book as well.

Other than his efforts and a few notable exceptions (e.g., Offutt 2011, Beyerlein, Adler and Trinitapoli 2011; Trinitapoli and Vasey 2009), much of the published research on STM has appeared as one facet of research looking at larger issues of Christian globalization, mission and religious transnationalism (e.g., Wuthnow 2009, pp. 164-75; Ammerman 2005, p. 202ff; Elisha 2011, pp. 214-22; Guthrie 2003, chap. 10). By producing a monograph presenting an historically and ethnographically grounded study of a short-term mission team, I hope to contribute a hitherto missing element to the conversation. Clifford Geertz (1973) popularized the notion of these studies as "thick description," in which the observable activities of culturally particular groups are unpacked for the layers of meaning, intentions, interactions and practices that can only be understood from the inside. Like Geertz (1973, p. 29), I do not imagine this work to move us toward "a perfection of consensus" on what STM is, or even less, what it *should* be. Rather, I hope to push the discussion forward, offer some helpful historical and cultural context, and contribute to the development of a vocabulary that other, far more accomplished scholars than I can use in sharpening our understanding of this complex, global, religious travel practice.

ACKNOWLEDGMENTS

Because this research sprang from my community, particularly my work at Wheaton College, it is there that I should begin with my acknowledgements. I used part of my sabbatical leave of 2008–2009 to begin writing this book. I also received an Alumni Foundation grant to support my travels to the Dominican Republic in 2006, and a Faculty Missionary Project Tim Phillips Memorial Grant in 2005 to support my entire family traveling to the Dominican Republic for seven weeks of short-term work. I appreciate the support of provost Stanton Jones, the alumni of Wheaton College and the librarians and archivists who aided me in my research. Colleagues at Wheaton and elsewhere have encouraged me in this work, and none more so than Robert Priest and Kersten Priest. Thank you both for your outstanding work on this topic and your personal encouragement to me during some rough going.

My family and I benefited immeasurably from the hospitality of the long-term missionaries in the Dominican Republic, identified by pseudonym in this book. They extended tremendous hospitality and care, and continue to do so to generations of travelers. I suspect some of what I have to say about STM will not be exactly how these faithful workers would say it, and I hope they will forgive any impressions they feel cast their work in an unfavorable light. It is not my intention to impugn anything being done in the name of Jesus; I only hope to encourage those working with the enormously gifted people of this ministry to listen even more closely to all that is going on there.

Of course, it was not only the long-term missionaries who blessed us with their care, but the many Dominican members of the ministry. While anthropological convention prevents me from mentioning them by name, there were teachers, school staff, directors of the children's home, drivers, cooks, construction foremen and many others who took time from their work for the children to extend their care and friendship to my family and me. *Muchisimas gracias por todo. Que Dios les bendiga en todas sus obras.*

The most important help came from Central Wheaton Church (CWC), the pseudonym for the congregation in Wheaton that afforded me extraordinary access to their STM program, and the Dominican Republic team in particular. Numerous members of the congregation graciously put up with the sometimes intrusive presence of an anthropologist in their midst, but none more than the high school members of the team I joined. I can't express how grateful I am to each one of the students for the patience, authenticity and genuine love they extended to me throughout our training and travels. I also thank their parents for permission to join them and use their stories and insights for understanding this work.

The adult coleaders on the trip were critical partners in this work, providing their insights and friendship to me as I joined in the work of our team. I regret that I have allowed these relationships to lapse as the research came to an end. Each one of these people, like the students and other STM leaders, were models of faithful service, honest inquiry, Christian love and thoughtful engagement. Even as I read my own research on our trip, I am struck by how little of the richness of character I am able to include in this short account. Please forgive the injustice that a study such as this inevitably does to the profound reality that these trips play in the lives of people.

Relatively little of this work has been published previously, although some sections of chapters five and six appeared in the article "Mission to Nowhere: Putting Short-Term Missions into Context" (Howell 2009). I have presented parts of this material at Hope College and the Interdisciplinary Christianities Workshop at University of California at San Diego. I thank Mark Husbands from Hope College and Joel Robbins and Naomi Haynes of the University of California, San Diego, for the invitations and the stimulating conversations these opportunities generated.

A number of friends and colleagues have engaged in conversations on this work and related topics; they have aided my thinking on many of these issues. Thank you to Rupert Stasch, Omri Elisha, Jon Bialecki, Eric Honenes, Tanya Luhrmann, James Bielo, Edwin Zehner, Ellen Moodie, Kurt Ver Beek, Terry Linhart, Mary Hancock and countless others whose discussion and wisdom have encouraged better thinking on these and many other topics.

I am grateful to my students at Wheaton College for their continued encouragement to get this work out and for their interaction with many of the ideas, which has sharpened my thinking at various points. On a very practical level, I have benefitted from the good work of several teaching assistants who worked on aspects of this project, compiling resources, formatting notes and working on the index. I am particularly indebted to Anna Porter, Josh Walton, Summer Holeman, Matt Jones and Stephen Paff. Thank you for your good work. Pamela Schnake, Rachel Dorr and Naomi Haynes, three former students who did collaborative or independent research on STM while I worked on this project, contributed excellent work to the topic of STM. I owe many thanks to their inspiration.

In the final stages, I have been grateful to the work of Al Hsu, my editor at InterVarsity Press, two "anonymous" reviewers (who revealed their identities to me later, but nonetheless provided blunt and invaluable comments on the entire manuscript) and the rest of the IVP team. Although it goes without saying, it must be said that in spite of the many excellent contributions all these people have made, a topic such as this is bound to elicit disagreement. Moreover, I have no doubt that I got some things wrong. Regardless of the many voices that have contributed, I take full responsibility for any errors contained herein.

Begun in 2005, it is obvious that this book has been a slow project, suffering from the fits and starts that afflict any project undertaken in the midst of teaching, committee service and real life. Unfortunately, it is often the members of real life who end up sacrificing the most to see these projects finally finished. My daughter, Hannah, who was ten years old when I began this work, bears the scar of a puncture wound obtained while playing in Linda Vista and then sutured by the physician missionary in place for just such a moment. My sons, Sam and Ben, went to the Dominican Republic with the family in 2005 as a kindergartener and preschooler respectively. Sam returned with scars from the egg-sized welts of bullous impetigo (on the bottoms of his feet). Only Ben seems to have escaped unscathed from his father's first foray into this research. Since then, they have all been supportive and encouraging as this book has come to light. God willing, we can all return to deliver this finished work ourselves and gain a new perspective on the many wonderful things happening in Linda Vista.

However, I suspect the people of Linda Vista would be most grateful not for my research, but for my wife, Marissa Sabio, to be back among them. As the director of the summer school there in 2005, she was blessed to work with the gifted staff of the school; she thrived in the context of education, service and Christian love we experienced. Since then, she has done more to support the final product of the research than anyone. To her I say thank you. And I love you.

Part One

◆

INTRODUCING NARRATIVES

1

"It Changed My Life"

SHORT-TERM MISSION AND
CHRISTIAN NARRATIVES OF TRAVEL

◆ ◆ ◆

MY FIRST EXPOSURE TO SHORT-TERM MISSION came through
my participation in such a trip as a high school junior in 1986. Our
church had recently purchased a comfortable, fifteen-passenger van,
and my youth leader and her husband were anxious to put it to work.
After a busy year of fund-raising, our Methodist youth group set out to
drive from our town in Washington State to the California-Mexico
border town of San Ysidro, where we would work with a Christian
children's ministry called Los Niños.

We stopped at Disneyland and Torrey Pines State Beach on our way
down, bonding through youthful hijinks and close proximity. I can't
recall that we had much in the way of preparation as to the cultural and
historical context of our destination, a theological rationale for the trip
or even a framework through which to understand our travels as part of
our faith. Perhaps my former youth group leader would disagree, and
we were offered more in the way of preparation than sank into my high
school mind. What I *can* remember is that as a sixteen-year-old, the
trip posed some challenges for me.

I clearly recall an evening when I joined a group of North American missionaries and the Mexican teen residents of a Catholic boys' home on an overnight camping trip to the beach somewhere between Ensenada and Tijuana. For much of the trip, I hung around with the other teenage boys, strolling up and down the beach. I spoke virtually no Spanish. Our "conversation" consisted of greetings and vague references to *chicas*. Eventually we ended up sitting with some bilingual *chicas* who were on a four-hour shore visit from their Los Angeles-based cruise ship. As a good Methodist boy from a small town in rural Washington, watching my Mexican compatriots interact with the girls, displaying their confident sexuality and vastly more mature self-assurance, I was intimidated and intrigued, but mostly confused. What in the world was I, a bumpkin from Walla Walla, Washington, doing on a "mission" to these guys?

Later in that trip, I had some time to talk with one of the adult chaperones, a man who was spending a year in ministry prior to entering the Catholic priesthood. A twenty-something Asian American who had grown up in the United States, he seemed to be someone who might provide some context, perspective or purpose to my trip. From my vantage point, I could not see what good I was doing, unable to communicate with the Mexican teens, feeling utterly disconnected from their experiences, lost in the midst of cultural, social and even spiritual dislocation. I have vague memories of him encouraging me to consider my own growth or to learn from the people around me. I doubt he answered all my questions, and I was likely unable to understand everything he was saying, but I recall it made me feel better at the time.

Approximately one year later, I did find a way to articulate at least part of the experience. I attached a photograph of me giving a piggyback ride to an adorable five-year-old Mexican boy, taken during a morning spent at a different children's home in Tijuana, to an application to Vassar College with a description of how meaningful the whole experience had been to me. For the purpose of self-representation, I assimilated my time with the littlest Mexicans into a narrative of service, personal growth and Christian virtue.

The confusing, even disturbing, experience with my vastly more experienced and sophisticated peers on the Mexican beach faded into a less salient part of the adventure.

Today, such travels have become regular features in college applications, particularly for Christian colleges.[1] Unlike me, with my halting efforts to find a narrative for my experience, the Christian college students I have taught for the past ten years seem ready to tell the story of their travel and articulate its effects in their lives. They frame their trips as significant—even life-altering—experiences, largely in regard to personal spiritual and emotional growth, and often related through one or two significant relationships, divine revelations or meaningful encounters.

In these retellings, there are often moments of epiphany, if not conversion, in which realizations of unity across cultures, gratitude for a relatively affluent life and self-discovery punctuate a week or ten days of manual labor, sacrifice and service in an unfamiliar cultural context. Those who traveled in middle or high school came to my college classes with well-developed narratives of growth and change, although not without misgivings. They seemed to have received clearer and far more involved preparation and structure for their trips than I ever did.

In particular, as I have interacted with these students over the years, I have been struck by how regularized the language used to describe these experiences has become. The question I began to ask myself was how the narratives of STM had come to take up such a predictable and seemingly powerful form in contemporary Christianity. How was it that students traveling to such diverse places as the Czech Republic, Mexico, Brazil and Kenya all returned with such similar experiences? What was the relationship between these narratives and the experiences themselves? Were students responding to the reality of their encounters, or were the narratives shaping their memories toward a common version of STM? It is toward answering these questions that I have undertaken this study.

---

[1]In 2009, Taylor University, a Christian college in Upland, Indiana, featured a short-term mission story on its home page. On its application, it did not ask about STM in particular, but included a space to talk about any "significant summer experience" of a spiritual nature. Parents of high school students at Central Wheaton Church (CWC) and other congregations in Wheaton expressed a widely shared belief that STM would help their children with admission to Christian colleges, if not college generally.

WHY STUDY SHORT-TERM MISSION?

For those unfamiliar with STM, it can most simply be described as short travel experiences for Christian purposes such as charity, service or evangelism, although such a definition probably obscures as much as it clarifies (see chapter two for a definitional understanding of STM, including a brief discussion of the distinction between *mission* and *missions*). At least within evangelical Christian circles, short-term missions have come to encompass everything from groups of high school students presenting the gospel through mime on the streets of Rome to major construction projects in the aftermath of the Haitian earthquake undertaken by teams of engineers and contractors.

But given recent statistics on the millions of U.S. Americans who have participated in STM travels, as well as the millions more who are exposed by encountering these teams in their own travels or hearing about their trips, I suspect that many of those picking up this book already have a mental image of STM.[2] My goal in this study, like much of anthropology, is to create some ethnographic distance for those who have been close to this phenomenon as participants, supporters or members of communities engaging in such travel, while bringing those at a distance—anthropologists, sociologists or other with little personal connection to the phenomenon—into the cultural world of STM. To do this, I focus in particular on the language—the narratives—of travel that STM participants create and use in making sense of the STM travel experience.

The stories I heard from individuals were quite diverse in many ways; some had powerfully transformative experiences, some had disappointments, some returned critical of what they did, and others were deeply in love with (or deeply disgusted by) the places and people they had encountered. But the similarities of phrases, expectations, disappointments or emotions were striking. From vastly different experiences, students were talking about their experiences within a common narrative framework of STM that helped them to think about these

---

[2]See Wuthnow and Offut 2008; Priest, Dischinger and Rasmussen 2006. Later in this chapter, I discuss the rates of STM participation a bit more.

diverse experiences as a single sort of thing, a type of travel they could all understand.

One definition of culture I have always appreciated is Anthony F. C. Wallace's (1970), in which he rejected the idea of culture as the reproduction of uniformity and instead considered it "the organization of diversity." It seemed that the evangelicals among whom I lived had found a guiding narrative—a metanarrative—by which they could organize the diversity of their own motives, experiences and interests. My questions were what that organizing narrative was, where it came from and how it became so influential among those traveling.[3]

To answer my questions, I needed to see how this overarching narrative was produced, consumed and experienced throughout an STM experience. I developed an ethnographic research project to explore the dynamics of narrative and experience at work. As I studied the narratives and experiences of STM travelers firsthand and through presentations in print and PowerPoint, I found a common understandings of what the trip was, or was supposed to be.

Most called these trips "life-changing" and "eye-opening," radically transforming the ways the travelers "saw the world." For many it was the first time "really seeing" for themselves the conditions of poverty and inequality in the world, evoking deep emotions, including sorrow, anger and compassion, in many of those who traveled. Narratives of connection and relationship—particularly with other Christians—were powerful positive experiences in which North American Christians, some of whom had never been outside the United States, "discovered" that "we're all the same" and "we are one in Christ," despite linguistic, cultural and economic differences.

---

[3]Anthropologist of tourism Edward Bruner (2005, p. 21) makes a distinction between *metanarrative* and "the tourist tales told before, during and after the trip." Bruner calls the metanarrative the "largest conceptual frame within which tourism operates. They are not attached to any locality or to any particular tour, and they are usually taken for granted." I would put the missionary narrative into the same category, but I find that the idea of a guiding narrative accomplishes the same purposes for my analysis. I invoke the term *metalanguage* later in this chapter to define what I mean by narrative (which overlaps a great deal with Bruner's term *metanarrative*), but I have chosen to remain with the term *narrative* to reduce the complexity of the prose. Historians have employed the terms *grand narrative* and *master narrative* to distinguish the various social influences of narrative, in which a master narrative is, generally, "a big story that makes smaller stories intelligible" (Cox 2005, p. 3).

In many ways, STM narratives resonated with, or reinforced, central theological commitments of Christian unity and the importance of service or sacrifice. The disappointments people expressed were often with their inability to see or experience these very things. I recall one of my students telling me that in her first STM trip, in which her group of high school youth traveled to Mexico, she felt as if the team was not needed. She told me she regretted the money and effort spent on the trip, because she felt the time serving did not make much of a difference. She contrasted this to a later trip she took to Africa (she did not name the country), in which she felt that the local people valued the presence of the team and that she was able to make "a real difference."

As I have spoken with people, particularly other Christians, about these narratives, I have found a great deal of familiarity with these themes, even among those who have not gone on STM trips themselves. Many can quote particular common phrases, almost verbatim, from testimonies I have heard in presentations and interviews I have conducted. These clichés are not simply familiar ways of expressing common experiences, however; they are culturally particular ways of framing those experiences. Anthropologists studying everything from race (Hill 2008), to gender (Schiffrin 1996), to tourism (E. M. Bruner 2005), to nationalism (Mattingly et al. 2002) have pointed out how familiar cultural narratives (or discourses) not only express experience but also shape it. Many setting out on their first STM trip already carry an arsenal of narrative structures through which they can interpret their trip.

This book is the product of my research, which draws together narratives from public presentations such as chapels and worship services, personal conversations and a two-year ethnographic experience with a particular STM team at a nondenominational congregation I refer to as Central Wheaton Church, or CWC. This 1,500-plus-member church has made STM trips a regular part of its missions program for more than twenty-five years.[4] STM travels, like other forms of travel, are

---

[4]Quotations from students or STM participants are used only with explicit permission or are taken from public presentations in which there was no expectation of privacy. In every instance,

cultural moments created through historical processes and institutions. Although it shares aspects of tourism and pilgrimage, STM can't be reduced to another version of either of these. Guided by theological commitments and embedded in a wider social context, STM is a type of travel unto itself in which particular guiding narratives shape the experiences of participants.

Although my study draws on the experiences of an evangelical congregation, STM is not exclusively an evangelical phenomenon. Orthodox, Catholic and mainline Christians, as well as Jews, Unitarian Universalists and other religious groups have expressions of short-term mission, often looking very similar to the evangelical versions described here (see Hefferan, Adkins and Occhipinti 2009; Wuthnow 2009; McAdoo and Principe 2010). Nancy Ammerman (2005, p. 143) has noted that virtually every religious group in the United States—conservative Protestants, Orthodox, Catholic, Seventh-Day Adventist, mainline Protestants, LDS, Jehovah's Witness, Jewish congregations—have increased the number of "direct connections" with missionaries through short-term trips. Similarly, in his comprehensive study of the ways religious congregations in the United States have engaged globalization, Robert Wuthnow (2009, p. 169) notes that while "evangelical churches are the most likely to sponsor mission trips . . . nearly half of mainline Protestants say their congregations do as well, compared with one-third of Catholics and members of historically black denominations."[5] No doubt, the practices and discourses of STM reflect the different theological and institutional contexts of these groups. Even among conservative Protestants and evangelicals, different congregations have idiosyncratic means of talking about these sorts of travels. What I believe is generalizable from the case of CWC is the process of narrative formation that occurs through the institutional and cultural practices that surround STM travels. Only when we see the cultural dynamics of these trips can we think about what, if

---

with the exception of historical and published accounts, names and identities are changed in accordance with anthropological convention.

[5]Wuthnow (2009, 293n29) gives the statistics as 54 percent of evangelical church members, 46 percent of mainline Protestants, 31 percent of Catholics and 29 percent of black Protestants.

anything, we might do in changing or reforming STM experiences.

The question of changing these trips in focus or practice is controversial, of course. For many who participate in these travels, significant change may seem unnecessary. Yet even some of the most ardent proponents of STM have written of the need for care and self-reflection (Morgan and Easterling 2008; Harris 2002). My purpose here is to provide the theoretical framework for understanding the ways we come to frame these trips culturally; my hope is that this will aid those who want these trips to accomplish the highest ideals of social and spiritual transformation, often said to be the trips' reason for existing (e.g., Anthony 1994; Peterson, Aeschliman and Sneed 2003).

In the case at hand, I demonstrate how a narrative of mission, emerging within the specific context of a congregation, reflects a history and social context, while providing the means for travelers to make sense of their experiences. At the same time, while this narrative provides a means to understanding, it also makes some sorts of understanding *more* difficult. I argue that in the case of this group, a personalistic missionary narrative serves a positive function to link these travels to a theological and spiritual understanding that the travelers and their supporters recognize and affirm, while obscuring aspects of the very things many of my team members wanted to understand: poverty, inequality and cultural difference.

By framing the encounter as primarily interpersonal, a service to "the poor," as well as having a theological motive of "sharing the gospel," the guiding narratives through which our team experienced these travels made it *more* difficult to see the structural, historical and cultural forces at work. As I explain in chapter two, narratives generally play a central role in Christian experiences of faith and life, but scholars have not always attended to the social life of these narratives—how they are created or recreated in the practices of faith.[6] For STM trav-

---

[6]Notable exceptions in the study of U.S. evangelicals include some of the excellent studies of conversion narratives (Harding 1987; Stromberg 1993), as well as ethnographies of congregational life that explore linguistic conventions and cultural logic in the kinds of stories evangelicals tell themselves about themselves (Elisha 2011, Bialecki 2009, Bielo 2011). Simply taking Christianity seriously as a cultural phenomenon in its own right is a relatively recent development in anthropology (cf. Robbins 2003).

elers, the narrative has cultural resonance that is both pragmatic and inspirational, enabling them to connect their trips and identity to a larger and longer theological narrative that is powerful and meaningful, though not always in ways that travelers and organizers seek.

Naming the experience of STM as a product of narrative does not mean I take these trips as *only* a product of narrative with no reality outside language.[7] In exploring the creation, reproduction and use of narrative in experience, though, I ask how these narratives reflect cultural context, practical action, theological commitments and history: how do they work in tandem with the experiences in the trip itself to shape the experience and rearticulation of the travel experience? Like all discourses, this language and practice is contested at many points, but the stories STM travelers tell of faith and mission are not simply reflections of an unmediated encounter in the "mission field," springing up from the countryside of Bermuda, slums in Mexico, megacities in China or chapels in Ghana. STM travels are cultural events embedded in historic, linguistic and institutional contexts through which we come to anticipate and, in some ways, construct our travel experiences before anyone gets on a plane.

SHORT-TERM MISSION AS A SCHOLARLY SUBJECT

Although those U.S. Americans who regularly participate in a Christian community of some sort are likely familiar with the concept and practice of STM, nonreligious people, including the majority of my fellow anthropologists, may be less aware of the phenomenon. As frequent travelers, many anthropologists have seen groups in the airport wearing matching T-shirts, preparing to board an international flight. They may have encountered a team surrounded by bags of medical supplies, or building materials being loaded onto buses in a Latin American capital. Even those who do not travel frequently or have not encoun-

---

[7]Readers familiar with postmodern literary and social theory will see in this my move away from radical versions of linguistic construction. Unlike theorists who privilege language to the point of at least potentially obscuring the material, I lean toward the position of someone like Bourdieu (1990; cf. Ortner 2006, 14-16), who argues that experience and the mediation of experience (through language and culture) can't be usefully distinguished, but both contribute to the structuring of social life and the reproduction of cultural practice.

tered these groups personally may have seen reports of the phenomenon in the media.[8] Major news outlets, such as the *New York Times* and the *Wall Street Journal*, have published articles about STM, including stories about Southern California megachurch pastor Rick Warren's plans for thousands of short-term volunteers to focus their benevolence on Rwanda in an effort to lift the nation out of poverty and expand the reach of Christianity (Kristof 2002). Partly depending on the perspective of the reader, these sorts of accounts inspire positive views of the phenomenon—medical personnel, dentists or skilled trade workers bringing their time and expertise to impoverished communities—or largely (even wholly) negative images: triumphalist Christians bumbling through vulnerable and remote communities engaged in neocolonialist projects of proselytism. Whatever the view or however it has been garnered, few of us have ever come to understand this phenomenon through scholarly literature, as relatively little research yet exists.[9]

Anthropologists and other social scientists who do study these groups often begin somewhat by chance. They encounter these groups in their field sites, where few North Americans are typically found, apart from the occasional Peace Corps volunteer. One anthropologist became intrigued when she came across a group of U.S. businesspeople teaching management and entrepreneurship in the small Baptist church in her rural Haitian field site. Another was drawn into translating for a group working among those speaking a minority Mayan language in the highlands of Guatemala. She later wrote a paper about her experience, but her initial motivation to assist the group was to minimize the potential damage she feared this wealthy, culturally naïve team of North American evangelicals might do in the small village where she

---

[8]Mainstream media outlets such as *USA Today* (MacDonald 2006), the *Wall Street Journal* (Sparks 2008) and the *Chicago Tribune* (Roth 2005) have all covered STM.

[9]While there is fairly substantial literature on the practice of short-term missions, debating its relevance or worth from a missiological point of view, there is very little published, research-based work. Notable exceptions include the work of Robert J. Priest, an anthropologist and scholar of missions at Trinity Evangelical Divinity School, who has guest-edited several theme issues of missiology or theology journals and a book (see Priest, et. al. 2006; also Priest 2008a, Priest & Priest 2008, all of which include several articles or chapters based on ethnographic or statistical research. In addition, there are a handful of articles (Montgomery 1993; Ver Beek 2008) and several brief mentions that appear as part of larger sociological projects on religion in the United States (Ammerman 2005; Smith and Denton 2005; Wuthnow and Offutt 2008).

worked. As I have presented on this phenomenon at professional meetings, many colleagues have approached me with their own stories of encountering STM teams around the world, occasionally with somewhat cringe-worthy accounts. Seen from the anthropological perspective, STM may seem to be the worst combination of religious fundamentalist zeal and touristic superficiality.

Yet just as anthropologists have argued for the relevance of scholarly—particularly ethnographic —attention to be paid to tourists, conservative Christians and missionaries, so too should both secular and Christian scholars turn an ethnographic eye to STM.[10] In the first place, it would be a mistake to believe that this is a marginal phenomenon involving a relatively small number of people. In their recent survey of transnational religious connectivity drawing on adult, church-based populations, Wuthnow and Offut (2008) put the number of U.S. Americans participating in STM at 1.6 million per year. Given that this number came from surveying only those church members over the age of eighteen, it is likely that the overall number is much larger.[11] Moreover, whereas Wuthnow and Offut asked only about STM trips abroad, significant numbers of junior high and high school students take domestic trips to urban areas or to regionally distinct cultural contexts (e.g., Appalachia) that my college students and members of CWC considered to be very much a part of the STM experience.[12] However the numbers are crunched, millions of U.S.

---

[10]Among many others, Sharon Gmelch (2004) makes the case for tourists; Susan Harding (1991) has written about the importance of studying "fundamentalist Christians"; and Bronwen Douglas (2001) has made the case for studying missionaries and missionary writing.

[11]Wuthnow, in his book (2009, p 171) published after the 2008 article, makes this point himself. Research by anthropologist Robert Priest (2011) provides statistical support for the higher numbers. For example, he observed that just over 50 percent of Christian college and seminary students surveyed in 2005 reported having gone on a short-term trip. With the population of Christian college students being over 300,000, and seminaries representing another 30,000, this alone represents nearly 175,000 travelers. A more precise figure would be dependent on the groups involved and the terms of inclusion. It is easy to suggest that the number, including teens and nonchurch-based participants, is over two million per year.

[12]Smith and Denton (2005, 43), using a wide definition of religious mission team or service project, found that 30 percent of religious (Christian and Jewish) teens surveyed had participated in one of these trips. Though this would include everything from serving in a soup kitchen to spending two years as a missionary intern in China, this represents an enormous number of teen participants and likely includes mostly trips of the one- to two-week service/mission variety discussed here.

Americans have participated in one or more of these trips, and millions more have heard from travelers through presentations at churches, youth group meetings and Christian colleges.

For many of the travelers, these trips potentially become a key moment for developing interpretations of social conditions such as economic inequality, cultural difference, racial dynamics, gender discrimination, globalization and social injustice. Within an STM encounter, however, these interpretations occur in an explicitly theological framework. Scholars of evangelical Christianity have long noted that while faith motivates charitable action and social engagement among its adherents, in some cultural contexts (e.g., white suburban evangelicalism), this social engagement is often in tension with any recognition of structural inequality, systemic injustice or geopolitical aspects of poverty (Emerson and Smith 2000; Emerson 2003; Elisha 2011; Bialecki 2008). Among those participating in STM trips, encountering and addressing poverty, learning about the culture of the place and people being visited and generally gaining a wider perspective on global Christianity are explicit goals of the travelers. Yet, after presenting how the missionary narrative comes to frame an STM trip, I argue that this narrative also *inhibits* these very goals. For this reason I offer, from an explicitly Christian point of view, a possible response to the pervasive narrative in STM.

There are also nonreligious versions of STM, known as "service tourism" or "voluntourism." Increasing numbers of people are paying big money to travel to remote villages and help install water systems, work in sustainable agriculture or learn about local health projects. All these forms of service/mission travel tend to follow similar patterns of activity, often taking place for a similar length of time and executing many of the same sorts of projects. What set the religious, and particularly Christian, version of these travels apart are the narratives created and employed around these trips. It was these narratives—culturally embedded discourses about otherness, mission, blessing and suffering—that drew me as an anthropologist of globalization and religion to want to study this phenomenon.

Mine is not, primarily, a project motivated by a strong support or critique of STM. I began my work wearing the hat of an anthropologist, a researcher interested in understanding what these trips mean for those who participate, how they reflect or refashion the practices and beliefs of participants and how they contribute to particular understandings of the world beyond those of STM travelers. As I thought more about this, however, I felt called to come also as a fellow Christian who is concerned for those receiving these teams as well as those participating, and to think more intentionally about how the church should be framing these travels. I believe the cause of missions is one Christians should support, even if particular methods or modes need to be critiqued, adapted or discarded. I hope this research will be a gift to the church in our efforts to be a more faithful witness to the gospel in local and transnational life.

NARRATIVES, CHRISTIANS AND CULTURE

Creating narrative is a universal feature of humanity, a process of such significance crossculturally that many anthropologists (along with literary critics, philosophers, historians, novelists and even "narratologists") have thought deeply about the dynamics of producing and consuming narratives as a common, and essential, human experience (Mitchell 1980; Rosenwald 1992; Ellis and Flaherty 1993; J. Bruner 2003). Arthur Asa Berger (1997, p. 10), a well-known scholar of popular culture, says narratives "furnish us with both a method for learning about the world and a way to tell others what we have learned." There are other ways of learning, of course, such as scientific experimentation and metaphoric association, but as Berger points out, narrative includes those forms of knowing as well. (Scientists must explain what they have learned through narratives of question, hypothesis, experiment and conclusion.) In this way, narrative is a kind of metalanguage, a way of using language that makes it possible to make sense of language and experience. Through shared narratives, culturally—or individually—specific experiences are made intelligible to self and other (see also Barthes and Duisit 1977, p. 79ff).

Narratives work as metalanguage because they are embedded in larger, shared frames of meaning and culture, what linguistic anthropologists often call "discourse." I considered presenting STM generally as a discourse, as I wanted to understand not simply the ways people talked about STM, but also how this talk forms and reflects relationships, understandings and institutional arrangements in the world at large. I decided to steer away from making discourse the central analytical frame for the study for two reasons: First, unlike *narrative*, *discourse* is a term smacking of anthropological jargon, one that shows up in pretentious philosophical conversations as well as technical linguistic and anthropological studies. I certainly do not want those reading this book to feel they must slog through any more unfamiliar theory than necessary.

Second, and more importantly, the notion of "discourse" has been most famously elaborated by Michel Foucault (1984) and his followers, who interpret discourse as always inextricably linked to power and domination. While I certainly suggest how the narratives/discourse of STM reflects power relationships as well as economic and social position, and may even serve to (re)create social hierarchy, I do not think that is all they do. As I have studied STM, I am convinced they are not always and only built around power and inequality. As I explore in part four, I believe the language of STM can be reformed, if not redeemed, to create bonds of unity, partnership and Christian fellowship in ways that can transcend, or at least make visible, relationships of inequality and social power.

My decision to concentrate on the language of the short-termers themselves as a key to understanding these trips came from ethnographic experiences and theoretical commitments I brought to the research. First, in ethnographic terms, I observed the high degree of convergence in the narratives and rhetoric of my own students who had gone on STM trips. Even before I was provided with statistical confirmation, it was clear that most of my students had been on at least one such trip.[13] These students used common phrases about how impoverished Christians were much closer to God, how the children "had nothing"

---

[13]Robert Priest (pers. comm.) conducted research on Christian college and seminary students generally. Among Wheaton students (n=147), he found that 66 percent reported participating in one or more trips.

yet were "so happy." Students routinely spoke of how the trip helped in "getting outside my comfort zone" and how the experience had "changed my life." In multiple conversations, I heard phrases like this one from a first-year student who had gone to Mexico to help build houses: "God just totally changed my world. When I saw how the church in Mexico worshipped God even though they had nothing, it just changed the way I see everything. Here we have everything, right? But there, they just trust God. I don't know, but seeing it for myself . . . it changed my life."

It was out of these interviews, along with an earlier research project on STM expectations among college students, that I began to believe that these narratives, embedded in themes of travel and return, drawing from the theological and cultural resources, and powerfully connected to evangelical priorities and cultural tools, made STM a unique form of travel.[14] Although they exchanged anecdotes, giving accounts of the unique features of their various trips and the particular dynamics of their countries and cultures, each could say that they had a common experience; all of them had "done a short-term mission."

The second reason I chose to focus on narratives sprang from the nature of evangelical Christianity itself. As both a scholar of evangelicalism and a Christian who has actively identified with and participated in evangelical communities since college, I am acutely aware of the importance and particularity of narratives of faith among my fellow believers. The ways Protestants generally, and evangelicals in particular, think about and use language has become a central concern among anthropologists of Christianity (e.g., Keane 2007; Coleman 2006; Engelke 2007; Engelke and Tomlinson 2006). Susan Harding (2001, xi), in her widely read book on Jerry Falwell and his followers, found that the "very site" of her fieldwork was not the physical locations of Christians, but the language they used to create an understanding of themselves.

This emphasis on language is not without its critics. For example, Harding's work in particular has been critiqued as overly focused on language at the expense of embodied practices by which Christians

---

[14]My earlier project (Howell and Dorr 2007), using the applications of students for the summer mission projects at a Christian college, focused on their expectations and motives for the trips.

come to understand their identity and faith (cf. Luhrmann 2004). Similarly, because Harding's work was focused on the language of evangelical elites (e.g., Jerry Falwell), some have argued that we can lose sight of the practices of Christian life that draw on and reshape the language of elites themselves (see Bialecki 2008, p. 376; Robbins 2006). To understand how the language comes to have an ordering effect on experience and identity, it must be examined *in situ* as it is used, formed, contested and shaped among rank-and-file believers, not simply as a top-down process.

As I show in part two, leaders of churches and nationally known authors writing about STM were part of shaping the travel narratives and nomenclature around the movement from the beginning. However, at many points, they seemed to be responding to the language of average Christians, rather than creating the language itself. It was at the level of congregational life that I thought I should understand how narratives were being produced, practiced and reproduced.

This is not to say that the narratives provided by elites are unimportant, either in the case of STM or in cultural phenomena generally. Anthropologists of travel have demonstrated how the authors of published guides or official spokespeople of cultural "authenticity" often play a particularly important role for travelers' interpretations of unfamiliar places and people. In various kinds of travel, be they pilgrimage to the Holy Land (e.g. Bowman 1991) or tourism in Athens (Travlou 2002), the descriptions and narratives produced by elites and brought to the traveler in text and tradition are powerful mediators of the traveler's experience (see chapter two for more on STM in relation to these other forms of travel). These interpretations, however, are never so powerful as to strictly delimit the range of personal interpretations and contestation made possible as real individuals encounter the world (cf. Eade 2000). To understand the experiences and interpretations of STM travelers, it would not be enough to know the narratives they used and may have internalized; I needed to understand the production and consumption of these narratives in the sites of influence. This sort of understanding is the strength of ethnographic research.

ETHNOGRAPHY AND SHORT-TERM MISSION

Ethnography is not the only way to study STM. Some studies look for measurable indices to determine the effect of STM trips on either travelers or host communities. For example, Calvin College sociologist Kurt Ver Beek (2006) designed a project to identify whether one particular claim to "transformation," namely that STM participants give more money to mission work, could be quantifiably substantiated. Using comparative statistical measures of giving rates, Ver Beek looked for evidence that those who participated in a given STM project (building houses in Honduras after hurricane Mitch in 1998) gave more money than those who had not participated or more than they had prior to their trip.[15]

Others have used survey research to test hypotheses that participation in STM makes participants less ethnocentric, increases participation in long-term missions or contributes to a more active prayer life (see, for example, Park 2008). Relying on self-reporting or measurable aspects of social life, these studies have been equivocal in their assessment of the particular effects of STM and silent on the constructed meanings STM is having among participants.

What ethnography contributes to the conversation is an understanding of STM that can't be gained through other methods. Unlike more detached methods of social research, ethnography provides a perspective on how people understand, interact with and construct the world. Attending to the personal, local and everyday interactions in a particular community or group, the ethnographer gains access to processes of subjectivity and the creation of cultural interpretation that are often difficult for people to describe about themselves (see Cerwonka and Malkki 2007).

The ethnographic method also allows for sustained attention to the wider context in which individuals act, speak and think. Sociologist Randall Collins argues that social analysis should always begin with the interactional context rather than with individuals themselves. De-

---

[15]Ver Beek found that over five years, there was little to no measurable difference in overall giving between those who had participated in the trip and those who had not (2006). For his exploration of other quantitative studies of STM, see Ver Beek 2008.

veloping what he calls a theory of "interaction ritual," Collins points our attention to the social dynamics of everyday life—the small social rituals—that shape individuals' experiences of their own lives and the lives of others (2004). Thus, throughout my research, though my attention is on the narrative, testimonies and stories individuals use and produce to understand their experiences, I link those to the historical and institutional contexts in which we find ourselves. In the final chapter, where I suggest interventions, my attention turns primarily to those institutional arrangements and interactional contexts in which these narratives are (re)produced. It is in transforming these interactions that the individual narratives will be most affected.

For this reason, it is not necessary that the examples that make up the focus of ethnographic research be "case studies" or representative examples; rather, they are a means of exploring processes and cultural dynamics invisible from other methodological vantage points. For this research, then, I sought a context in which I could engage in long-term fieldwork with an STM team, attending to the processes by which narratives were embraced, created, modified, employed or rejected. By becoming part of the process (what anthropologists call "participant observation"), I hoped to gain some insight into what these participants understood as "transformation," how that was experienced and what that might mean for and about their faith. Therefore, while I was not attempting to find an archetypal STM team, based on what I had heard from my Wheaton students over the years, there were a number of characteristics I sought in finding a "site" for my research.

SELECTING A SITE

To prepare for my research, I spent the summer of 2005 as a kind of short-term missionary myself, during which my family and I worked in a summer school program with the ministry my Dominican Republic team would visit the next year. During that time I took a one-day side trip with an STM team from Tennessee into a small *batay* (a village of sugar cane field workers) in the middle of the sunbaked sugar cane fields near the North Coast city of Puerto Plata.

I met up with the Tennessee team at a gas station on the side of the

road. I explained my research, and they were warm and accommodating. Not having my informed consent forms on hand to sign, I assured them I would only observe. The team seemed to have been fairly
well prepared for their trip. The girls wore modest skirts and the boys
long pants, and everyone respectfully took in what our North American
missionary guide had to say. Before arriving at the mission agency's
housing project of modest cement homes, where clean water ran and
sanitation was available to all, we stopped at a "company village," a
virtually uninhabitable collection of rundown, dirt-floor barracks,
where single men and families were squeezed together in cinderblock
rooms with little ventilation in the stifling heat. Toilet facilities were
virtually nonexistent, and although the residents clearly did all they
could to maintain a livable area, fetid trash lay in piles not far from the
living quarters.

As we walked between the buildings toward the home of a family
our missionary guide knew, the members of the group greeted people
along the way and comported themselves carefully. If anyone expressed
distaste at the environment or behaved in a way other than friendly, I
did not see it. We even came upon a funeral, being conducted according to traditional Haitian religious practices, where the body of
the dead man was being prepared for burial. While our group undoubtedly looked a bit odd in the setting (a collection of white people
standing around between the houses, occasionally breaking into quiet
hymns such as "Amazing Grace" or "How Great Thou Art"), no one
expressed anything negative about the religious practices so different
from North American evangelicalism. I watched carefully to see if any
facial expressions or comments would suggest revulsion, distaste,
shock or even pity, and I saw nothing but interest or a kind of respectful awkwardness.

After finishing our tour of the poverty-stricken company village, we
reached the mission community in the *batay*. Our truck pulled up to a
large church, where we could already hear the lively music of the
Dominico-Haitian congregation. We filed into the building to see that
two other STM teams were already there. One, a small group of eight
to ten adults—medical professionals who had come to work at the

health clinic—sat quietly toward the back of the church. Our group sat across the aisle from that team, behind the men of the congregation, who wore suits or dress shirts, separated from the women of the congregation, who were likewise modestly dressed, many with the head coverings associated with ultraconservative Christianity.

Our group clapped along to the music being played by a band with an electric keyboard, guitar and percussion, and sang along as best we could with the Creole lyrics. I sat with the other members of the Tennessee team, singing along and listening to the preacher, who mixed Haitian Creole and Spanish for his congregation of mostly Haitian cane workers. He greeted our group, which at one point was invited to the front with its adult leaders to sing an English worship song. One of the team leaders played guitar. At the end of the song, the Haitian congregation, which had been nodding and clapping throughout, burst into applause and shouts of "amen." The pastor put his hands on the group leader's shoulders and, in Spanish, thanked her for coming and being part of the service.

A third group, which may have shared a song earlier or perhaps had sat through much of the worship already, was not engaged as the Tennessee team was. Instead they were in the back of the church and outside on the front steps—a group of some thirty to forty white, U.S. teenagers, several wearing bikini tops or shirtless (boys), playing with the Haitian children, who were dressed in Sunday clothes and who had presumably come to church with their parents. A number of the U.S. girls wore their hair in the cornrow style with small braids ending in colorful beads done for tourists by Haitian women, who walk up and down the beach, charging five to ten U.S. dollars for a process that could take several hours.

While the Haitian churchgoers seemed unconcerned by their movement, several members of this team played with kids in the back of the church or walked in and out as laughing children took their hands to lead them into the yard for piggyback rides or games of tag. Perhaps the parents of these children were happy for the distraction the visiting teens provided; I did not ask any at that time. I had a hard time believing, however, that the immodest attire or casual approach to participating in the worship service was appropriate for guests.

For me, the defining moment of this team's visit came as they left on an open-sided truck that had brought them to the village. Several of them gave out candy as the truck began the drive back to the all-inclusive resort where they were staying, their bright pink wristbands clearly visible. As someone already thinking about the issues of neocolonialism, patronage and even exploitation potentially involved in these short-term missions, the sight of these beautiful North American teens shouting "Adios" and "Hasta la vista" to the swirl of Haitian children running away from the church in their Sunday clothes, hoping to get a piece of American candy, was a bit disturbing.

The point of this story is to contrast these two images, particularly the latter, with what I would eventually seek out for this project. I had seen or heard accounts of enough variation in these sorts of teams to know that the more egregious examples of North American indulgence or insensitivity were not necessarily more common than respectful, well-prepared teams. As an anthropologist, my first interest is not in constructing a case for or against, but in providing understanding and interpretation. Toward that end, I deliberately sought out a program that, while not necessarily representative in a statistically verifiable way, would not be an obvious outlier or exceptional case, either good or bad. That is, I did not want to focus my study on a church that was doing something remarkably cutting-edge or distinctly different from what I perceived to be the patterns of short-term missions.

I have heard of churches that engage in "bilateral mission," where they bring members of non-Western churches to their U.S. congregations, and others that engage in long-term relationships with particular congregations, developing deep connections with non-Western leaders, learning the local language(s) in the U.S. congregation and working according to some of the best practices of holistic economic development. I have likewise heard of others who routinely send unprepared teenagers into rural villages, where they engage in all sorts of insensitive and culturally inappropriate behavior. For the purposes of this study, I felt neither sort of trip would be helpful.

I also sought a group that was not planning to engage in remarkable or extraordinary activities while abroad. In terms of the explicit objectives of STM trips, there is a great deal of variety, although among trips not bringing professionals, such as dental or medical missions, particular projects seem favored. Priest's (2010a, p. 99) research among U.S. megachurches confirmed what I heard from the students in my classes: the most popular activity for these trips is construction projects, followed closely by work involving children such as Vacation Bible School (VBS) and "backyard Bible clubs." Evangelism remains an important element of the discourse, but for those going to non-English-speaking countries, which are a majority, direct evangelism remains difficult (see also Priest 2006). Other, more personal, goals also played critical roles in organizing the purpose and expectations of these trips—expectations that I discuss in detail later in this book.

Likewise, in terms of the amount of time distinguishing a short-term trip from a long-term or "mid-length" trip, there is no standard. For some, anything under two years is "short term," while others would see trips lasting more than one month as providing something distinctly different from one-week excursions. My own definition of a short-term mission, which I explain in chapter two, doesn't make time a definitive criterion. But relying on the testimony of my college students and on research done by Priest and Priest (2008), I observed that trips that were around two weeks long seemed to be common, particularly for high school students.

Finally, although I knew teams traveled to a wide variety of countries, one element of the STM narrative characteristic of many travels concerned language and communication across language barriers. Trips to Spanish-speaking countries constitute the vast majority of short-term trips, with Mexico being the country receiving the highest number of such teams, and the Dominican Republic being in the top five (Priest, Dischinger and Rasmussen 2006; Priest 2010a; see also Gilbert and Hamilton 2009).[16] Thus, finding a team in which language barriers had to be negotiated seemed to be relevant to understanding the narratives so common to these trips. In the end, when I set about se-

---

[16]In Priest's research, the country receiving the most teams *per capita* was, perhaps unexpectedly, the Bahamas.

lecting a team to study, I found myself imagining a ten-day to two-week trip of construction and children's ministry, in which a high school group would travel to a Spanish-speaking country as part of what they and their church explicitly framed as a short-term mission.

As I began to conceive of the project, I learned of a woman who would soon be leaving her job on staff at our college to spend three years with a Christian organization in the Dominican Republic, known here by the pseudonym *Ayuda para Niños*, or Help for the Children. I had heard something about this organization from one of my students, and in talking with the woman preparing to go, discovered that several churches from the Wheaton area regularly sent short-term teams to work in the children's home and the elementary school, and to do construction projects. I approached one of those supporting congregations where I already knew the missions pastor to see if it would agree to allow an "outsider" access to one of its teams for two years of research. A charismatic man in his thirties, this pastor at CWC was a former missionary who had an M.A. in mission studies. I knew this congregation to be a place with a venerable commitment to long- and short-term missions. Similarly, I knew this pastor had developed a relatively thoughtful and carefully planned short-term missions program. It seemed a great place to start.

I began studying the team before it was a team, during the selection phase when prospective leaders were interviewed and student applicants were vetted and assigned to one of the five teams (Mexico, Costa Rica, the Czech Republic, Spain and the Dominican Republic). I went through the preparation with the team, including the logistical preparations, cultural training, theological/spiritual discussions and team-building times. I also interviewed each member, usually in groups of two or three, before we traveled. During the trip itself, I spent virtually all my time simply doing what the team did. Except for two afternoons when I visited with Dominican leaders or community members, I worked on the building, helped conduct the VBSs, participated in devotional times and hung out with the team. Upon our return, I joined in the occasions to gather and remember the trip and present our pictures. I also interviewed all members again individually, generally eight

to twelve months after we had returned, to understand how they remembered their experiences.[17]

ORGANIZATION OF THIS BOOK

My goal with this book is to demonstrate the ways a particular narrative that has become important to many peoples' religious lives was
created and used in understanding the STM travel experience. This
narrative began long before any of the individuals presented in this
ethnography started thinking about this trip, and it came to each of
them in the institutional context of CWC. It is my intention to offer
something more than just a study of a particular STM trip, but to
present a larger framework for understanding STM generally and the
ways narratives are created among Christians to understand themselves
and others.

To set the stage for the ethnographic study of the team, chapter two
lays out the theoretical framework I used to understand the development
of STM travel. I address the definition of "short-term mission," with an
extended discussion of how STM represents a particular mode of travel.
Reflecting on the anthropological work done on related forms of
travel—specifically pilgrimage and tourism—I argue that while STM
overlaps with both, it is a unique phenomenon referencing a unique
social encounter. From there, I present a history of STM in part two,
with a focus on the emergence of the term and concept of the "short-
term mission." I divide the history as a way to demonstrate a movement
from the more adult and mission-agency aspect of the history to a youth
and teen phenomenon, and finally explore its church-based focus. Such
a history has not yet been undertaken, and a full history of STM is a
project deserving far more attention than I am able to give here.[18]

---

[17]There was one student who, due to schedule conflicts, was not able to have the final interview.
I did, however, have follow-up interviews with several students in the year after they took a
second trip to Linda Vista in the summer following our trip.

[18]Peterson, Aeschliman and Rasmussen (2003, pp. 241-55) give a brief history in which they
chronicle a number of initial STM projects undertaken by various organizations. Their focus
is on the practice, rather than the language, but is very helpful for establishing the emergence
of STM in deed if not word. See also C. M. Brown, "Field Statement on the Short-Term Mission Phenomenon: Contributing Factors and Current Debate" (unpublished paper, Trinity
International University, June 9, 2005), online at <www.tiu.edu/tedsphd/ics_research>.

In particular, as I looked for the ways the idea of short-term missions, marked as a distinctive activity, appeared in various publications, I tracked rather closely with the heritage of my ethnographic subjects in the evangelical church. Unfortunately, this means Catholic, Orthodox, Mormon and mainline histories of the movement are neglected. For the discussion to follow, however, it seemed important to trace the genealogy of the language and ideas leading up to the evangelical manifestation I encountered at CWC.

Happily, Wheaton College, in addition to being a hotbed of short-term mission activity, is home to an extensive evangelical mission archive. Exploring recent records of groups formed to send short-term teams abroad, along with the speeches or presentations of significant mission practitioners and theorists, I use part two to illustrate how the emergence of STM as a practice was accompanied by a shift in the very definition of *missions*. That is, since the earliest years of the Christian movement, there have been those who travel to other places for brief periods to engage in missionary work, but the contemporary short-term mission phenomenon with its focus on sending average laypeople, and particularly young people, abroad for the length of time generally reserved for a vacation is a contemporary movement indeed. The archival data reveal a fascinating emergence of the language that today contributes to the expectations and interpretations of short-term missionaries.

From there I move into the ethnographic study of the team itself. Part three begins with a presentation of the process in which I participated while preparing for our trip to Linda Vista. My purpose in chapter six is both to explore the processes of narrative construction as well as to consider how the wider cultural context of U.S. evangelicalism contributes to the ways team members would interpret the experiences of the trip and process the experience when we came home. From the first church interviews with prospective leaders and students to the writing of support letters and evangelism workshops, and even to the informal rhetoric of our team leaders, each of us was gradually brought to a common discourse of our trip and our purpose in travel.

Chapter seven moves to the trip itself and the ways our narrative was extended to the experiences in the Dominican Republic. At times members of the team resist the constraints particular narratives provide; at other times they fall comfortably into the themes and tropes laid out by these narrative structures. I focus in particular on ways that members of our trip interpret or construct particular aspects of the experience anticipated in the pretrip phase, specifically difference, community and poverty. I also consider the relationship I observed between times of "mission" and times of "tourism" experienced on the trip. Although, as I explore in chapter six, no one on our team wanted our trip to be confused with tourism, there were several moments in which we understood our activities to be touristic in nature.

Chapter eight focuses directly on the articulation of the trip in the months after our return. I revisit the themes of poverty and community as they emerged in the narrative of "transformation" for our post-trip lives. As I explored the varied personal narratives of our team, as well as my college students and earlier participants or leaders of CWC's short-term missions programs, the shaping and even constricting role of the guiding STM narrative became clearer.

While my goal in this research has never been primarily prescriptive, the more I worked with this material and the more I talked about it with other Christians, the more I came to believe that simply presenting my research was not what I needed to do. As the most vocal critics of STM and its sharpest observers, Christians themselves wanted tools to think about how these narratives could be refashioned, strengthened or otherwise imagined toward the highest goals of Christian life and mission. Thus I use part four to think about how these narratives, in their creation and practice, could be viewed in theological and missiological terms. Thinking about the nature of narrative and travel as anthropological concepts, as well as mission as a theological mandate, I propose a few thoughts on how Christians might think about changing STM as a process of *cultural* change. Following the argument that STM is a particular cultural experience, in chapter nine I consider what it means to talk about cultural change and how (as well as why) this might take place. I draw primarily on the theological language and perspective of my own evangelical context, but I hope these will offer resources for fellow travelers in other Christian traditions in which

STM has also become a significant feature of religious life.

The final chapter lays out some of the directions I hope this book might lead. In terms of continuing research on STM, I suggest that anthropologists, along with other social scientists, theologians and perhaps even some poets, have a great deal more to contribute to our understandings of ourselves. In theological terms, I encourage us to think together about how STM might fit into a larger and more robust understanding of God's work in the world as we join his redemptive work.

2

"Are You for Them or Against Them?"

DEFINING SHORT-TERM MISSION

Whenever I tell someone, particularly a fellow Christian, about my work on short-term missions, the most common response is the question "Are you for them or against them?" This is a natural question to ask about what has become an enormous—and somewhat controversial—movement. Should our churches continue putting considerable resources toward these trips if they don't "work"? Are we simply financing foreign travel for privileged teens, or are we making a difference in the world? While it is not my intention to quantify the worth of short-term mission definitively, the question does raise the issue of what, exactly, a short-term mission is. How is it differentiated from other types of mission or from travel generally? To be "for it" or "against it" suggests we know what "it" is.

Those asking me to provide a thumbs-up or a thumbs-down on STM likely have a view of what they believe a short-term mission to be. This may be the (stereo)typical high school, international service project in a developing country during a few weeks in the summer, but it could just as easily be one-day trips to the so-called inner city, a Habitat for Humanity building project or a two-year stint as a "missionary intern" working alongside a career missionary in another country. The term "short-term mission" has come to encompass a wide variety of travels, activities, places and time frames in the context of Christian theology and practice.

For my purposes, developing a singular definition of STM was not immediately crucial to my research. I already knew that, as a way to explore the creation and use of narrative alongside experience and practice, I wanted to focus on the one- or two-week trips in which high school students went out in a team. I could confidently argue that this high school trip was a *type* of STM without defining STM as a whole. But thinking about the nature of a short-term mission trip compared and contrasted with other forms of travel led me to some understandings of the trips that proved helpful in thinking about the cultural dynamics of this sort of travel experience.

Additionally, having a definition of STM helped give shape to how I structured the research project and the methodological theory and practice I used to explore my subject. I was convinced that an ethnographic approach would yield insight not available through other methods, but I also knew this would not be a traditional ethnographic study, such as those classic monographs of isolated island societies, small groups living in remote forest villages or other images of heroic anthropological lore. Some consideration of what sort of methodological approach was appropriate to this particular subject required consideration of anthropology and STM in more precise terms.

WHAT IS A SHORT-TERM MISSION?

Given the modifier *short-term*, it might seem that the duration of a mission defines a short-term mission from some other sort. However, not only is the question of what constitutes "short" a debated point, but the definition of *mission*—and its differentiation from *missions*—is often contested as well.

First, among our CWC team, a distinction between *mission*, as a singular noun, and *missions* in the plural, was never made. Looking through my notes and reviewing interview transcriptions, I see the terms appearing interchangeably. I have had conversations, in the context of STM and at other times, in which college students have asked about the difference between the plural and the singular terms, but it was typically a more academic conversation, with little pressing relevance to how the team members thought about their travels.

Many mission theologians distinguish *mission* as "the *missio Dei* (God's mission), that is, God's self-revelation as the One who loves the world," while employing the plural *missions* to "refer to particular forms, related to specific times, places, or needs, of participation in the *missio Dei*" (Bosch 1991, p. 10; see also Wright 2010, p. 23). Those I observed participating in STM did not make such a distinction, either narratively or conceptually. At the time, this was merely an ethnographic reality that I did not consider particularly significant. Later, as I reflected on the way an understanding of what "real mission(s)" was in the narratives of STM travelers, I found this to be an important consideration with ramifications for the ways these trips were constructed and interpreted. I address the importance of this theological and definitional consideration for the STM narrative in chapter eight, but in the historical and ethnographic analysis, this distinction was not an aspect of our travels.

For those outside missiological studies, attempting to create a definition of short-term missions focuses less on the idea of mission and more on the length of time and what should be considered "short." Today, in thinking about the popular image of the STM team as a group of relatively untrained laypeople traveling for one or two weeks to a Latin American country, most people would likely view a two- or three-year service commitment to be an activity different in *kind* and not merely degree. Yet even the two-year term is unlikely to require the kind of language learning, financial support and cultural or theological training common among career missionaries. A researcher with the Overseas Ministry Study Center who explored the data reported in the fifteenth edition of the *Mission Handbook*, noted that in 1988, one mission research organization excluded anything shorter than two months from its statistics on the number of missionaries going out from the United States (Coote 1995). It excluded trips such as the one I would take from being counted as missions at all. Others have created categories of "short-term," "mid-term" and "long-term" to distinguish varying lengths of service, divided in a variety of ways (see Moreau 2008). Among those who keep statistics on missionary activity, no consensus definition of *short* has emerged.

Some advocates of STM have used a combination of theological and temporal criteria to identify a short-term missionary. Missiologists Enoch Wan and Geoffery Hartt (2008, p. 65) use a combination of duration and practice to define STM as "intentionally limited, organized, cross-cultural mission efforts for a pre-determined length of time without participants making a residency-based commitment of more than two years." Roger Peterson, founder of Short-Term Evangelical Ministries (STEM Int'l), and his coauthors add a strong theological element, defining a short-term mission as "the God-commanded, repetitive deployment of swift, temporary non-professional missionaries" (Peterson, Aeschliman and Sneed 2003, p. 110). They call this a "practitioners definition," but readily admit that this can't be a definitive definition, as they identify eight "defining variables" (e.g., length of time, mission philosophy, demographics of participants) as possible characteristics of a particular short-term mission. In all the possible combinations they identified, they suggested that there are more than 777 million configurations of a short-term mission (2003, p. 68).

For my purposes, rather than trying to determine a specific configuration of time, motivation or activity as categorizing a short-term mission, I was interested primarily in how people experienced these trips. This led me to consider not simply (or primarily) the physical realities of travel, but the kinds of social relationships or cultural context engendered by the travel. The focus, in other words, would be less on what people did or how long they stayed, and more on the cultural context and meaning of the trip, particularly for those making the trip.

The element of time is not irrelevant to how these trips are understood and experienced, but it is the cultural significance of these travels, as opposed to the time itself, that is important. Many STM trips today are designed to fit into the windows of time North Americans (particularly U.S. Americans) have for vacation travel. For working adults, this typically means a maximum of two weeks. For college and high school students, the time may be longer, but it is likely to fit into a summer break. Working adults choosing to spend a month or more doing ministry in another country generally have to shift their mindset from one of suitcase travel to steamer trunk adventure. Likewise, students spending six months or a year doing ministry away from home typically frame the trip as a more profound commitment—something akin to study abroad or a gap year—rather than a summer vacation-length experience. In other words, what defines a short-term mission trip is the cultural and social location of the traveler, rather than the trip itself.

Making the analogy of STM with vacation travel is not to make those equivalent categories. There is no question that for many of those participating in STM, tourism is also the foil to their travels. One of the most withering critiques of STM I have often heard is to call it "Christian tourism." One prominent resource for STM preparation advertised by voicing the provocative question "Real Missions or Christian Tourism?" and invoked all the negative associations of tourism as shallow, self-centered and trivial, versus the substantial work of "real missions." My purpose in comparing STM with tourism, or even specifically religious travel such as pilgrimage, is not to denigrate STM or to suggest that it is something other than what people think it is. My definition should not be seen to suggest that STM is not "real mission," since I argue that the notion of what a real mission is comes from a changing and dynamic narrative itself. At the same time, looking at the structure and narratives of STM in light of research on tourism and pilgrimage does illuminate cultural aspects of travel generally that help explain STM as a cultural travel narrative.

SHORT-TERM MISSION AS TOURISM

From the beginning of my research on STM, it was clear that those going on short-term mission trips did not want to be confused with tourists. For example, soon after I began to consider STM as a research topic, I took a trip to Asia to visit several student interns in our college's development studies program. On the longest leg of my journey, from Los Angeles to Bangkok, I encountered a group of short-termers from Southern California. Some twenty-five members of the college group from a large congregation in Fullerton were on their way to Kolkata (Calcutta) to work among the poor.

During the long flight, I had several occasions to talk with the leader, an Asian American pastor with an obvious passion for what the group was about to do. When I asked what inspired him to choose Kolkata as the site for their work, he explained, saying something like, "I wanted to take them to the hardest place. Calcutta is the most difficult city in the world. We didn't want to head off to some tropical paradise or just hang out somewhere; I wanted a trip that would be right to the heart of what ministry is about, so we can do ministry and not just a vacation."[1] Similarly, in a recent conversation with a college student, she compared her three STM experiences (the first to the Caribbean island of St. John and the second two in Zambia and Ghana), noting that the first was disappointing because she did not think people "really needed [the STM team]," and it was "too much like a vacation," whereas "in Africa you can really just see the need. We could really make a difference."[2]

Over time, I found that this distinction—service versus vacation or missions versus tourism—was a common one, often made strongly by those preparing for an STM trip. College students with whom I have spoken, those participating on our Dominican Republic team and many others who have participated in STM trips often take pains to clarify how the trip was different from other kind trips they had taken for personal reasons. Paul Wright, one of the adult members of our DR team, was a businessman who had traveled internationally quite a bit

---

[1] I was just beginning to think about studying STM at this point, and I realized this conversation would yield interesting insights into the phenomenon. Although I did not record this conversation, I wrote down as much as I could remember when I returned to my seat. Using informal conversations as ethnographic data is stock-in-trade for anthropologists, and depending on the circumstances, I was occasionally able to transcribe particularly memorable phrases word for word. In other cases, I put words in quotations marks to indicate they were speaking, but preface the remarks with qualifiers to note that these may not be perfectly accurate transcriptions of their words, but represent the tone and content of their remarks.

[2] The astute reader will note that this is quite similar to the words of a student cited in chapter one who had been to Mexico and "Africa." In fact, these two students were together telling me about their trips. I did not manage to write down the words of the first student, but I was able to recall the words of the second more exactly. They were struck (as I was) by the similarity of their experiences.

before taking his first STM trip to Wales. When I spoke with him early in our preparations for the Dominican Republic, he reflected on the differences between these kinds of travel.

> We spent a lot of time preparing, maybe too much. But it's not like you're going to just visit, or you're going to do business. We didn't always even know what to expect, how to prepare. So, we're planning out all these great events, but didn't start thinking about the spiritual end of it until . . . I started thinking, "I should prepare for this." . . . It's a really different thing, to be a spiritual leader and be ready for whatever they need you to do.

Some of the kids preparing for the DR trip were even less sure of what to expect, having not been on an STM trip, but they were similarly committed to the notion that this kind of trip would be different from "just travel." Prior to our trip, I talked with the students who would be traveling, meeting with them in groups of three or four, usually in a coffee shop or on the campus of Wheaton College. Each time I asked some version of the question "Why do you want to go?" the answers invariably referred primarily to missions, service and other theological categories, although the students did not dismiss the fun of travel, a sense of adventure, being in a new country and the other aspects of travel. What they did reject, universally, was a conflation of the trip with tourism.

In one interview, Jeanie, one of the younger members who had not been on an STM trip before, said, "I guess I just want to see for myself, what it's really like . . . " Then she paused, and Amina, an outgoing girl who had traveled more and seemed to have a stronger sense of purpose jumped in: "But not like a tourist or anything. I mean, it's not like we'll just be staring at them." The group laughed at the image of our group gawking at Dominicans for thirteen days, as well as Amina's acted-out version of a gawking tourist with wide eyes and mouth agape. The point was clear; this was a different kind of trip.

The ubiquity of this distinction and the forcefulness with which it is often expressed betrays the awareness travelers have that STM trips share a lot in common with tourism. The infrastructure needed for travel—the airports and airplanes, buses and hotels—are the same for the two groups. The logistics of international travel such as passports, vaccinations and visas are common experiences, but there is no doubt that it is not the physical similarity that unnerves STMers when it comes to defining their travel against that of the tourist; it is the cultural implications of the "tourist" they reject.

STMers are not the only ones with an aversion to the tourist label. Anthropologists and other scholars of tourism often begin their articles or books with an apologetic about the importance of their subject, anticipating the objections of their fellow anthropologists and perhaps readers generally, who might scoff at the study of a seemingly trivial and even distasteful activity. One well-known anthropologist of tourism, Sharon Gmelch (2004), entitled the introduction to her widely read anthology of tourism research "Why Tourism Matters." She notes that her students doing ethnographic fieldwork in Barbados are "always horrified" when mistaken for tourists (2004, p. 3). Scholars, too, first encountered the study of tourism as "barely respectable," given its seeming superficiality. Gmelch also notes, however, that some of the initial reluctance on the part of scholars to study tourism came from the uncomfortable closeness of tourism to anthropological research: Westerners venturing to remote or "exotic" places to see the other for themselves can make the anthropologist appear suspiciously similar to the tourist, but with research grants (2004, p. 7; see also Crick 1995).

It is a mistake, however, to think that comparisons of STM with tourism are necessarily negative or that tourism is only a boorish, insensitive exercise in personal indulgence. Anthropologists who have studied tourism have been able to use these forms of travel to demonstrate many aspects of globalization, modernity and cultural change generally. They argue that many tourists are, in fact, more like modern pilgrims, searching for (or creating) meaningful experiences of encounter and otherness, leaving the everyday world of their lives for something "more real" to be found somewhere else. By comparing the research on tourism and pilgrimage with STM, we can see how STM is also a cultural journey, informed by a practice and narrative of movement from the margins to the center, where Christians have a chance to experience something different, new and, in many respects, "more real" than the lives they temporarily leave behind.

One of the early serious studies of tourism came from Dean Mac-Cannell, professor of sociology and critical theory at University of California, Davis. His book *The Tourist: A New Theory of the Leisure Class* (1976, p. 42) argued that tourist travel was not simply a pleasure-seeking activity of a moneyed society, but also a cultural ritual, structured in ways "precisely analogous to religious symbolism of primitive peoples" in order to create a sense of connection and respond to the pervasive alienation of modernity. Feeling disconnected from a sense of place and relationships at home, tourists seek to recover a connection to "authentic" life. He argued that tourists are particularly drawn to performances of authenticity in which people around the world determined what would be best perceived as their "authentic" culture and then created displays for tourist consumption.

What counted as authentic, or came to fulfill this role, were those sorts of performances, places, sites and experiences that had received "ceremonial ratification" by tourists themselves. In other words, the visits tourists make, the ways they interact with particular sites and experiences, and the ways they talk about and represent those experiences become a kind of ritual of authenticity, making particular places more real and authentic than others.

As MacCannell (2001) continued to study this interaction of expectation and experience, he argued that this led to changes in the places tourists chose to visit, suggesting that the practice of tourism has caused the emergence of a "tourist culture." Travelers to various places come to expect a particular experience, enacted in locally distinct terms, but this is not necessarily a real product of that place. As different localities around the world are drawn into the tourist structure, their distinctive local identity becomes a patina over a uniform tourist culture. He writes, "When the culture of tourism succeeds in replacing local culture, it becomes increasingly difficult to distinguish between destinations" (2001, p. 388). The tourist culture is a "total experience," a type of ritual itself, in which the values and expectations of the traveler shape the experience to fulfill the expectations, in a closed cultural feedback loop. The quality of these experiences, as noted by Norwegian anthropologist Ovar Löfgren (1999), are rated and assessed based on how "magical" or profound the experience, not unlike how a participant in a religious ritual characterizes the feelings and experience of participating in a worship service.

Since MacCannell's work was published, this idea of tourist travel as a kind of ritual has been picked up by a number of scholars who have studied the interactions, language, photos and consumption of tourists, uncovering the patterns and processes that make them meaningful, just as rituals take everyday objects or common experiences and elevate them to special or sacred status. Nelson Graburn (1977) has likened the tourist experience to an altered state of consciousness in which departure from the "workaday" world produces a sort of "high" before the traveler is forced to descend back to daily life. He went so far as to call them "sacred journeys" that took on a cast of transformative movements toward centers of authenticity, human engagement and vitality, as world-weary workers from the "developed world" found oases of respite among the "simple," "primitive" and "isolated" worlds of beach-dwelling natives. In these ways, tourists, unlike those going on retreat or up to a summer cabin on a lake shore, set out not simply to exploit the beauty of the landscape and relax, but to have an experience, even a transformative one, that has transcendent, if not spiritual, dimensions.

This is not to say that tourists necessarily set out with some sort of religious experience as their objective. It may be the surprise of finding something meaningful in "mere travel" that makes the experience meaningful at all. Lofgren, writing on the history of vacationing, notes that

> in the history of tourism there is a strong normative element in discussions of experiences. They are not only framed, localized and memorized, they are also weighed, measured and ranked. They can be described as rich and poor, deep or shallow, full or empty, strong or weak to name a few of the metaphors used. How do we know when we have had an experience or even a peak experience? (1999, p. 95)

The answer, he argues, comes from the narrative framework and the subsequent experience that create meaning for the traveler. These are not conscious rituals or planned moments; indeed, they only work if they "take us by surprise" and "send a shiver up [our] spine," such as when we see the famed Mona Lisa for ourselves or gaze at the Grand Canyon in just the way we had always imagined it or suddenly find ourselves "lost" in Venice only to "stumble upon" the most picturesque café or delightful vendor we had only imagined in our dreams. Yet while these moments (or at least the feelings that accompany them) are not planned, they are anticipated and expected, desired and described, long before the trip begins. Travelers anticipate a transcendent experience in which they are "renewed" in the temporary (and sacred) space of holiday, vacation or getaway.[3]

When taking tourism as this cultural process, surrounded by its own narrative of travel, discovery and personal growth, it is not hard to see the connection to short-term mission. While the label of tourism strikes many as anathema to the spirituality and theological significance implied by the idea of Christian mission, as anthropologists of travel began to take seriously the deeper significance many so-called tourists invested in their travels, they began to question the distinction of tourism and other, seemingly more profound, types of travel. In particular, this explication of tourism as a kind of secular travel ritual caused anthropologists to look at the more developed literature on pilgrimage as a sort of analogy, if not an overlapping subject (see Badone and Roseman 2004; Coleman and Crang 2002; Swatos 2006; Timothy and Olsen 2006). Scholars of STM, including me, have considered it more closely connected to pilgrimage than to tourism.

SHORT-TERM MISSION AS PILGRIMAGE

Pilgrimage, as a consciously ritualized practice, has been the subject of anthropological study longer than tourism, but as in MacCannell's 1976

---

[3]These very terms suggest the sacred, transcendent nature of tourist travel. Holiday comes from the word *holy*. *Vacation* implies something is vacated, or emptied, of what it contained. The idea of a getaway is self-explanatory, but the notion of escape implies a kind of freedom or boundlessness that does not exist in everyday life. This is right in line with anthropological notions of liminal space as a social space "betwixt and between," emptied of encumbering social norms or outside normal social life.

book, key texts in this research came from the anthropology of the 1970s. Victor Turner, often writing with his anthropologist wife, Edith Turner, published several influential works analyzing pilgrimage as a social process, a "sequence of social dramas and social enterprises," whereby the movement from staying at home to living temporarily abroad, from the familiar to the strange, secular to sacred, and the exchanging of normal social relations and hierarchies of the whole society for the shared community and unity among the small team is embedded in religious language and beliefs, and experienced in embodied practices.

Turner developed a structuralist theory of pilgrimage, comparing a wide variety of pilgrim processes to other ritual processes, such as rites of passage (*rites du passage*.) Following the social theory of Emile Durkheim and the theories of ritual developed by Arnold van Gennep and Turner, Turner suggests that pilgrimages were structured around phases of separation, liminality and reincorportation for the purposes of heightening religious awareness and anchoring social structure.

By way of example, Turner draws on cases of pilgrimage from many religious traditions and cultural contexts, but devotes a great deal of attention to the Catholic pilgrimages of Europe. In these examples, he argues, are the elements of structure and "anti-structure" in which pilgrims use the physical movement of the trip as a way to experience a social reversal away from the everyday hierarchies of social life to a new, temporary space in which they can experience unity and equality—what he calls *communitas*. Often characterized by physical hardship, bonding created through commonality (such as common clothing, ritualized language or behaviors that mark the pilgrim off from those of "normal" life) and the voluntary submission of the individual will to that of the group, the pilgrimage is structured to strip away worldly distinctions to allow for a heightened sense of the spiritual through the experience of unity with other pilgrims. When pilgrims return to their lives, they bring with them an increased sense of faith, drawn from the temporary experience of spiritual awareness, social equality and freedom from social constraint experienced in the journey (see Turner 1974, pp. 166-230).

Early in my own studies of STM, I could see a clear parallel between the structure of pilgrimage in Turner's accounts, and the rhetoric—and often experiences—of short-termers. My first research assistant on this project had gone on a number of short-term mission trips as a teen. She told of one trip in which the staff began the journey with a ritual moment of separation in which every student handed over his or her cell phone, music player, personal food and spending money to the staff. To further emphasize the separation phase, during the flight to Peru, the STMers were not allowed to watch the in-flight movies, listen to the radio, accept the meal and drinks being offered or even talk to one another. They spent the five-hour flight in prayer and personal Bible study, she recalled.

Once they landed in Lima, wearing their matching T-shirts, the team carried their bags several miles to where they stayed during the mission. The dorm was deliberately stripped of material comforts, such as mattresses. Their time was tightly controlled, spent entirely on a work project and in evangelism. She recalled that, even then, she was a bit dubious about the methods, but it had the effect of creating powerful bonds between the team members and with the leaders. By emptying themselves and giving up the privileges of their wealth, they could experience the "authentic missionary life" and bond with each other and the poor among whom they lived. She recalls that she left with a sense that they had endured and sacrificed for the sake of the kingdom, and drawn closer to God as a result.

The comparison of STM and pilgrimage is one that several researchers have noted. Priest writes,

> Like pilgrimages, [STM] trips are rituals of intensification, where one temporarily leaves the ordinary, compulsory, workaday life "at home" and experiences an extraordinary, voluntary, sacred experience "away from home" in a liminal space where sacred goals are pursued, physical and spiritual tests are faced, normal structures are dissolved, *communitas* is experienced, and personal transformation occurs. (Priest, et al. 2006, pp. 433-34)

Similarly, Don Richter (2008, p. 36) suggests that

the mission trip has emerged as a contemporary form of pilgrimage among Christians of every stripe. Mission trips draw on the structure of classical pilgrimage: traveling away from home, shared liminality and practices on the road, communion with "saints" in distant lands, and returning with a transformed heart. Mission-trip veterans yearn for the life-centering community they've encountered while on the road.

What both comparisons suggest is that, like tourism and pilgrimage, STM is a culturally mediated form of travel with particular dynamics. But considerable overlap notwithstanding, STM is a separate phenomenon. Narratives of pilgrimage and tourism emphasize the individual and her or his experience of travel and transformation. Even where group dynamics are intrinsic to the experience of the journey, the narrative of personal transformation remains at the center of the tourist *cum* pilgrim narrative (e.g., Holmes-Rodman 2004, p. 27). For the STM traveler, personal transformation, adventure and spiritual growth can only ever be by-products of the trip. As I heard many times at Central Wheaton Church, what makes STM different—the reason it is *not* tourism—is that at its heart, its essence, it is about sacrifice, service and calling; to be done correctly, STM had to be "real mission."

Short-Term Mission as Real Mission

When talking with a colleague who also studies STM about the central argument of this book—that the missionary narrative serves to shape and, in some ways, inhibit the expressed purpose of STM—she enthusiastically inquired, "So you've figured out the missionary narrative?" Of course, I had to backtrack quickly to explain that I certainly had not figured out the *singular* missionary narrative, but I did think I had a handle on how the view of missions within evangelicalism (if not Christianity more broadly) shapes the STM narrative. While many historians, missiologists and anthropologists have devoted their careers to telling the historical events of particular missions and missionaries, including magisterial works covering everything from the apostle Paul to the present day, history is not the same as narrative. Certainly particular histories are narratives, but the missionary narrative through which the short-term team of CWC learned to view our travels was a larger, guiding narrative that provided a framework for thinking about ourselves and our travels rooted in history, culture and institutional memory(ies).

At its most basic, a narrative is a story, a sequence of events in which one event leads into another. Narratives may be short or long, true or fictional. Within every culture, narratives are important means of teaching about the world, understanding right from wrong and thinking about people, nature, life and God. Jesus primarily used narratives (e.g., the story of the old woman who lost a coin and the parable of the sower) to teach his disciples, although he did not use only narratives. A statement such as "blessed are the peacemakers" is a teaching without a narrative context, and we certainly live with a great deal of nonnarrative in our lives. (Single images, such as a photograph with no caption, a single-panel cartoon or a work of visual art do not, in themselves, carry a narrative.) But all societies live with a great deal of narrative—be it myth, sacred scripture, fairy tales or epic histories—to explain the world to themselves (see Berger 1997).

Contemporary U.S. life is awash in narratives dispersed through television, print media, national myths, electronic rumors and classic novels. We use these more than ever to explain the state of the world to ourselves. As philosopher Michel de Certeau (1984, p. 186) wrote, "Our society has become a recited society, in three senses: it is defined by *stories* (*recits*, the fables constituted by our advertising and informational media), by *citations* of stories, and by the interminable *recitation* of stories." Since he wrote, we have become only more immersed in the stories and retelling of stories as media have developed to make it easier to communicate.

For many Christians today, the telling of a missionary narrative is a significant part of understanding faith, the Christian community and, as I argue, the STM trip. The missionary narrative I found in the ethnography of my team, in the testimonies of my students and in the self-representations of various STM groups is not simply a history, or a retelling of experiences, though it is not disconnected from either. The missionary narrative I encountered at CWC and have heard with regularity among my own students flows out of a missionary identity and history, particularly in the U.S. context, to become a Christian story that powerfully shapes the framework of the STM trip.

The contours of this narrative will emerge in the chapters to follow, but in brief, the narrative follows something of the Great Commission, in which Jesus commanded his followers to "go therefore and make disciples of all nations, baptizing them in the name of the Father and of the Son and of the Holy Spirit, and teaching them to obey everything that I have commanded you" (Mt 28:19-20). Thus the mission involves something of a "go" element. This is typically imagined spatially but can also be imagined socially. "Make disciples" and "baptiz[e] them" translates into "sharing the gospel," evangelism or building the church. In other words, mission is a theological enterprise that should result in an increase in Christian faithfulness among those to whom you have gone. The element of going to "all nations" invokes the typically foreign, or at least crosscultural, implication of the word *mission*.[4]

My point here is not to argue that the missionary narrative internalized by the members of my team or by Christians generally is consciously drawn out of this particular Scripture, but rather that Matthew 28 provides a neat device for demonstrating the elements of the narrative. The narrative itself is rooted in the processes described by de Certeau of telling stories, citing stories and reciting stories.

Central Wheaton Church has an annual mission festival in which long-term missionaries return to give testimony of their work. I had the chance to attend in 2008 when the theme was "All Scripture to All People." The evening service I attended began with a visiting women's choir from a midwestern Christian college singing songs in Swahili and Hindi, and a "South African" song (in English). The sanctuary was festooned with flags from the nations in which supported missionaries were working. After the initial songs, Pastor Nate introduced the fourteen missionaries (of the nearly one hundred supported by the congregation) who were present for the festival. They processed up the central aisles in their national garb, carrying a Bible. The first was an Ethiopian couple, followed by white U.S. Americans working in such

---

[4]Numerous histories chronicle the development of mission as an activity and idea in the church throughout the centuries, including how these terms have come to evoke particular activities and theologies. See Neill 1964; also Ott and Tennett 2010, pp. xiv-xviii.

places as the Czech Republic (wearing rugby jerseys and soccer shirts), then those from India and Japan (in full kimono). Included in the colorful procession was a single woman working on a "Midwestern college campus." She wore typical U.S. fashion. In the final spot, a Bangladeshi man supported as a missionary of the congregation came carrying an empty bookstand representing the lack of Scripture translations for many languages.

The "story" told throughout the service was that because of the faithfulness, sacrifice and obedience of the missionaries and their supporters in the congregation, millions of people around the world now had translations of Scripture in their own languages. Most importantly, however, there remained "much to do." After the parade of missionaries, Pastor Nate cited statistics about how many languages lacked any or all of the Bible, how many adults are illiterate throughout the world and the degree to which many governments suppress the distribution and teaching of the Bible. All this was the concern of missions and missionaries.

There was more to the service, which could be broken down for the ways it told a narrative of missions as the means by which God and his church are to be involved in growing the church around the world. It was not a triumphalist screed or a nationalist agenda in which the United States and the church were conflated. Nor was there much aggrandizement of U.S. culture or of that particular congregation. One prayer specifically referred to missions reaching into "the darkness near to us and the darkness far away from us." The idea of going to "darkness," bringing light and returning to tell the story was very much part of the narrative.

This might be seen as a contemporary version of what Jeffrey Cox (2005, p. 4) calls the "providentialist master narrative" of Western missions, in which "global Christian expansion is not inevitably triumphalist or celebratory or even heroic, but always focuses on the documentation of God's providential work in the world." This narrative also provides a way of understanding global Christianity and how the North American traveler is already connected to Christians elsewhere through missionary activity. Simon Coleman (2000, p. 6), an anthropologist who studied a Charismatic congregation in Sweden, observed that the language of global Christianity "involves the creation of a multi-dimensional yet culturally specific sense of reaching out into an un-bounded realm of action and identity. Seen in these terms, globalization is not merely a broad sociological process; it is also a quality of action, a means of investing an event, object or person with a certain kind of translocal value."

Mary Hancock, an anthropologist at University of California at Santa Barbara, explicitly connected this sense of globalism as a "quality of action" to the language of STM. In her insightfully argued paper, she suggests that by seeking to get outside their "comfort zone," a phrase endemic to STM narrative, travelers anticipated their en-gagement with others and with God in a qualitatively different place, a "global" space in which barriers of culture and everyday life could be transcended. "Mission," writes Hancock, "implies the encompassing frame of the global" (2011, p. 8).

For the team of short-term missionaries who would be going out from this large congregation well known for its vigorous support of mission work, the guidance stemmed from this idea of moving into "the darkness" of a global space characterized by spiritual and economic poverty, sharing the gospel, supporting "our missionaries" and returning to inspire others with the work. It was never stated plainly or as unam-biguously central to our trip, and the particular recitations of the trip various members of the team would have on our return complicated this narrative in various ways. But throughout our preparation, travel and return, this STM narrative, linked to global mission, figured promi-nently in the ways we would experience and reconstruct our travels.

What distinguishes the STM narrative from being simply a mis-sionary narrative is the awareness travelers have of their limits. We knew we would be in the Dominican Republic for only thirteen days, and several of those were to be spent enjoying the tourist activities for which the island nation is well known. We were acutely aware that we were a group primarily composed of high school students, most of whom did not speak the language of the people to whom we were going, had not done construction work and therefore could struggle with the labor or culture. It was clear that the missionary narrative would need to be slightly reoriented if we were going to imagine our travels in missionary terms.

NARRATING MISSION IN THE SHORT TERM

At the VBS held at a large Baptist church in Wheaton to which I took my children one summer, the week included a "mission project." The words were painted on a large, brown square of butcher paper and taped up in the main meeting room. At the end of each session throughout the week, the emcee reminded the kids about the mission project they were carrying out for "those in need." The project was bringing canned foods for the food bank serving low-income families in the apartments next to the church. It was a bit incongruous with the Jerusalem Market theme of the week, but certainly an effort worth supporting.

I recall being somewhat uncomfortable, however, as the emcee presented the drive to collect food. The congregation had made an effort to invite the children of families living in a neighboring apartment complex to attend the VBS, so throughout the crowd of mostly white, middle-class children were Asian, African and Latino kids, many of whom were from the families regularly receiving help from the food bank. As she presented the needs of those the food collection would benefit, she spoke as if those families were not present: "There are a lot of families that can't afford food, and God wants us to help them and reach out to them, so this week, we'll be just collecting the food and taking it to the food bank so we can be a blessing to those families who just need some extra help sometimes."

Although the mission project was to share with families sitting in the room, the rhetoric was that of missions somewhere else ("reach out") to others ("them" and "those families") to whom God calls "us" to be generous. This is not to suggest that this woman or anyone in the room did not recognize or welcome the families from the apartments (they had, after all, made a concerted effort to include them in the week's activities), but that the language of mission was about serving the poor somewhere else, who are different from us.

Mission as economic aid with moral dimensions and relational position was similarly grounded at CWC and among my college students. Many of the applicants for the college summer STM trips I have studied made reference to how they were looking forward to addressing the poverty of other countries in practical ways (Howell and Dorr 2007). Even those traveling to Europe often invoked the language of poverty and need, talking about the "spiritual poverty" and "cultural poverty" of Europe compared to the United States (or at least to the largely Christian communities in which they grew up). One of my students told me how some questioned her STM trip to Japan. She reported many of her questioners as saying something like, "I didn't know there were any poor people in Japan." Like the darkness referenced in the CWC's mission festival, poverty and alleviating physical need have become strongly attached to the notion of mission work generally and short-term missions in particular.

Addressing poverty, something that can be done on an STM trip without significant relationships or linguistic abilities, then becomes part of the narrative of a mission that meets spiritual, emotional and physical needs. Terry Linhart presented a particularly compelling example of this in his study of high school STM travelers to Ecuador, noting how they viewed their context through a narrative of poverty and spirituality, interpreting the actions of Ecuadorians as those of a people bravely carrying on in the face of desperate need. Sharing the particularly poignant experience of "Lauren," Linhart (2006, p. 457) offered her testimony of seeing a little boy who "lived with five brothers and his mother in a hammock," bringing the gift of a bag of fruit to the visiting North Americans—giving "all that he had"—just because "he wanted us to have this fruit and to serve us in a way." This little boy represented all the poverty she perceived as she characterized him (and others) as "these kids (who) have nothing. No food. No house. They just live in a hammock and that's it."

As with the members of my team, a narrative of mission became the rubric by which Lauren interpreted the actions of the boy, the nature of her relationship with him and the circumstances of his life. She saw this boy as the poorest of the poor behaving in a way reminiscent of the widow in Jesus' parable. Recognizing the Christian nature of the North American team's service, the humble gift becomes an offering to God, like the widow's mite, representing his poverty and the team's godly witness.

Linhart goes on to note that the little boy did not, in fact, live in a hammock, but lived above the store behind the hammock the family set up each morning for the children. The family sold the fruit, along with other consumables, and brought them to the team as a courtesy for the work they were doing in the community. But less important than the reality of the boy's circumstances (at least for this member of the STM team), the example "shows how the visual and experiential aspects during a brisk cross-cultural trip dominate how interpretations are made" (2006, p. 457). I would expand Linhart's conclusion to suggest that it also demonstrates how prior narratives of poverty, crosscultural encounter, service and mission mediate the interpretations and experiences STM travelers make.

MEDIATED TRAVELS

In his book exploring representation, travel and tourism in Calcutta, John Hutnyk (1996, p. 1) describes Calcutta as a "cipher" onto which travelers can inscribe virtually any idea they have heard, read or imagined. On the first page, he quotes a Frommer's travel guide as saying, "Everything you've heard about Calcutta is true!" His point is that visitors encountering Calcutta do so only through the "rumors" of its existence: writings, testimonies of others, representations in film, television, print and photograph. He does not suggest that Calcutta exists *only* in these representations, but that the "pre-encounter" with Calcutta profoundly shapes the encounter itself. "The 'rumour' of Calcutta refers to that imaginary Calcutta of guidebooks and charitable Western sympathies, but also to the experience of Calcutta which sometimes impinges upon those who visit *despite* the guidebook protocols" (1996, p. 3, emphasis in original).

Naturally, as I read Hutnyk's work on tourism in Calcutta, I thought of the team I met while flying to Asia. Had they read the guidebooks? What rumors had they heard? Clearly, the pastor leading the group had a notion of what he was leading his group into—the "hardest place" he could think of—but he didn't talk as if he had been there himself. Had he been inspired by Mother Teresa? Had he seen *City of Joy*, the 1992 film starring Patrick Swayze about a missionary doctor in Calcutta? However he had come to his understanding of Calcutta, it was clear that his trip—his missionary journey—was motivated most of all by the desire to sacrifice for the sake of the needy and the gospel.

For some of the members of our team, the Dominican Republic was a cipher as well, but even those of us returning to the DR learned to set aside what we knew and start fresh. For us, our whole trip was a cipher. We did not go primarily because we wanted to see the Dominican Republic. We did not go, first and foremost, to grow or learn or have fun. Our whole trip was a cipher, and deliberately so. We were going because God wanted us to. We were going because there were needs in the Dominican Republic that we could, and thus should, meet. We were going as a way to give something of the blessing we enjoyed as relatively wealthy North Americans to those living in a context marked by poverty and deprivation. To whatever extent personal benefits would be realized, and even valued, they would be made secondary in our understanding of what it meant to be on a short-term mission.

This understanding of mission, however, was not unique to CWC, nor was it something that grew up only in the context of STM. The notion of missionary work—what it means to do "real missions"—is an idea with a history in which we found ourselves. It is to this history that we turn next.

Part Two

THE HISTORY OF A
NARRATIVE

3

"That's No Missionary!"

REDEFINING MISSION AND
THE MISSIONARY ESTABLISHMENT

◆ ◆ ◆

IN 1967, WADE C. COGGINS, assistant secretary to the Evangelical Foreign Mission Agency, wrote an article in the journal *Evangelical Missions Quarterly* titled "Whither the Short-Termer?" When the STM movement was in its relatively early stages, Coggins was on the leading edge of asking where this new practice might go within the established evangelical missions community. More than forty years later, we can venture an answer to that question, but our vantage point should prompt the reverse query: Whence the short-termer? Specifically, how did the notion of the short-term missionary in the form seen today come to occupy this prominent position in the imagination of so many U.S. Christians? What were the roots, in terms of language and practice, of this widespread phenomenon? How did trips lasting no more than two weeks come to be called missions?

The next three chapters explore the history of the STM narrative through the lens of the established North American evangelical missions community, the growth of parachurch youth movements and the development of STM programs at CWC. This is an admittedly limited

historical study of a much broader shift in mission practice and thought
in the United States. A book-length history of this phenomenon deserves to be written, bringing together Catholic, Orthodox, Mormon,
Mennonite, evangelical and mainline Protestant practices. Certainly,
among the parachurch organizations and even the avowedly evangelical
mission boards examined here, there were participants and influences
from across the Christian spectrum.

Moreover, STM did not develop exclusively in the North American
context. Today there are hundreds of similar programs around the world,
drawing in countless participants, expressing a historical development
and narrative context quite different from—and even at odds with—
North American narratives (see Priest and Priest 2008, pp. 66-67).
Thus, by focusing on North American evangelicalism, I do not mean to
imply that these were the only, or most important, strands in the growth
of STM practice and narrative. It is for more practical reasons that I
have chosen to focus on the evangelical threads of the story.

First, my own location when beginning this project was Wheaton, a
center of evangelical intellectual life in the United States. The Billy
Graham Center Archives on Wheaton College's campus contains the
records of numerous evangelical mission agencies, interviews with hundreds of missionaries, board minutes, magazine clippings, newsletters
and correspondence. Organizations such as Short Terms Abroad
(STA), an early advocate of short-term missionary service, have do-
nated boxes of correspondence, memos and minutes. As a repository of
evangelical writing on twentieth-century mission, these archives are
surely among the best in the world.

Second, it was this evangelical history that led into the context for
my own experience with the Dominican Republic team at CWC in
2006. In 1985, the twin movements within evangelical missionary organizations and a more diffuse Christian youth movement came together in the life of CWC. The history surveyed here is meant to con-
textualize the ethnography of our team within the evangelical
missionary past of the twentieth century, as well as illustrate the historical processes of narrative formation common to Christian communities more generally.

This first of the three chapters in this section focuses on the institutional context of evangelical missions and the emergence of STM as both an innovative practice and a conceptual shift in the wider missionary community. While the nodes of influence are diffuse, this survey of writings from and about STM (and STM-like travel) from the mid-twentieth century suggests that the practice of STM grew around ostensibly pragmatic and theological reasons. What began as a movement to respond to needs and opportunities of mission, however, became the occasion for a significant shift in the understanding of what a missionary is.

SHORT-TERM MISSION AS A RESPONSE TO CRISIS

In an introduction entitled "Age of Crisis," mission scholars Arthur Glasser and Eric Fife (1961, pp. 9-10) characterized the end of the 1950s as "a time of unparalleled crisis in world affairs; a period when crises have developed in every corner of the globe." The book, dramatically titled *Missions in Crisis*, argued that political challenges such as communism and nationalism, social challenges of racism and inequality, and ecclesial and theological challenges in the form of the World Council of Churches and liberal theologies of Europe and Latin America required a radical rethinking of missionary methods and revitalization of missionary zeal.

The declaration of crisis at the beginning of that decade foreshadowed what seemed to be a period in which evangelical missions experienced the best of times and the worst of times. Writing on the era from 1945 to 1969, evangelical mission scholar Ralph Winter (1970) called the time "Twenty-Five Unbelievable Years." This somewhat ambiguous characterization encompassed what he perceived as the negative and positive trends among mission work of that era. On the negative side, he, like Glasser and Fife (1961), pointed to the political and social turmoil of the world as inhibiting the ability to recruit and deploy missionaries. He likewise pointed to what he perceived as the theological challenges of the National Council of Churches (NCC) and liberal theology generally. He noted a "deepening pessimism" about missionary work throughout the mid-twentieth century.

On the positive side, Winter cited statistics demonstrating growth in the number of missionary organizations affiliated with the relatively new National Association of Evangelicals. "By 1968," he wrote, "the initiative in fundraising and personnel recruitment was clearly in the hands of a host of new agencies. Almost all of these were in the cultural and theological tradition of the Evangelical Awakening and, for the most part, expressed their interests outside of the historic denominations" (1970, p. 55). Winter went on to present tables illustrating the growth in the number of missionaries being sent out by these organizations. Notably, while several of the NCC affiliated mission organizations demonstrated a decline in numbers, conservative (evangelical) groups such as the Churches of Christ, Southern Baptists and Wycliffe Bible Translators experienced significant growth (1970, p. 53).

In spite of these bright spots, holding on to a sense of embattlement is a noted characteristic of evangelicals (see C. Smith 1998). In the nascent world of evangelical publishing of the late 1950s, the good news of missionary activity was often subsumed under the concerns of political and social change. The lead editorial in a 1960 edition of *Christianity Today* magazine declared, "Today no enterprise is so thwarted and threatened by forces all around it as the missionary venture" (F. Bruner 1960, p. 3).[1] Throughout the 1960s, articles appeared in evangelical missionary magazines expressing concerns for a flagging missionary zeal. The first issue of *Evangelical Missions Quarterly*, launched in 1964, featured the article "Hand Wringing or Hard Questions?: An Approach to the Candidate Shortage" (Fenton 1964). At the end of the decade, such concerns persisted. Herbert Kane (1973), a professor of missions at Trinity Evangelical Divinity School from 1967 until 1975, published a cautionary text with chapter titles such as "Missions at the Crossroads," "What Happened to the Halo?" and "Where Are the Candidates?" It is not surprising that a movement theologically undergirded by a sense of urgency and needing to raise human and financial

---

[1]*Christianity Today* was founded in 1956 by leading figures in the evangelical movement, including Billy Graham. The purpose was to bring a level of cultural engagement to the conservative movement that had, under Fundamentalism, made social withdrawal a noted feature of its identity.

resources would turn to a language of crisis to motivate its constituency. Whether this sense of crisis was warranted or universally shared, it was in this context of global social transition that mission organizations began developing the practice and language of short-term missions.

MISSIONARIES IN THE LONG AND SHORT TERM

The appellation "father of modern missions" is often applied to William Carey, a British Baptist who established an early presence of Protestantism in India in 1793 (cf. Neill 1964, p. 222). The modern missionary movement across denominations, regions and eras is far too complex to lay at the feet of one person; nevertheless, the model Carey practiced of learning local languages, translating Scripture and significantly adapting to the cultural context in which he worked had a profound influence on mission theology and practice in the English-speaking world. By the time of the World Missionary Conference in Edinburgh in 1910—an event mission historian Stephen Neill (1964, p. 402) credited with creating "the first permanent instrument of international Christian cooperation outside the Roman Catholic Church"—the missionary was overwhelmingly conceived in terms of lifetime service.

That is not to say that other models did not exist at or near that time. The LDS church had supported missionaries committed to fixed terms of service since the publication of the Book of Mormon in 1830 (Church of Jesus Christ, 2007). Mennonites and American Friends instituted a similar service term in the 1920s. In both cases, this pattern had explicit and implicit corollaries to military service and, like later STM trips, was geared toward youth (see Shepherd and Shepherd 1998; 2001). Mainline mission organizations approved a similar service term some time later. The United Methodist Church, for example, launched a program for recent college graduates in 1949, emphasizing development work, medical service and missionary support roles (Priest 2011). All these organizations, however, had different understandings of the missionary vocation. The LDS church certainly shared the evangelical concern with evangelism, but unlike the missionary rhetoric of evangelical groups, did not invoke the notion of a missionary call as being necessary or relevant to the role of mission work (Shepherd and

Shepherd 2001). Mennonites, American Friends and mainline Protestants had moved away from evangelism as the driving force of missions, adopting a more humanitarian focus for missionary work.

For those who remained committed to the Edinburgh definition of the missionary vocation, the idea of the short-term missionary was an oxymoron. It was not merely (or perhaps even primarily) the idea of missionary work being for a short time that contradicted the missionary category, but rather the notion of a missionary beginning with a specified term of service and explicitly serving in areas outside evangelism and church planting. From 1910 to 1960, a number of evangelical mission organizations developed or recommitted themselves to the recruitment and support of missionaries for career service and evangelistic efforts. By the end of the 1950s, however, a variety of factors converged to stimulate a reevaluation of traditional missionary categories and narratives.

It goes without saying that in the decades of the 1960s a lot more was changing in the United States than simply Christian missionary language. These wider social and political changes affected religion and missions in the United States in countless ways, but there were several aspects of technological and social change that would relate directly to STM. The success of youth movements, manifested in large-scale institutional forms such as the Peace Corps or Operation Mobilization, as well as more informally through college campus organizations, had profound effects on the conceptualization and realization of short-term missions. Technologically and economically, the growth of STM practice was made practical by the development of mass commercial air travel.[2] An economic emphasis on tourism as a growth industry in the Caribbean and Mexico combined with gains by U.S. labor movements and a competitive labor market offering greater paid vacation time

---

[2]The history of air travel clearly correlates with the growth of STM. As several historians of air travel have noted, it was only toward the end of the 1960s and into the 1970s that flight technology, air travel infrastructure (particularly in the developing world) and the growth of disposable income converged to make long-haul travel practical for the mass public (Heppenheimer 1995; Hudson and Pettifer 1979). Particularly significant in terms of the North American experience and arguably in the explosive growth of STM in the 1980s was the deregulation of the airline industry by the Carter Administration in the late 1970s (Sinclair 1998, 15).

brought millions of new visitors to the tropical countries near the United States (G. Gmelch 2003, pp. 5-7). The popularity of spring break as a travel opportunity for college students, though inaugurated in 1936 as an opportunity for northern athletes to train in the sunny southern climate, exploded in the 1960s as a mass youth movement (Bohn 2009).

Many more social, economic and political changes could be identified as relevant to the rise of short-term mission travel. Yet, as critical as the material and wider social conditions were for the development of STM, equally important was the reconceptualization of mission work that would open the way for the inclusion of our Dominican Republic trip in the orbit of missions in the twenty-first century.

REIMAGINING MISSION

At the close of the 1950s, Harold John Ockenga, a founder of the National Association of Evangelicals and widely known pastor of the influential Park Street Church in Boston Common, gave an interview to *Christianity Today* headlined "Rising to the Missionary Task." The interviewer was particularly interested in the success his congregation had had in both recruiting and financially supporting foreign missions. At one point, the interviewer asked about the practice in which "some churches send young people to work camps abroad during vacation time, or they have some of their young people suspend college courses for a year to help out at a mission station." Ockenga replied,

> I think that can all be used as a means of recruitment, provided you don't become wasteful of resources for we have so many desperate needs on the mission field. I hear of a church that sends 25 young people to the foreign field for a summer yet has a roster of only 10 permanent missionaries. That's all out of balance. We never sent anyone on a trial basis. Our young people got to the mission field by listening to the Word of God and seeing the need. (Ockenga 1959, p. 3)

For Ockenga, these short-term volunteers were only potential missionaries, rather than missionaries themselves. Recruitment was, in his mind, the only good reason to use such a strategy, and always as a supplement to "real" missionary work.

By the end of the 1960s, it is clear that practices such as the one that concerned Ockenga were more widespread. At the same time, many continued to feel as Ockenga and balked at the notion of encouraging prospective missionaries to *begin* their service with a term in mind. John Gration (1964), associate home director of Africa Inland Mission (AIM), wrote a newsletter column in 1968 that extolled the virtues of short-term work, but only if the short-termer started with a commitment to long-term service. His article "a.i.m's [*sic*] First Short-Termer" notes that by the end of the 1960s "short-term missionary service has become one of mission's current phenomena."

> Young people spend a year or two on the mission field right out of college, or even during their college career. Grandmothers fly to distant lands to assume missionary responsibilities. Doctors take a year from their busy States-side practice to cover for a furloughing medical man. AIM has had all three of these cases in addition to a number of other interesting short-termers. (1964, p. 86)

He goes on to point out that for AIM, none other than Peter Cameron Scott, the founder of the organization, first practiced a short term in the mission field. However, Gration makes it clear that he is making his point only in the most literal sense. After noting that Scott spent "only a little over a year on the AIM field of Kenya [and] four years before this he had spent a few months on the West coast of Africa," Gration gets to the point:

> Yes, Scott, AIM's founder, was a short-termer; but he didn't plan it that way. God called him home as he was just beginning his missionary career. It was God who chose to launch AIM through a short-term missionary. Does this maybe tell us that in missions God is more concerned with the commitment of a life than even commitment for a lifetime? (1964, 1)

Like others addressing STM, Gration goes on to point to the needs for skilled workers—nurses, teachers, doctors—who are needed in long-term missionary projects. But unlike those who are beginning to advocate for explicitly short-term service, he discourages those who would begin with the short-term timeline in mind.

> If you are just looking for an interesting couple of years in a foreign land, we can guarantee it, but we don't plan to provide it. . . . If a short term on the mission field is for you a substitute for what you know God really wants from you, then don't apply. Furthermore, if you are enlisting simply to get "missionary service" out of the way (like one's military service) so that you can follow your own plans for the rest of your life, please forget it. We are not convinced God wants this kind of a "volunteer army." (1964, p. 10)

In the end, he tells the potential volunteers to enlist without a timeline in mind. "We'll leave the time element up to Him. . . . He alone determines the length of one's service." (1964, p. 10)

Even when comparing Ockenga and Gration, responding almost ten years apart to the question of missionary term limits, it is striking that the earlier language from 1959 does not use the phrase "short-term mission" or even seems to have a handy phrase to employ. The interviewer gives instead a somewhat wordy description of the practice. By 1968, the phrase is readily available, though it has a slightly different tone. Perhaps responding to such relatively recent phenomena as the founding of the Peace Corps and the growth of Christian youth missions (discussed in more detail below), Gration seeks to maintain a distinction between the missionary vocation and the sorts of travel increasingly available to lay Christians. He acknowledges the short-term missionary work as a thing unto itself, but as the representative of a missionary sending agency, he is troubled by the implications.

MISSION BOARDS AND THE SHORT-TERM MISSIONARY

Mirroring the change from Ockenga to Gration, the short-term category emerged in the work of the larger evangelical missionary organizations as they began to recognize the practice of short-term missionary travel and sought to incorporate it into their network in some way. One example of this development appears in the records of the Evangelical Foreign Mission Association (EFMA). Founded in 1945, the EFMA (renamed the Evangelical Fellowship of Mission Agencies in 1992 and "rebranded" as The Mission Exchange in 2007) was established by the National Association of Evangelicals two years after its own inception to coordinate mission groups identified with the nonfundamentalist conservative Christian movement in the United States. This group chose not to merge with the venerable Interdenominational Foreign Mission Association (IFMA) over differences regarding the inclusion of Pentecostals (the EFMA was for it; the IFMA not so sure) and nervousness on the part of the EFMA that the relationship of their counterpart with older, so-called mainline denominations made them susceptible to liberalism. In spite of the decision to maintain its identity, however, the EFMA and IFMA had very similar objectives: to coordinate the missionary work of multiple agencies, assisting with logistical and administrative tasks.[3]

In 1952, the EFMA held a missionary retreat in Palos Park, Illinois. Among the dozens of pages of archived letters, notes and event descriptions were summaries of the training sessions and conversations on the agenda for the weekend. The discussions ranged from personal and family issues, such as how to educate children on the field, to structural issues, such as how best to navigate visa procurement regulations. One of the topics addressed in some detail was the recruitment and training of new missionaries, including the need to provide "a definite period for practical experience" prior to a long-term assignment. Embedded in a longer passage, "Qualifications for Missionaries," the conversation covered such things as education in linguistics and the need for more Bible and theological training. At this point in their history, however, there is no reference to "short-term missions" or short-term experiences as being a way to provide this "definite period" of practical experience.[4]

---

[3]During revisions of this manuscript in 2011, the IFMA (CrossGlobal Link) and the EFMA (The Mission Exchange) announced their merger effective October 1, 2011. The new organization is now named Missio Nexus.

[4]An argument from silence does not mean that no one within the organizations represented in the EFMA was talking about short-term assignments. R. Peterson et al. note that the Conservative Baptist missionary organization CBInternational sent "one couple . . . as MAC [Missionary Assistance Corps]" workers in 1958 to provide technical assistance to long-term missionaries (Peterson, Aeschliman and Rasmussen 2003, p. 244). Undoubtedly, conversations about the feasibility, economics and theological implications of such activity would have been discussed in the years prior. However, the lack of mention of these activities by EFMA leaders in 1952 suggests that, at least at that point, these ideas had not filtered into the wider evangelical missionary consciousness.

In the subsequent decades, the notion of short-term travel and service being used for the promotion of missions as well as the recruitment and training of missionaries appears in both conversation and institutional structure. In an "Advance Information" sheet dated November 1968, the EFMA announced a "future full-time director" whose responsibilities would be to "design . . . mission station tours planned specifically for your own mission, church or denomination" as well as "student tours for promotion of missionary recruits and study tours for colleges, seminary students and others." In pursuing a formal response to the desire for visits by supporting churches to the missionaries they support and viewing these visits as a recruitment strategy, the EFMA was reflecting the larger conversation going on among member agencies.

In 1965, the general director of Sudan Interior Mission (SIM), Raymond Davis, wrote of "A New Dimension in Mission" (Davis 1965), describing the newly established Sudan Interior Program (SIP). This program of "short-term assignments" for "specified need" was promoted primarily in terms of how it might help long-term missionary efforts and the national church in the countries served by SIM. "Short-term service," he wrote, "is first and foremost a missionary program. Its objective and goal is the calling out and development of the Church of Jesus Christ. It is not a substitute for, but a complement to lifetime missionary service" (1965, p. 26). In the article, Davis uses the term "short-term missionaries" alongside such labels as "short-term missionary service" and "short-term assignment." In a theme that continues into the present, Davis testified to the transformative effect of these trips on those who go: "Their entire remaining years," he averred, "will be totally different because of this short-term assignment overseas" (1965, p. 28).

Davis, like other missionary executives of his time, was not talking about high school youth groups traveling with a few adult lay leaders to do manual labor or VBS for twelve days. He presented the SIM program as one that brought needed skills to the mission field with short-term volunteers who, like career missionaries, applied as individuals who perceived a call from God to be missionaries. The language and design of the program reflected a strong commitment to the missionary as an adult who heard a "call" to give time, skill and resources to missionary work, still conceived as primarily evangelistic in nature.

The Southern Baptists established their own program for a kind of short-term service with the introduction of missionary "journeymen" in August 1965. A two-year term to "free career missionaries from routine jobs or help them begin new work" was aimed at recent college graduates and other young, generally unmarried Baptists, to expose them to missionary life while serving established goals of career missionaries. In a short piece introducing the program in their journal *The Commission* (October 1965, p. 4-9), the Southern Baptists provide a mostly pictorial depiction of the people going out in the first group. Four paragraphs of text accompanying the photo spread describe the earnest young men and women engaged in classroom preparation, in acts of service and in what appear to be mentorships with older missionaries; the term "short-term missionary" or even "short-term" does not appear. The use of the term "journeyman" evokes the guild relationships of the Middle Ages, suggesting a hierarchy of the short- and long-term missionaries, as well as the training, education and recruitment valued by mission agencies.

Coggins (1967) addressed the question of short-term versus long-term missionaries head-on. Noting the various programs that mission agencies had established to provide opportunities for short-term volunteer assistance to career missionaries, he reported on the burgeoning interest among groups such as SIM, Youth for Christ International and the newly formed interdenominational agency Short Terms Abroad. He noted that in an SIM survey of fifty-one agencies associated with the EFMA, "none of them viewed short-term service as unscriptural. Twenty-two of the fifty-one are now using 'short-termers' to some extent, while four others have used them, [but] currently do not have anyone serving this way. Of the twenty six who have been or are involved, seventeen promote it, nine use it but do not promote it" (1967, p. 157).

Coggins raised the objections he had heard or anticipated in response to the phenomenon: "1) Will short-term divert funds from long term? 2) Will short-term trips 'sidetrack young people from making a lifetime commitment?' and 3) is the service of the short-termer worth the cost?" (1967, pp. 158-59). He addressed each question in turn with testimonies and counter-objections from advocates of the movement; it becomes clear that he was not opposed to the practice. He did not, at any point in the article, refer to the "short-term missionary" or "short-term missions." He reserved that term for career, vocational missionaries. In other words, in 1967, some in the missionary community were ready to consider short-term work as laudable or useful, but not as "missions." For that conceptual shift to occur, the community of evangelical missions needed a shift in their understanding of the missionary.

SHORT TERMS ABROAD

One organization that formed exclusively around the vision of promoting short-term work, and ultimately redefined the notion of the missionary, was Short Terms Abroad (STA). In its Memorandum of Incorporation, filed in 1967, STA defined its purpose as being "solely for charitable, religious and benevolent purposes: including for such purposes, assistance to Christian missions in the United States and in other countries by recruiting and selecting personnel for special short-term service, and the making of distributions to organizations that qualify as exempt organizations under section 501(c)(3)" (1967, p. 1). What this meant, in practice, was encouraging their evangelical audience to reconsider the definition of missionary itself—apart from the exclusively career-oriented model—to include the short-termer as a missionary.

Judy Barr, who is only described as a secretary of STA, produced the most comprehensive discussion of how the organization wished to define the idea of short-term missions. In 1969, Barr wrote a manifesto in the form of a short book entitled *Overseas Short-Term Service*. Although throughout the work she continued to refer largely to "short-term missionary service," she spent much of the work defending the idea of the short-termer as a legitimate missionary. After giving the "biblical validity" of short-term work (including the examples of Noah and Abraham cited earlier) and criticizing the overprofessionalization of the missionary enterprise, she wrote,

> What *really* is missionary work? Generally people do not know that the work and responsibility of a missionary are the work and responsibility of every Christian. This misconception has arisen because somehow the call of God has been equated with a call to overseas missionary service. The results of this emphasis have been detrimental to the cause of Christ. Laymen have failed to understand and grasp their responsibilities as Christians, and potential candidates for overseas service have been confused and misled. (1969, p. 13, emphasis in original)

As STA moved ahead in the 1970s, the sorts of testimonies shared, promotional pitches made and language evoked by it stick to the concerns of mission agencies in the years prior, namely recruitment of long-term missionaries and provision of specialized skills for the aid of those career missionaries already on the field. At the same time, STA began to lay the groundwork for these short-term workers to be considered full-fledged missionaries.

In their inaugural newsletter of 1968, STA published the testimonies of several who had taken advantage of short-term opportunities with various mission agencies through the referrals of STA. In each case, the success of the experience is given as the desire of the short-termer to return as a career missionary. A letter from Marlene LeFever, who traveled to Japan to teach at Christian Academy for one year, came from Tokyo as she began her (unanticipated) second year of service. She ended the letter, "I'd be happy to write to any girls who might be considering Japan. Mostly I'd warn them to bring twice as much stuff as they think they'll need for a year's stay. Short terms have a way of multiplying!" (Short Terms Abroad 1968, p. 5).

In this early push for the practice of short-term missions, it is clear that the vision remains at some distance from the meanings that would come to be attached to that language in the twenty-first century. In one newsletter column, STA leaders define the word *short* as "a relative term. In this instance, the short-term of missionary service is compared with the involvement of the career missionary. In this context a short term designates a period ranging from a few months to two years" (1968, p. 4). In the following year (October 1969), STA produced an application to be used by mission organizations to list possible jobs for prospective short-term applicants. The time frames listed are one to three months, three to six months, six to twelve months and up to two-plus years. There was nothing shorter than one month.

Later in that year, STA published in a color, trifold brochure for wider distribution at missionary conferences and other promotional opportunities in which the shortest length of time was listed simply as "summer." Few of the trips promoted by STA could be considered as analogous to the vacation-travel model adopted in later years. While the practice of STA remained a more significant commitment of time and energy than it would be twenty years later, by reorienting recruitment away from lifetime commitments, STA began advancing a discursive change that would open the possibilities for thirteen days in the Dominican Republic to be "real missions."

REDEFINING THE MISSIONARY

As STA developed its vision and structure in the years after its incorporation, it began forming strategic alliances with other organizations working to connect potential missionaries with appropriate opportunities, including the group with which it would eventually merge, Intercristo. Intercristo began when *ABC News* producer Phill Butler volunteered to produce public service-style announcements for a mission organization that needed to recruit teachers for the Belgian Congo in 1967 (Intercristo 2009). From there, Butler founded Intercristo, which today has expanded beyond mission referral and recruitment to Christian job placement generally. Short Terms Abroad began contacting Intercristo in the 1970s for assistance in promoting the idea of short-term missionary service.

In a letter dated June 29, 1973, Butler wrote to STA director Irving Philgreen that of the eighteen thousand applications being processed for mission work, "many of these" were looking for short-term opportunities.[5] In his correspondence, Butler, who regularly connected missionary applicants to many mission sending agencies, noted that the area of short-term assignments was growing to the point that mission agencies needed to consider structural and staffing changes to accommodate the change. At one point in the letter, he stated,

> There is a real need to encourage mission boards to assign a full-time staff member to the area of short-term service. Someone is needed to develop projects, provide orientation, give on-the-field direction and, finally, follow-up the participants. Without this specific assignment of responsibility within the mission boards there is going to be an increasing confrontation and dilemma surrounding this whole area of short-term service.

Part of the strategy, particularly for a former producer and media operative like Butler, became to redefine the image of the missionary in the Christian imagination. Like the mission agencies themselves, many Christians of the 1970s defined the missionary as a long-term or career worker in crosscultural Christian ministry. In forming a strategic partnership, Butler and Philgreen began to work together on recasting the term *missionary* to include more than career service and the tasks of evangelism and church planting. For example, the following is a radio spot proposed by Butler to STA in a letter dated May 30, 1973. Scripted as a conversation between two friends (with a few lines of voiceover), it is titled "PICTURES."

A. I'd like to show ya some pictures . . .
B. Of what
A. Missionaries!
B. Oh! All right!
A. Here! This is the first one . . .
B. That's no missionary . . . !
A. What?
B. That's no missionary, that's a mechanic! Anyone can see that!

---

[5]Throughout the letter, Butler uses "short-term service" and "short-term opportunity" rather than the phrase "short-term mission," suggesting that although some, like Barr, had published materials arguing for the short-term assignment as "real missions," there existed an indeterminate vocabulary, even among its proponents.

A. They can?

B. Sure. He's got grease on his hands . . . !

A. Well, that's because he IS a mechanic.

B. But you said he's a missionary

A. W'll [*sic*], he is! But he's also a mechanic—you might call him a "missionary mechanic" . . .

B. Wait a minute. . . . How can someone be a mechanic and a missionary?

A. The same way a person becomes a NURSE and a missionary.

B. Howzat?

A. By writing a letter

B. By writing a letter???!!!

C. 5,600 [originally 4,000, but crossed out and written in pencil] openings for SHORT-TERM Christian service. Openings for professionally-trained people as well as those with general aptitudes. To find out how you can be part of the SHORT-TERM service, simply write to INTERCRISTO, box 9323 Seattle.

B. Here, let me see another one of those pictures . . .

A. OK, here's one of another missionary

B. But this one shows a lady takin' care of some little kids. You tryin' to tell me that she's a missionary too?

A. (disparingly) I'll tell you what—why don't you drop a note to INTERCRISTO. . . . they'll explain SHORT-TERM service to you.

C. INTERCRISTO, box 9343, Seattle 98109

The effort to expand the semantic range of the word *missionary* suggests that a new agenda was emerging in the mission community. While most agencies and agency leaders still seemed primarily interested in short-term assignments as a support for long-term work and a means of recruitment, they were beginning to accept—indeed promote—the notion that to call these short-termers *missionaries*, the definition of that call would need to change.

There is no question that during the 1970s, the practice of STM (even as that term took shape) expanded in the evangelical mission community. In his report on the EFMA conference held in Overland,

Kansas, dated September 29, 1975, Coggins suggested to the board of directors, "We need to decide whether to include short-term missionaries in our report. If so, How short? Shall we show various categories, or shall we exclude those shorter than a certain duration (say two years) from the statistics?" The next year, the EFMA changed its dues structure to count short-term missionaries for the first time. The dues structure had for decades been determined by the number of missionaries a given agency supported; the EFMA charged per missionary. Although it is not clear from this report how the definition of short-term came to be delimited, in addition to the number of what they called "career missionaries," the EFMA added to the dues structure, charging member organizations $1.25 for each of the "short-term missionaries" they supported.[6]

At the same time, mission agencies, mission scholars and agency administrators were addressing the growth in short-term missionary work, student-oriented groups were riding the crest of their own wave of short-term foreign Christian ministry. It would not be until the 1980s and 1990s that these two streams would converge in institutional and intellectual work across the country, but the power of the youth in pressing for short-term missions was, without a doubt, a major factor in the explosion of STM today.

---

[6]From the Board Minutes, September 27, 1976, Overland Park, Kansas, submitted by Lester Westlund, p. 95.

4

"Youth Try the Impossible!"

Youth Movements
and Short-Term Mission

♦ ♦ ♦

Don Moore, a campus minister at Briercrest Bible College,
published a seventy-eight-page booklet in 1982 titled *Youth Try the Impossible!* The cover features four men working on a cinderblock wall,
dressed in the jeans and cowboy shirts still seen at worksites around the
world today. A man atop a high wall wears a hat in a style more like a
Latin American worker than a North American volunteer. His face is
obscured by shadow. In the center of the photo is a tall, handsome
blond guy in his late teens to early twenties, visibly straining as he holds
a cinder block over his head, presumably handing it to the worker on
top. Two other young men in denim shirts and work gloves stand on the
stacks of cinder blocks below, waiting to hand more to their hard-
working colleague.

The booklet uses a breezy narrative style, giving a third-person account of the adventures of various teams on "summer mission opportunities" in Europe, Latin America, Africa and Asia. With chapter
titles "Help Yourself . . . Help Others," "Expanding Your Horizons"
and "Making Your Mission Possible . . . Now!," the book aims to break
down the resistance youth and youth leaders have to leading groups on

service trips overseas. Moore is clearly convinced that crosscultural travel represents some of the best opportunities for Christian education (i.e., spiritual formation), developing group cohesion and personal development. He declares, "God can use your summer in missions to give definite direction as to what he wants you to do with your life" (1982, p. 42).

At the end of the book is a chapter devoted to promoting Missions Outreach, Inc., a Missouri-based short-term travel agency founded in 1976 to organize "summer youth work teams," connecting them with career missionaries around the world. Aside from the hyperbolic title (which, with the addition of a comma, would be a challenge to youth, rather than a description of their work), Moore's booklet is filled with encouragement to step up to the hard tasks ahead: "Have you got what it takes to go with the proper motive?" (p. 59); "You can make your mission possible now!" (p. 64).

Moore's work appears at the beginning of a decade in which the summer youth mission trip would gain enormous acceptance as it began growing into the massive phenomenon of the 1990s and 2000s. His booklet, while designed to promote a specific agency, addresses the questions of raising funds, convincing church leaders the trip is worth the effort and speaking to parents of the importance of such travel for the spiritual lives of their teens. Moore presents numerous anecdotes to heighten the expectations for prospective travelers in a way that later books and websites would repeat.

While a booklet in 1982 is on the early edge of promoting these travels among high school students, the travels of youth, particularly college and young adults, goes back to the middle of the century. In the transition of U.S. evangelicalism from the post-World War II era into the social change of the 1960s, young evangelicals were drawn to develop forms of STM on college campuses and as evangelistic outreach. Employing the rhetoric of evangelical fervor, spiritual calling and the power of youth, this movement would develop parallel to the mission board program until the mid-1980s when it would merge into the missions community through the institutional and discursive lives of churches and colleges across the country.

YOUTH MISSIONS IN THE EVANGELICAL MOVEMENT

Calls to youth for the cause of Christian missions have been woven into the U.S. missionary vision since the rise of U.S. missions at the end of the nineteenth century (Neill 1964, p. 312; see also Hutchinson 1987). With the founding of the Student Volunteer Movement and the Young Men's/Women's Christian Associations in the years prior to World War I came a new vision for youth to advance the kingdom of God worldwide. These new movements drew from the ascendant liberal theologies of the day, challenging the mission leadership of the 1920s to "heighten their concern for social reform and world reconstruction, to lessen their preoccupation with personal evangelism, and to begin meeting other world religions in 'humble dialogue'" (Hutchinson 1989, p. 157). Students in the first half of the twentieth century pushed to make missions a more comprehensive activity, embracing humanitarian as well as, or in place of, evangelistic work.

After 1945, conservative Christians, particularly young people, found many of the established mission agencies to be insufficiently evangelistic and, judging by the rapid increase in new organizations, unable to respond to the enthusiasm and ideas for innovation brought by a generation exposed to foreign travel and culture as never before. David Howard (2001), writing "the story of cross-cultural missionary outreach from Wheaton College," begins with the end of World War II and the influx of former soldiers under the G.I. Bill. Himself a student at the college from 1945 to 1949, he recalls the new students as more mature, wiser and more serious than their younger compatriots, but also with a strong concern for the spiritual condition of the world they had seen during the war.

> These men had seen the world as no previous generation of students had ever seen it. They had been around the globe in Europe, North Africa, and Asia, and they had a worldwide perspective never before seen among collegians. As Christians, many of these men had a great desire to go back and help restore the countries that had been so devastated. . . . As a result of this experience, these veterans returned to Wheaton with a vision to establish mission societies for the specific purpose of returning to the lands where they had fought. (2001, p. 4)

In these years (1946–1960), an enthusiasm for evangelism drove these young Christians into missions; short-term practices appeared more as consequences of life-stage than as an explicit embrace of missionary term limits. Two organizations in particular, Youth with a Mission (YWAM) and Operation Mobilization (OM), typified the rhetorical, theological and practical elements of these movements as they arose at the end of the 1950s.

YWAM. The founding of YWAM (pronounced "why wham") is recounted in the memoir of its founder, Loren Cunningham, published by the organization in 1984. This heroic autobiography was a bestseller portraying the inspirational story of how a young Assemblies of God pastor received a vision to begin a ministry in which "waves of young people" would go out to every country in the world in explicitly evangelistic mission work. Beginning with an evangelistic motive, combined with the awareness of social need that was part of the *zeitgeist* of the 1960s, Cunningham worked throughout the decades of the 1960s and 1970s to launch a ministry of young (post-high school) missionaries to travel throughout the world before beginning college or careers that may or may not involve missionary work. By the year 2000, YWAM boasted a staff of over eleven thousand worldwide who engaged in medical work, refugee resettlement, literacy training and other humanitarian work alongside their first focus on evangelism and conversion. In telling the story of how he came to envision this ministry, Cunningham (1984, p. 30) recalls a literal vision he had while visiting the Bahamas with a Christian vocal ensemble in 1956.

> That night after our singing engagement, I returned to the missionary's guest room with its white walls, unadorned except for an island scene in a cheap wooden frame. I lay down on the bed, doubled the pillow under my head and opened my Bible, routinely asking God to speak into my mind.
>
> What happened next was far from routine.
>
> Suddenly, I was looking at a map of the world, only the map was alive, moving! I sat up. I shook my head, rubbed my eyes. It was a mental movie. I could see all the continents. Waves were crashing onto their shores. Each went onto a continent, then receded then came up further until it covered the continent completely.

I caught my breath. Then, as I watched, the scene changed. The waves became young people—kids my age and even younger—covering the continents. They were talking to people on street corners and outside bars. They were going from house to house. They were preaching. Everywhere they were caring for people. . . .

Was that really you, Lord? I wondered, still staring at the wall. Amazed. Young people—kids, really—going out as missionaries. . . . If this strange picture really had come from God, there must be a way to avoid problems yet harness youthful energies.

The practice of young people, or old people for that matter, traveling for missionary terms was not unheard of at this time, as Ockenga demonstrates in his 1959 interview. In fact, Cunningham's concern with "a way to avoid problems" refers to the account of three young men who had gone to the Bahamas just before his own trip. He reports that, according to long-term missionaries living on the island, the Bahamas was "full of damaging rumors" due to these young men. At the same time, Cunningham (1984, p. 29) reports his response to their story as thinking, "What a neat idea they had—young people coming here to do missionary work!"

In the years following his vision, Cunningham would found his organization while facing some resistance to his passion for young people traveling for summer ministry. In his first conversation with the mission leaders of the Assemblies of God, he was convinced to send "vocational volunteers," that is, those with specific skills useful to current mission work. Later, the Assemblies of God would sever ties with Cunningham's new organization over his plan to send out hundreds of youth in teams to work on projects of their own. According to Cunningham, the denomination wanted to stay with the model of individual youth (ten to twenty per year) traveling to work with established missions for a time. What he was beginning to articulate, however, was a case for the trips being considered missionary work in themselves, rather than a means of recruiting future, career missionaries or directly supporting the work of current ones.

Operation Mobilization (OM). Similar to YWAM, Operation Mobilization grew up around the same time from a common evangelistic passion. George Verwer, who transferred to Moody Bible Institute from a small Christian college in Tennessee in 1958, was one of many college students inspired by the evangelism of Billy Graham and the newly established evangelism organization Youth for Christ (YFC). After participating in evangelistic crusades and door-to-door evangelism in the United States, Verwer was inspired to bring the practice to Mexico during a summer vacation in 1957.

Like Cunningham's Bahamian vision for YWAM, Verwer's trip to Mexico and his subsequent challenges for others to follow in his footsteps represent the "faith mission" in which prospective missionaries raise funds through their own networks (having faith that "God would provide") rather than through mission sending agencies. He challenged young people to throw themselves into whatever evangelistic or ministry opportunities were available during their breaks from school, and they shared stories of radical acts of generosity, mass conversion and miraculous healing as evidence that their travels were indeed within the will of God (Randall 2008, pp. 9-17).

Unlike YWAM, OM began with the idea that short-term trips should properly lead to career missionary commitments. As participation rates, staff and budget grew for both organizations in the 1960s, however, parachurch organizations such as these began to set goals for the distribution of literature, the number of countries visited or the number of doors knocked on in a given amount of time, seeing these as the evangelistic work in themselves, rather than as the prelude to long-term missions. Enthusiastic teams of young people sent to countries around the world for specific amounts of time no longer seemed ineffective or unreasonable as missions of their own.

These organizations coupled their goals to distribute "25 million pieces of literature" (Randall 2008, p. 31) or knocking on every door on every island in the Bahamas (Cunningham 1984) with strict moral injunctions against dating and sightseeing. Both organizations forbade participants from bringing spending money or other creature comforts that would accentuate the difference between the North Americans and those whom they evangelized. In its early years, OM did not allow participants to bring cameras "as if OMers were tourists" (Randall 2008,

p. 238n18). Though a new form of mission, these organizations began with an awareness of the overlap with other emerging forms of travel.

In addition to the strong spiritualized climate that YWAM, OM and similar groups created through their language of evangelism and action, these organizations benefited from another movement gathering steam at the end of the 1950s. The argument for the power of young people on term assignments to have a real impact in countries around the world gained a powerful advocate in John Kennedy as he ran for president in 1960. He made the use of young people as agents of good will and humanistic development a key part of his campaign. Early in his administration, after his election victory, he established what would become an inspiration for a generation of all U.S. Americans, but with particular resonance among Christians.

A CHRISTIAN PEACE CORPS

Presidential candidate Kennedy first publicly proposed the idea of the Peace Corps in a campaign speech to students at the University of Michigan on October 13, 1960. Building on ideas proposed by legislators such as Hubert Humphrey and Richard Neuberger, Kennedy told his youthful audience that "on your willingness to contribute part of your life to this country, I think will depend the answer whether we as a free society can compete. I think we can and I think Americans are willing to contribute, but the effort must be far greater than we have made in the past" (as quoted in Ashabranner 1971, p. 12).

As with the calls to sacrifice and the promise of youth heard from the leaders of YWAM and OM, Kennedy moved the notion of two-year service by young people for the betterment of so-called undeveloped countries to the center of the national conversation. He did not have to build his vision *de novo*, however. Early histories of the Peace Corps note the work of various Christian organizations sending young volunteers to work with their established missionaries as "forerunners" of the Peace Corps (Adams 1964, p. 4; also Ashabranner 1971). Charles Wetzel, writing in 1966, called Christian missions the "obvious antecedent" of the Peace Corps. He notes that Kennedy himself cited an innovative program founded by the Reverend James Robinson, an African American pastor in the tradition of what some would characterize as the social gospel (Sarkela and Mazzeo 2006, p. 45ff). Robinson founded Operation Crossroads Africa, an organization still working to bring U.S. and African youth together for summer work-study tours as a means to "bridge interracial as well as international misunderstandings" (Wetzel 1966, p. 7). As a church-based group, raising their own financial support and focusing on the development of interpersonal, crosscultural relationship with impoverished communities, Operation Crossroads Africa bears a striking resemblance—phenomenologically, if not theologically—to the practice of contemporary short-term missions.[1] When President Kennedy pointed to Crossroads as "the progenitors of the Peace Corps," he intentionally drew on the developing Christian impulses to combine youthful energy, Christian virtues and anticommunist, democratic American values to promote civic youth service in the twentieth century.

Public response to the Peace Corps was enthusiastic, to say the least. Within a few years of its inauguration, some ten thousand volunteers were being trained for service in over forty countries (Armstrong 1965). Major stories in *Time* magazine, the *New York Times* and elsewhere portrayed the volunteers as America's best and brightest, bringing democratic idealism throughout the world. Parades and gala sendoffs marked the sending and returning of the first waves of volunteers. Enthusiastic endorsements came from world leaders, U.S. politicians of both parties and media personalities.

Though Christian work served to inspire the creation of the Peace Corps, the success of the government program inspired many with the church to call for a redoubling of Christian efforts in line with Peace Corps practices. Roger Armstrong, a student of missions at Yale Divinity School in the early 1960s, wrote a comparison of Christian mission and the Peace Corps meant to encourage the church to look on the new movement favorably and to adopt many of its principles, such as living at a standard close to local population, sending young people for fixed terms of service and embracing humanitarian work. At the

---

[1]The quotation of Kennedy, as cited in Wetzel (1966, p. 7), is attributed to a self-published book from Operation Crossroads Africa, titled *Ambassadors of Friendship and Freedom*.

end of his introductory chapter, he said with palpable excitement,

> A new American is overseas, symbolic of a new movement that is taking
> place all over the world—a revolution of human advancement in which
> young persons are playing a key role. Few innovations during the past
> five years deserve as much attention, command as much respect, or will
> prove to be a significant as the Peace Corps. (1965, p. 36)

While not everyone in the missionary community or society at large
was as passionate about the Peace Corps as Armstrong, the Peace Corps
became a regular reference over the next decade as a symbol of the potential and promise of short-term assignments. Coggins specifically
cited the Peace Corps as a significant factor in the growth and interest
in short-term service (1967, p. 156).

Two years later, STA's future partner Intercristo conducted a survey
of college students at three Christian colleges in the Pacific Northwest.
In an effort to ascertain attitudes toward missionaries (assumed to be
career service), the survey asked which was more "relevant" to current
social needs around the world: Christian missions or the Peace Corps.
Eighty-four percent of respondents chose the Peace Corps over
Christian missions. An article by Baptist pastor Raymond Prigodich
(1969, p. 16), published in *Eternity* magazine, pointed to the founding
of the Peace Corps as having "stimulated expansion of existing short-
term programs and led to several additional mission organizations
into the field." He mentioned missionary leader Robert Moffitt as
endorsing the Peace Corps for offering "opportunity for meaningful
humanitarian service."

Also in 1969, an article appeared in *Evangelical Missions Quarterly*
presenting "What Missions can learn from the Peace Corps." The article suggested, in part,

> Most mission agencies place emphasis on lifetime or vocational com-
> mitment rather than short-term service. Young people are generally un-
> willing to sign for long terms—especially when needs are nebulously
> defined. Missionary service is often such an unknown that recruits have
> little basis for predicting success. Long-term commitment is simply too
> big a gamble.

A Peace Corps term is set at two years. Volunteers, I know, say two years is enough to identify real needs and to make a genuine contribution. Some mission leaders feel that mission programs can't be built on short-term service. Significantly over half of all returned Peace Corps volunteers have changed vocational plans while in service. Would it be presumptuous to anticipate similar changes with short-term missionaries? (Moffitt 1969, p. 236)

This combines the arguments that short-term service is long enough to make "a genuine contribution" with the idea that it is significant in shaping the life choices of participants. The language reflects the long-term missionary community's concern with recruitment, but it also echoes the concern suggested by Intercristo's survey results: many young people did not have a positive view of Christian missionary work generally.

In addition to providing inspiration for the development of short-term assignments within missions, many involved in the short-term movements of the 1950s and 1960s cited the Peace Corps as a model for training, purpose and philosophy. In her handbook for short-term missionary work prepared for STA in 1969, Judy Barr pointed to Peace Corps training methods and general expectations for volunteers as analogous to those that would work for short-term missionary assignments. She compares the work of potential short-term workers to Peace Corps and Christian Service Corps (an existing short-term missionary organization), emphasizing how the preparations used by those groups should inform agencies preparing to send out their own volunteers (1969, pp. 25-27).

This awareness and positive endorsement of the Peace Corps encouraged mission leaders to adopt the rhetoric of the Peace Corps, notably through the positive assertion of the ability of young people to make a difference in the world (*Youth Try the Impossible!*). Evangelicals, like U.S. society generally, were concerned that young people would grow complacent or rebellious without a challenge and purpose. The language of short-term mission, then, and the perspective of why and how it would proceed, began to flow from the social and spiritual concerns of a generation seeking to restore a positive image of the missionary, unleash the power of youth and challenge the potentially wayward generation to give their lives to the cause of Christ.

HIGH SCHOOL MISSIONS

The Peace Corps and Christian organizations such as OM and YWAM made the focus of recruitment on recent college graduates and young, typically single, adults in their twenties. It was not until the 1970s that high school students began pursuing opportunities for international travel, while mission agencies and congregations began to extend the initiatives of short-term missionary work to this younger set.

Including high school students in the work of short-term missions was an innovation of practice, necessitating a shift in rhetoric. No longer could these trips be promoted solely on the grounds of re-cruitment for long-term service or in a vision of the efficacy of vital young people pouring themselves out for the non-Christian world. Those impulses, along with the Peace Corps-like challenge to enter into a difficult but rewarding service of something significant, were not abandoned in the move toward youth trips, but they were married to the language of personal growth and spiritual development appropriate to thirteen- to eighteen-year-old students.[2] The move to bring teen-agers into the orbit of STM provided a reason to bring a far more con-scious appeal toward the personal and formative dimensions to the center of STM language and practice.

One of the first organizations to actively promote the use of teens in short-term (summer) missionary service was Teen Mission Interna-tional, Inc. (TMI). Founded in 1970, TMI recruited thirteen- to seventeen-year-old students to participate in teams traveling outside the United States for service projects or evangelistic outreach. Founder Robert Bland, who first participated in a version of STM through Christian Service Corps, gave his vision for the organization in an ar-

---

[2]Though the language of personal spiritual growth was not entirely absent from the summer missionary service programs of the 1950s and 1960s, the emphasis on missionary recruitment by the mission agencies, on the one hand, and the rhetoric around the power of youth on the part of early STM organizations such as OM and YWAM, on the other, kept personal consid-erations of learning about the world or experiencing personal growth out of the public appeals for support.

ticle appearing in *Christian Life* magazine in 1974. In addition to the familiar rationale that short-term trips would inspire young people to consider missionary work as an eventual vocation and the assertion that youth had the vitality needed in contemporary missionary work, Bland added a third element to the call: "Above all, [Bland's] young contacts represented the future of missions. They should be exposed to the urgent needs of foreign fields and sense the burden of a lost world during their crucial teen years. God seemed to be saying, 'You are somebody'" (Hardaway 1974, p. 67).

The final section of the article lays out the personal benefits of STM work even more clearly. "Does the impact last?" article author Gary Hardaway asked. He answered the question by first asserting that "a whopping percentage" of the students participating in a trip took second and third trips with TMI. Moreover, many of those decided to enroll in Bible colleges rather than liberal arts institutions, presumably testifying to their desire to abandon worldly pursuits and be devoted to Christian vocation. But the most convincing evidence seemed to be the changed attitudes and actions of former participants. With examples including returned short-term missionaries leading revivals in a high school and raising money for Nicaraguan earthquake victims, the article highlights the effects of travel on the travelers themselves. Parents were encouraged to support the participation of their children by quotations from other parents impressed by the impact of these trips. "Our daughter has come back a different girl," enthused one mother quoted in the article. "We are just thrilled" (Hardaway 1974, p. 68).

The same year, Kay Oliver, writing in *Moody Monthly*, encouraged teenagers to "beat that summer slump" by becoming involved in short-term missions. Like earlier appeals, hers encouraged the young Christian in her or his ability to make "a greater contribution to [God's] cause far greater than you ever dreamed," telling potential participants that they may "be taking the next step in discovering His will for your life." She led off, however, with the promise that teenagers participating in summer mission trips would "not only . . . see the mission field first hand, but also . . . experience the difficulties as well as the rewards of mission work" (1974, p. 80).

The rewards include the sense of significance drawn from the work and the satisfaction of knowing that the missionaries have been assisted in material ways, but her emphasis lies on the personal growth of the students in spiritual insight and relational life. Oliver quoted Joan Mc-Nichols, a participant in a teen team to Guatemala, as representative of what the teenage participants can expect:

> The first week we went to a service in a small Indian church. Some of the Indians had walked for two hours in the rain barefoot to stand in an over-crowded church and listen. These people and everything else we saw really heightened my love for other people, and I've begun to realize that wealth and money are of little importance. Love—especially God's love—is what is important. (1974, p. 80)

McNichols's language mirrors many of the sentiments that would be expressed more than thirty years later among the CWC students traveling to the Dominican Republic: a new appreciation for material blessing, admiration for the faith of the poor, renewed spiritual life. Hers is a familiar testimony of God working in a believer's life, but in this case, she brings that testimony to her experience of travel and mission.

The language of personal growth and spiritual formation begins to appear among college-aged participants in STM as well. *HIS* magazine, a now-defunct publication of InterVarsity Christian Fellowship, ran a story in 1976 titled "What I Did Over My Summer Vacation" to highlight several college students who had participated in the Student Training in Missions (STIM) summer mission program. Although the article began with a three-fold apologetic—promote interest in missions, serve others, personal development—the testimonials focused squarely on the facet of personal development. Susan Beyerlein (1976), a student at Michigan State University, wrote about her time in Austria, where her "mission" consisted of working at a Christian retreat center. Her story read, in part,

> Other than the beauty of the location, my expectations for the long-awaited summer were somewhat different from the summer itself. I was prepared for difficult things to happen to me, time of adjusting, and

times of coping in foreign situations. I would work this all through with God and thus become more dependent upon him. However, I was placed in a situation with many mature *American* Christians! I wondered how I could be a "student missionary" under these circumstances. Because I knew a bit of German I was assigned to work with Martha, one of the Austrian workers, in the mornings doing maid work. This pleased me because it gave us something in common, and a way for a friendship to begin. My other jobs around the castle consisted of waitressing (part of the castle was a hotel), working in the bookstore, library and Kiosk (a small snack bar).

After a few weeks I saw that God could use me in many different ways, and for me to limit him with *my* expectations was just wrong. I now have a better idea of how I can pray for the missions work taking place in Europe. God has been raising up a few committed Austrian Christian students which is encouraging, yet many more are needed.

Martin Luther once said, "We ask for silver and often God gives us gold in return." That's very much how I feel as I look back on my summer in Austria. (1976, p. 12)

In these articles, and throughout Christian publishing, the phrase "short-term mission" had yet to become widely used to describe what was variously coming under the heading "summer missions projects," "short-term missionary service," "student missions" and "youth missionary service," but the narrative was taking shape. Throughout the decade of the 1970s, these trips were becoming a means for relatively affluent U.S. Americans to expose their kids (or themselves) to mission work. They were opportunities to gain spiritual insight through experiencing the simple faith of the poor, encountering non-Christian/non-evangelized communities firsthand while enduring a taste of the hardships of living outside of the United States. For youth ministers, this would become a preferred method of bringing about their goals of spiritual maturation and emotional growth in their youth.

At the end of the 1970s, congregations were picking up the work of organizing their own short-term missions programs. Individual congregations saw value in these trips for their youth and adults. Two ministry leaders working at Central Wheaton Church (CWC) in the 1980s, one with youth and the other in adult missions ministry, each felt these trips would serve to promote missionary support while developing their members. Like the separate discursive streams running through the evangelical world, these two pastors saw their purposes somewhat differently, and even twenty-five years later, they used subtly different language to talk about the first trips that members of the congregation took in their separate spheres of ministry. In the early 1990s, however, the two streams had come together at CWC and the evangelical world in general, with all the turbulence to be expected at the union of mighty rivers.

5

"It *Will* Change Your Life"

SHORT-TERM MISSION AND
CENTRAL WHEATON CHURCH

SAM JOHNSON CAME TO CENTRAL WHEATON CHURCH fresh
from his seminary program. He had studied for a traditional pastorate
position, but with a few classes on youth ministry under his belt, he
joined the staff of CWC as its youth pastor, a logical first job for a
young man planning a career in ministry. When he started in 1984,
CWC had been taking youth group members on service trips to various
places within the United States, including to the mostly African
American communities on the West Side of Chicago, as well as some
further afield to rural Mississippi, New Orleans and New York City.
Many of these trips, particularly those involving air travel, were multi-
generational teams in which families brought their children so they
could serve together. The youth group leaders were taking high school
students on trips themselves, but they had not yet launched a foreign
mission program in which a team of high school students would spend
time in a foreign country.

I interviewed Sam by phone more than twenty years after the first
trip of CWC high school students in 1986. Now serving as a church

pastor in another Midwestern city, he recalled the CWC's first foreign mission trip for youth as a great success: "One of the best I have ever had." The trip had been a relatively long excursion (twenty-one days) to Ecuador with seventeen of the high school students in his youth program, and represented a significant expansion of the previous tradition of summer youth travel. Sam's inspiration had come from the work of several high-profile youth leaders who were regularly contributing to resources such as *Group* magazine and the publications of Youth Specialties, widely read resources for youth ministers at the time. Accounts of how these foreign mission trips affected the youth who went, and how such trips could be conducted, prompted Sam to believe that this could be the perfect opportunity for the youth of CWC.

One of the inspirational leaders whose articles Sam was regularly reading was Paul Borthwick. An early and widely published advocate of short-term missions with high school students, Borthwick was the youth pastor at Grace Chapel, a large congregation outside Boston that was an early entry in the megachurch movement of the 1990s. In 1981 he published a short booklet through his own congregation's publishing arm. As might be expected from something entitled *How to Plan, Develop, and Lead a Youth Missionary Team*, it's a highly practical thirty-five-page book with advice about everything from how to make contact with missionaries reluctant to welcome groups of high school students to the sorts of pictures the group should take in order to make a presentation upon their return. (He suggests twelve group shots, ten touring shots, various people photos, working pictures and "general shots," including unique animals, markets in the area and weather patterns [Borthwick 1981, p. 22].)

Unlike later books presenting much more by way of rationale (i.e., narrative) for the trip, this early publication sticks largely to practical matters. However, in the foreword, head pastor (and celebrity evangelical author) Gordon MacDonald notes the "extraordinary number of successful outreach projects" their church had been able to support through Youth Missionary Teams: "Parents have remarked over and over again that they sent their children off and received them back as men and women. But the payoff has been to hear one young person after another report that they yearn to hear God call them into some form of ministry or missionary service" (MacDonald, as quoted in Borthwick 1981, i).

Borthwick himself, in introducing the idea of youth missionary teams, gives "three principle (*sic*) reasons for tailoring these short-term opportunities for high schoolers," which he describes as "modeling," "memories" and "missionaries." Borthwick picks up on the earlier decade's emphasis on spiritual growth (modeling), personal development (memories) and recruitment, "plant[ing] seeds of desire in students which will bear fruit in the form of cross-cultural servants of Jesus Christ" (1981, pp. 1-2).

The tone and content of the book make it clear that Borthwick was on the leading edge of making these trips part of the youth program in a church. Although youth retreats, camps and even service work projects were widespread in evangelical churches in the 1980s, foreign travel was relatively rare. *Group* magazine, a publication for evangelical youth leaders founded in 1974, had a half-page advertisement in its 1987 spring issue promoting "workcamps" that *Group* magazine itself was sponsoring. In places like Romney, West Virginia, and San Marcos, Texas, leaders were encouraged to provide these experiences where "your group members will grow [by giving] them an unforgettable week at a *Group*-sponsored workcamp" (*Group* 1987, p. 78).

There was not, in that issue or volume, any mention or advertisement for foreign travel or "short-term missions." Within two years, however, the back page of the magazine featured a full-page advertisement for "an international workcamp mission of Christian service and love" in Xocenpich, Mexico. Like the West Virginia workcamps, this opportunity was also sponsored by *Group* magazine; the ad employed a similar pitch to encourage leaders to bring their groups to participate in the camp.

> Reach across international boundaries to change lives. Inspire a deep and lasting faith in your senior high group. Travel to the back-country of Mexico's Yucatan Peninsula. Heal the wounds of poverty by rebuilding crumbling homes for rural people. Watch your kids' understanding and compassion expand as they work to serve others in Christ's name. Plan now to put your faith into action. (*Group* 1989, p. 118)

Unlike the text accompanying the domestic workcamps, the international opportunity includes the word *mission*. The entire phrase "short-term missions" was not yet part of the appeal, but the model was there: a two-week trip to a rural, impoverished area for service and ministry. Moreover, the emphasis on personal growth was clear. In these advertisements, the rationale of missionary recruitment was absent, although for Borthwick, Sam and my own team at CWC, that remained part of the motivation. The vision of vital Christian youth creating lasting material change in the face of profound poverty *is* part of the *Group* magazine appeal, yet it is consistently linked with the changes youth leaders can expect to see in the youth group members themselves. This juxtaposition of the good done for others and the benefits to ourselves remains a source of tension in the language and motivation of short-term mission into the present. At CWC, it was particularly when the youth mission work came together with the adult mission program that the appeals of personal growth and the call for selfless service would be brought together.

"THEY STILL TALK ABOUT THAT TRIP"

Sam recalled that at CWC "the idea of getting kids overseas was not a slam dunk." Some members were concerned that it was "too much too soon" for high school kids to have international travel experiences. Sam was convinced, however, that this sort of experience would deepen the students' faith, teaching them something about themselves and the world. By the time he left with his seventeen students for Ecuador, Sam felt confident that this would be a trip with significant consequences for the students' faith. When we spoke, he narrated the memory of his anticipation of the changes he and other leaders believed they would see.

> We went wanting to get a bigger picture of what God's doing around the world. We wanted to go into those contexts really supporting and encouraging those who were there. It was really important for us that it wasn't just a work team, but that these kids could use their time, their gifts, their energy to further God's work in these places in another setting. That was a big part for me, for us. For a better sense of how God was working, you know, this whole idea of having a Christian worldview

and sense of God in the world—encouraging kids individually to deepen their commitment to Christ.

It is clear from Sam's overall account of preparing for the trip that he was not alone in his optimism. Raising money, he recalled, was not difficult, although each student only received a third of the money needed from the church budget; two-thirds had to be raised from friends, family and congregation members. Moreover, he noted that, though the trip to Quito, Ecuador, had no problem attracting seventeen students, shorter, less expensive trips to do service and mission work in Chicago had drawn only seven to nine participants the previous year. "[Some] parents were more freaked out taking the kids to the West Side of Chicago than they were about taking the kids down to Quito, Ecuador," he explained. "[Chicago] didn't have the travel glamour of an international trip."

The trip itself took the group all over Ecuador, beginning in the mountain city of Quito, to lowland Amazonian areas, through tributaries of the Amazon and along the Pacific coast. Although he had not taken a group on a trip like this, Sam had a clear idea of which elements to include.

> We had a real balance of ministry. We visited a public school, prison, churches, orphanages. . . . We got those kids up in front of five thousand people; we had our kids doing ministry with HCJB [an evangelical radio ministry in Ecuador] to paint their building. We were getting to know the culture of the country and a lot of face time with people everywhere we went—and getting down into a tributary of the Amazon. We went to Pizo and Papayapa, went to a retreat center. You know we had those kinds of things built in. It wasn't just work, work, work, but I was riding on the experience of Ridge [Burns] and Paul [Borthwick], and we did a lot of training. And all those things got our kids prepared. It's not like we didn't have things. We had those kinds of breaks and experiences that you need in a situation like that. It made it a really complete experience for us.

Sam and the team worked with a long-term missionary supported by CWC in Ecuador, but unlike the emphasis in earlier descriptions on short-term work, there was only a muted element of missionary recruitment in his narrative. That's not to suggest he didn't see the work itself as making a contribution to the work of the missionary. Sam remembered the effects of the students' ministry as successful and effective.

> We got set up with an Ecuadorian evangelist so while we were working the mime [performance], he was there to present in Spanish.[1] All the kids prepared their testimony.
>
> Q: In Spanish?
>
> A: No. No, in English. I forget his name right now; we had this wonderful evangelist translating. When we did ministry together, I think all the teams—we were all together. Wherever we went, we did the puppets; we did the music; we did the mime, in all those settings the kids were sharing their stories.

As the youth leader, Sam felt the strongest indicator of success was the testimony from the students themselves, even years later, about how meaningful the trip was to them.

> There was this general feeling of enthusiasm. One of the things people noted right away was the kids' excitement to be involved in something in that part of world that they were actually doing ministry in that kind of context. The kids came back completely different. The most significant thing that happened: seeing how God could use them in another place and coming back realizing that. Wow, God can use me and God did use me. . . . They still talk about that trip.

LIVES CHANGED, OR YOUR MONEY BACK

The plan to institute a short-term missions program for adults at CWC emerged just slightly earlier than Sam's first youth trip. Barney Torrance came to the church in 1975 as the director of Christian education. In the early 1980s, he and his family took a sabbatical as a chance for him to explore missionary work for himself. At the time, he didn't have a plan to investigate missionary work as a way to inform the establishment of a short-term program at CWC. Barney recalled that in

---

[1]In situations where the STM team does not speak the language, it is, at least today, common to prepare a performance in mime to communicate the gospel story, particularly the passion of the Christ, which is the central focus of evangelism for most of these teams.

1983 "short-term missions were not yet in vogue."

During his sabbatical, Barney and his family spent ten months in Manila, followed by several months in Japan and Taiwan. "I hated it," he stated bluntly. "I was living with a family in Metro Manila and [I had] culture shock big-time." It was something of a disappointment to his mother-in-law, who dreamed her daughter and son-in-law would become foreign missionaries. I didn't ask where his mother-in-law got her passion for missions, whether from personal experience or from her own romantic ideals of the missionary life as the pinnacle of Christian life, but her commitment to foreign missions inspired Barney to make "a deal with the Lord to run the missions program" at CWC.

Although he had been responsible for the missions program as the director of Christian education at CWC since 1979, Barney had not pursued sending laypeople abroad on short-term experiences. Only after his own experience outside the country did he see the value in personally "witnessing the mission field . . . and experiencing life overseas for themselves." Soon after his return, he arranged for the first trip of adults to travel to Bolivia to build an addition on the home of a long-term missionary supported by the church.

The work itself, he recalled, ran into several problems. "We didn't know what we were doing," he said. After digging the foundation, they realized they had forgotten to arrange for the municipal housing in-spector to visit the site and approve the work. At one point, they had to refill the hole they had dug for the foundation, complete the necessary paperwork and redo the work—all by hand. Although the rest of the project seemed to go smoothly, Barney recalled that the experience set the precedent, in his mind, for the future of these trips.

> At that point it was so new, people were saying, "What are we going to be doing?" People were concerned about the political climate and were they going to be sick there and were they going to end up in the hospital. That trip was eighteen or nineteen people, so we took a lot of people with us. We came back and it really became a seismic change when I finally understood that the purpose of the trip was not to do the work; the purpose of the trip was to change the people who went, because that's what happened to me when I went to the Philippines. How do we

not do the work? But the work is really secondary to the purpose of [the program, which] is to change people who go. So don't look at the importance of what we are doing; the importance is that you come back changed.

In establishing the program at CWC, Barney emphasized the aspect of personal change to the point that he convinced the mission board of CWC to "guarantee" the experience.

> Four years into this I went to the board of missions with a resolution that we would refund anyone's cost if it didn't change their lives. It doesn't mean you're going to be a missionary, but it will change your life. It will impact your life, and if it doesn't, we'll give you your money back.

Barney did view the trips as having material and social benefits for the long-term missionaries, including socialization with American teenagers for the children of missionaries and stronger social support for the missionaries when they returned for periodic yearlong furloughs in the Wheaton area. For the adult program, however, the idea of missionary recruitment was not the focus.

In those first years, there were some who questioned the expenditures, Barney recalled. The "real hardliners," as he called them, "were saying we were wasting money. They would say, why don't we spend seventeen thousand dollars on long-term missions. It wasn't a huge group, but they were there." For Barney, however, there was no question; the benefit for those who made the trips outweighed the financial costs. "The trips," he said to me, "become your best tool for discipleship at the church. If discipleship is becoming a deeper follower of Christ, there's almost nothing you do in the church [that is better] than these trips."

Barney recalled that in the late 1980s, when he and Sam were developing these travel programs, there were no other churches in the area with a foreign, short-term missions program.[2] He found himself invited to national conferences to speak about the program at CWC. Reflecting their newfound passion for short-term missions, as well as the

---

[2]Without contacting other congregations in the Wheaton area, I'm not sure if this is true or simply represents Barney's perception. There are several other large congregations in the Wheaton area that are quite active in STM today, so it seems likely there were other congregations at least beginning to develop their programs at the same time as CWC.

demographics of an unusually affluent and well-connected community, the congregation eventually made a commitment to get 50 percent of its members on a short-term trip. Some years after the program was well established, and the church was at or near its 50 percent goal, Barney moved to a church on the East Coast, where he was asked to reproduce the program.

The growth of STM in Wheaton corresponded to a growth of a wider movement toward international service trips, or "voluntourism," that began in the late 1980s and blossomed in the 1990s. In 1987, Bill McMillon wrote the first edition of *Volunteer Vacations*, a guide to international travel volunteerism that came out in its eleventh edition in 2012 (McMillon 2012). Groups such as Habitat for Humanity (founded in 1976 and receiving a tremendous boost in popularity when former President Jimmy Carter joined his first work project with the organization in 1984), Global Volunteers (founded in 1984) and Cross-Cultural Solutions (established by a former Peace Corps volunteer in 1994) developed models of using volunteers in vacation-length times to do service domestically and internationally. These and many other groups experienced significant growth throughout the 1990s and into the twenty-first century (see S. Brown 2005, pp. 23-27). Often employing a narrative of mission and frequently having some affiliation with Christianity (as in the case of Habitat), these organizations grew as ecumenical or secular parallels to the STM movement.

A key contrast between these movements and the growing STM phenomenon was the degree to which STM increasingly brought junior and senior high students into the work. In the 1990s, several books appeared promoting short-term mission trips for youth groups (Burns and Bechetti 1990; Anthony 1994; Aeschliman 1992). Throughout the decade, the wider missions community began to discuss the phenomenon much more vigorously. As the diffuse practices of STM gained wider recognition in the Christian world, the discursive context began to take shape. From the beginning of the decade, when several terms and phrases were advanced, until the turn of the century, when a more fully formed rhetoric existed, the language of STM would be engaged as a site of contestation over the nature, meaning and purpose of the trips.

The scattered efforts of parachurch and congregationally based short-term mission advocates emerged as a major phenomenon of evangelical life in the 1990s. Quite dramatically, the number of books, articles, guides and dissertations addressing STM went from a trickle to a flood. By the end of the decade, short-term mission, *sui generis*, had arrived. The challenges to STM language seen in the 1990s reveal the contested nature of narrative as various leaders sought to advance particular versions of the STM narrative. The terms that rose to the top created a discursive form that would carry through for another ten years.

NARRATIVES OF SHORT-TERM MISSION IN THE 1990S

Kim Hurst, with her coauthor Chris Eaton, published her short-term mission guide in 1991. She was the leader of a ministry at the large and nationally influential University Presbyterian Church near the University of Washington in Seattle, long a congregation associated with InterVarsity and youth/college ministry generally. Hurst had started a ministry there that she called Vacations with a Purpose. In their guide, Hurst and Eaton made a conscious effort to promote the use of the label "Vacations with a Purpose," or VWAP (pronounced "vee whap"), as a kind of synonym for short-term missions.[3] Certainly evocative of YWAM (Youth with a Mission), VWAP trips were intended to promote the goals identified by many others as central to the short-term mission experience: (1) experience a different culture, (2) interact personally with individuals of that culture, (3) serve the nationals and/or Christian workers in the culture, and (4) become "world Christians" through personal and spiritual growth derived from the experience. In the introduction, Hurst gives a narrative of the birth of the idea (and, in particular, the name) as coming from several dissatisfied vacationers who had recently returned from a trip to Mexico.

> Vacations with a Purpose began for me in 1985 at University Presbyterian Church in Seattle. Two members of the U.P.C. singles de-

---

[3]Hurst and Eaton gave the pronunciation in their introduction: "VWAPs (pronounced Vee-Waps) are short mission trips that give people the opportunity to meet new friends, live in community, experience a different culture, and best of all, see God at work" (1991, p. 16). The VWAP pronunciation is very similar to YWAM ("why wham").

partment commented on the beauty of their recent vacations to Mexico. But they felt frustrated that they had been unable to appreciate and know Mexico's finest asset—its people. Was there a way to get to know the people in a short vacation? What if UPC singles could spend their vacation with Mexican Christians? Six of us began to meet and pray about where we might begin. (1991, 17)

The narrative goes on to tell of a return trip, during which the vacationers spent time working in an orphanage and with internal migrant farm workers near the resort town of Ensenada. In what would become a familiar phrase, she concluded, "We went to serve and returned to Seattle profoundly served."

What has not become nearly such a familiar phrase is the term Vacations with a Purpose. A Google search in 2009 turned up one Christian organization based in Western Pennsylvania named Vacations with a Purpose, in which members take cruises or other explicitly touristic travels while agreeing to perform humanitarian tasks along the way. One other use of the phrase appeared in a headline within a Southern Baptist organization website promoting family short-term missions as "Vacations with a Purpose."[4] University Presbyterian Church, however, no longer has any mention of VWAP on its website. (Its short-term missions program is now a part of its larger Global Missions ministry.) Very few churches or organizations promote VWAP or similar language in their materials. No preparation materials or handbooks published after Hurst and Eaton's book make the term central to their title or concept. It seems that the notion of these being "vacations," albeit with a purpose, is not amenable to the concepts and ideals embedded in the emerging STM narrative.[5]

---

[4]As web-based resources are notoriously ephemeral, what has remained or appeared in the months since I did my search has undoubtedly changed. It is worth noting that several secular organizations used the phrase, either as an organizing concept or a promotional phrase (see Bell and Bell 2009; Demko 2009), but very few evangelical groups make use of it. (Note: Reach Ministries provides a link to "Vacations with a Purpose," but in 2009 that page was blank except for the heading.)

[5]Hurst continued to promote the language of VWAP through her own speaking. In 2005 she presented a workshop at St. Stephen's church in Sewickly, Pennsylvania, on VWAP. Interestingly, in her 1991 book on VWAP, she uses the phrase "short term mission(s)" only about half

The term that does capture these ideals is *mission*. However, this term reemerges as a site of struggle in the 1990s. In the October 1992 issue of *Evangelical Missions Quarterly*, two articles on STM appeared. One was by Seth Barnes, a former long-term missionary who had founded Adventures in Missions, a parachurch organization to organize short-term trips. Leslie Pelt, a missionary with SIM, authored the other. Barnes began his article arguing that STM may save the evangelical missionary movement. Citing the pessimistic view of a missionary agency leader, Barnes (1992, p. 376) wrote,

> Barring a reversal of current trends, the North American church may virtually drop out of the world missions enterprise in the next 20 years.
>
> Hope does exist, however. The short-term missionary movement is perhaps the most powerful force mobilizing new missionaries today.

Barnes went on to address the definition of *mission* head-on. In 1992, he wrote, "The changes are forcing a redefinition of our concept of a missionary. No longer is the mission field viewed as the province of an elite few. Increasingly, ordinary lay people are finding that they can be empowered to contribute to the missions enterprise with their time and talent" (Barnes 1992, p. 376).

In her response, Pelt (1992, p. 388) reasserts a traditional definition of *mission* as referring to long-term/career commitments to evangelism.

> If we are to reach the world's 1.3 billion unevangelized people, we need more full-time workers. When you think about all the lofty goals that missiologists and mission agencies have set for themselves, you realize that such things can't be accomplished by two-week or two-year missionaries. Mission organizations must require commitment from their candidates and challenge thousands of potential missionaries to biblical discipleship.

Tellingly, Pelt refused to use the term *missionary* in referring to short-term workers. "Short-termer," "short-term program" and "short-term trip" are all she'll allow in the description of these ventures.

Yet even then, Pelt must have known she was fighting a losing battle.

---

a dozen times. In her pamphlet of approximately one thousand words advertising her workshop fourteen years later, she uses the phrase four times.

The expansion of the missionary narrative was well underway, and the notion of the short-term mission was gaining considerable momentum. In the area of youth work, the writings of such leading authors as Borthwick (1988, 1991, 2003), Ridge Burns and Noel Bechetti (1990) were encouraging youth pastors to make the foreign mission trip a central event in the yearly youth group calendar.

Prior to the 1990s, most youth programs had some sort of summer trip as a significant event designed to promote group cohesion and spiritual growth among their members. Cooped up in a bus for fifteen hours, traveling to rural Mississippi for a work camp or to Colorado for a spiritual youth jamboree at Estes Park, was a staple of the youth group leader's repertoire.

In 1996, *Group* magazine published a special advertising section that listed over forty pages of ski resorts, retreat and conference centers, whitewater rafting companies and general trip planning tips. In 1997, the section had swelled to nearly one hundred pages and included eight pages devoted to "summer missions," listing companies dedicated to arranging short-term mission/summer service projects for youth groups. Some were domestic, but about half the offerings were international trips or had international options.

By the year 2000, one of the three cover stories for the May/June issue of *Group* was "The Summer Tripping Section." The first of the two articles in the section was about summer Christian music festivals; the second was entitled "Mission-Trip Prep: How a Seasoned Youth Leader Prepares Youth Groups for Summer Outreach Trips" (Bidwell 2000). As evangelicalism moved into the twenty-first century, the use of the terms *mission* and *missionary* in the context of youth work ceased to be problematic in these sorts of articles.

That is not to say that critics didn't continue to wrestle with the wisdom of STM. Throughout the 1990s and 2000s, articles questioning the expenditures and efficacy of such travels for youth or adults continued to appear (see, for example, Adkins 1991; Winter 1996; Fernando 1999; Loobie 2000; Adeney 2006; Priest and Priest 2008; Livermore 2004). The argument shifts ground, however, from the missionary nature of these trips—that is, the main argument is not primarily whether these trips should be called missions—to conversations about how helpful, effective or worthwhile they are in their own terms.

In 2000, two major evangelical mission publications, *Mission Frontiers* and *Evangelical Missions Quarterly* (*EMQ*), put short-term missions on their covers. The articles generally took an analytical-critical tone, arguing that STM should not be "an end in itself" (Hartford 2000) and that "short-term service is no substitute for the bedrock of long-term missionary commitment" (Bush 2000, p. 16; see also Slimbach 2000). Yet after rehearsing the critique of short-term missions in his introduction to the *EMQ* theme issue, editor Gary Corwin concluded,

> So what is the message? Short-term missions, both within the agency rubric and the more direct church-to-church variety, are not going away any time soon. Get used to it. Adapt. Innovate. And most of all, quit complaining and make yourself useful. When and if the Lord wants to change the emphasis, he's more than capable of changing the context. (Corwin 2000)[6]

The "accept or die" message comes through in several of the articles geared toward the established missionary community. The acceptance was geared toward the practice of STM; it seems that the language of STM—that short-termers are "real" missionaries—is becoming fairly settled. From 2000 on, debates about process, method and motive continued, but the semantic range of STM had become clear. For Corwin, the success of STM at drawing participants provided powerful evidence that the STM phenomenon, like mission work throughout Christian history, must be a work of God. Others, particularly educators speaking directly to the youth-oriented side of STM, seemed less convinced of the theological imperative (Slimbach 2000; Linhart 2006), yet saw their role as pushing the inevitable growth of STM in positive directions. Regardless of the presence of a divine imprimatur, the uniting of youth work with missionary concerns brought together the missionary narrative and the STM trip.

---

[6]Much like my argument here, Corwin notes, "The meaning of [STM] is bound up with what it reflects about our culture and time. Eras in missions, like eras in anything else, grow out of a context" (2000, p. 422).

EMBODYING A NARRATIVE

This short history of STM language, like most history, is largely that of leadership and the language of the elite. It is also, at many points, centered on the white, evangelical, Midwestern context of Central Wheaton Church and the particular contextual concerns familiar there. But in the particularity of this account are a number of notable features. First, as the STM phenomenon developed as a youth group staple, the dominant voices in the formation of the process were familiar figures of the evangelical community: white men with theological degrees firmly established within recognized, even prestigious, institutional locations. There are few women and no non-Western voices among those writing for the burgeoning youth STM movement.[7]

Second, within the history of CWC, the STM program began and largely continued through the connections of the congregation with their supported missionaries rather than through partnerships with local congregations. This pattern has not persisted across the landscape of congregations involved in their own STM programs, where many churches have established church-to-church partnerships with congregations in the countries to which they typically send teams (cf. Priest 2010). Yet, within the partnership model, the problems of uneven power relationships, unexpressed or unrecognized expectations, and dominant narratives often inhibit or even derail efforts to bring in the voices of those outside the context of the North American congregation (see C. Brown 2008, pp. 216-23).

Recognizing the institutional and contextual formation of the STM narrative assists in efforts to reform the interpretation of experience. But the history leading up to our trip in 2006 is only half of the story. Even at the level of CWC, rank-and-file members can't automatically take up the STM narrative offered by the leadership. The power of the STM narrative to shape the experiences of individual travelers comes from the embodied and encompassing prefiguring of the experience.

---

[7]Notably, Leslie Pelt, who played the "con" to Seth Barnes's "pro" STM article, is a black woman who graduated from Moody Bible Institute and Wheaton College's Graduate School with a degree in Intercultural Studies, and had published on the importance of diverse perspectives and experiences in the wider mission community (Pelt 1989).

How does the narrative become convincing, important and persuasive for the travelers? The next chapter explores how a particular narrative of STM becomes dominant in a particular team.

Contemporary anthropologists work from the understanding of culture as more than the worldview, values or ideas people have in their heads. Rather, a culture is found in the dynamic interplay of words, ideas, actions and reactions that shape individuals in community. Our lives are governed by a logic of practice, in which the ways we orient our bodies, put together our words and (re)shape our notions of the true, good and real are partly a product of the individual choices we make and of the cultural materials available, which constrain our choices. This dynamic of constraining structure and individual action (or "agency") is profoundly problematic for anthropologists, something that keeps us up at night and employed during the day. It also means that it is not enough to know what people think—or what they say about what they think—but we must also attend to what they do: how they create environments in which particular conceptual frameworks (narratives) become influential, persuasive, accepted and, often, taken for granted.

When I joined the preparation process for CWC's Global Outreach teams in 2006, I stepped into a process of embodying the narrative of our mission. Through a variety of particular practices—interviews, letter writing, informal conversations and formal lessons—our travels were framed, given a narrative and prefigured in ways that would shape how we experienced and retold the experience. The narrative was rarely explicit and never complete, but as we participated in its construction, it became powerful nonetheless.

Part Three

◆

TRAVELING
NARRATIVES

6

"Remember, These Are Real Missions"

EMBODYING A MISSIONARY NARRATIVE
AT CENTRAL WHEATON CHURCH

♦ ♦ ♦

IN EARLY OCTOBER, A LITTLE MORE THAN nine months before
Central Wheaton Church would send its Global Outreach (GO) teams,
the congregation was invited to gather to hear from the leaders of the
short-term mission program at CWC. This kickoff event featured
Pastor Nate, Charlie Gimble, the chairman of the GO leadership, and
Glenn Cantor, the leader of the adult short-term mission program
(Servant Teams Engaged in Mission, or STEM), each of whom would
present the plans for our summer 2006 STM trips. Not all the students
who ended up on the Dominican Republic team were in attendance
that night, but more than half of those who would eventually be in
Linda Vista with me were there to hear these leaders describe the different teams and the process of selection, organization and team formation. By the time that night's program began, more than one hundred
people sat at large, round tables spread around the room. Three tables
accommodated mostly high school students, while a mix of adults and
teens gathered around the other eight.

As I would learn was common at this tech-savvy congregation, the

evening began with a video. One of the leaders briefly welcomed us to
the evening before turning our attention to the large screen set up at the
front. The lights dimmed and music filled the room. Images of exotic
scenes began to play across the screen—giraffes silhouetted by the
sunset, zebras looking warily at the camera—and quickly transitioned
to photos of dark-skinned Africans engaged in daily tasks, some looking
at the camera without smiling in photos reminiscent of *National Geo-
graphic* and others wearing wide grins. The photos mixed in scenes of
what I assumed were CWC work teams putting up concrete walls,
playing with groups of children and posing with local people, white
arms slung around black shoulders, displaying the affection and af-
finity found among new friends met during their short-term trip. We
learned at the conclusion that the photos were taken from an STM trip
to Uganda the year before.

Behind the photos, cycling through in a Ken Burns-style montage,
were several popular worship songs. The first included references to
"the African plain," "the Amazon rain" and "Asian believers" singing
together with the rest of the world, "He reigns." The next songs also
had themes of foreign travel and Christian unity, creating a powerful
sense of God's calling and the missionary motive behind the images on
the screen. From the start, the tone was set, visually and musically;
among the unfamiliar foreignness of the places depicted, these trips
were being framed from the beginning as mission.

This was just the beginning of a nine-month process of forming
teams, preparing the members, raising money and arranging for trip
logistics. It was also the beginning of a process of embodied narrative
construction and cultural framing that would give our trip a particular
shape and meaning. As I discovered over the course of our preparation,
placing these travels in the context of mission work conditioned our
expectations of what this trip should be about as well as our narratives
of what it ultimately was.

I am not arguing that any member of our team came to assert a personal missionary identity in a full-orbed meaning of that term. Indeed,
several members found the missionary calling to be one almost too
high to be pursued. Yet the sense that our work was part of a missionary

calling surrounded our preparation and experience, affecting our interpretations of culture, poverty and tourism. Moreover, these narratives
were not merely ideological or linguistic constructs, but embodied dis-
positions created throughout our preparation, travel and return.

In the focus here on the preparation process itself, I explore how our
activities became the site of narrative adoption and creation, such that
these narratives would become powerful in shaping our later experiences. I explore particular aspects of this missionary narrative—as a
"cross-cultural encounter," as a sacrificial calling and as service to the
poor—to understand how the process of preparing to travel shaped
both the experience and the renarrating of our trip.

REAL MISSIONS AT CENTRAL WHEATON CHURCH

I had certainly heard a number of people at CWC and Wheaton
College, and even anthropologists familiar with the phenomenon,
question the link between short-term trips and the monikers *missions*
and *missionary* attached to them. At one point in the years before
starting my formal research, before I had read much of the critique
from within the missionary community about short-term practices, I
spoke with another anthropologist undertaking his own research on
STM. As we talked about the phenomenon in general, we began to
discuss the terminology and rhetoric involved, discussing what it meant
that these trips—so different from long-term missionary endeavors of
the past—had come into the discursive category of mission. Why were
those who were most committed to evangelism and the growth of
Christian churches embracing the inclusion of construction trips and
Vacation Bible School (VBS) programs in the orbit of missions?

This colleague had written several works constructively critiquing
and engaging STM, so he didn't find himself opposed to the general
practice. Yet, as we talked about why these trips were not framed primarily as educational travel, discipleship or some other Christian activity, his assessment was blunt and to the point: it was only by invoking
the term *missions* that congregational members were able to approach
others for funding in a traditional missionary fundraising model. As he
said at the time, "*Missions* is the money word."

Needless to say, the leaders at CWC did not consider the mission label from such a pragmatic angle. They understood missions to be theologically defined and practically effective service. Their interest was in making sure that each STM trip rose to the level of "real missions" they had in mind. In one meeting of the GO program's board of directors, I listened to a conversation planning for the recruitment of GO participants. In reviewing the post-trip evaluations submitted by participants, several members of the board remarked on how much people reported having learned about God, themselves, their team members, the countries they visited and so forth.

One member of the board, who had sent children on previous trips, enthusiastically noted how much her children had learned on the trip. The youth group leader echoed her comment, praising how much the students learned about "God's work around the world" and "the real differences in cultures out there." The conversation went on a bit, with various members suggesting how these educational benefits could be highlighted for prospective participants—until the most senior member of the board, who served as a representative of the congregation's overall board of mission said, "But it's important we remember this is real ministry. This isn't just travel, I mean, it's important that the kids are learning, right? But they're doing real missions. People need to see that these kids are with the missionaries, working alongside them. There is real benefit; these are real missions."[1]

These trips are meant to be understood in sharp contrast to tourism,

---

[1]This comment effectively ended the discussion of learning and personal growth. Everyone in the room seemed to grant assent to this notion that "real missions" was a priority over any secondary benefit. This board member's comment brought up a discussion of the long-term missionaries and how they were affected by these trips and how they went about requesting short-term teams to be sent to their sites. This was when I learned that short-term teams were sent only to those long-term missionaries who requested them and that there was some competition among those missionaries for the teams (not every career missionary who requested a team would get one). My first thought, when hearing this, was that this was an important way for the long-term missionaries to maintain support for their work among the more than one hundred missionaries supported by this congregation. In their subsequent discussion, various members of the board emphasized how much the long-term missionaries must need the help the short-term teams were thought to provide. Given that many of the long-term missionaries, such as those who served through *Ayuda para Niños*, had structured their work around the presence and contributions of short-term teams, both financial and practical support were likely important components of STM work, but the aspect of using STM teams for institutional support was not emphasized.

pleasure seeking or even educational travel. At CWC, this contrast—
"real missions" versus educational or leisure travel; "missionary work"
over the perceived or real benefits to those traveling—were themes
shaping how the process of preparation guided the development of our
narratives throughout the six months leading up to our departure.
Through the institutionalized and linguistic practices of the congregation, we were inducted into a particular way of understanding ourselves and our travels, reflecting a wider understanding of what a missionary really is and what it means to do STM.

MISSIONARY APPLICATIONS

At the end of the initial presentations in October, those of us in attendance were encouraged to pick up materials and an application at
the table on the way out. This marked the beginning of the next phase
of the preparation process. Students would submit their applications
for spaces on one of the five GO teams, while adults would apply to
become leaders. Many of the adult leaders of the various trips were
actually recruited to the position, since it invariably meant using vacation time or at least time away from family members. Even those
traveling with their own children on the trip were typically leaving a
spouse and younger children behind for the ten to fourteen days of the
trip. Nevertheless, adult leaders were likewise asked to fill out applications and sit for an interview with members of the church board over-
seeing the GO program.

　　These applications and interviews had a very practical purpose: to
learn more about the individuals and their abilities in order to put together teams in which various strengths and weaknesses could be bal-
anced. Charlie, the lay leader of the GO board, explained to me that
they wanted to

> make sure we can spread out the gifts. You know, we don't want all the
> Spanish speakers going to La Paz (Mexico), and some people are more
> administrative or take charge. You don't want all the administrators—
> people who can focus on details and getting things done—just on one
> team while all the kind of leaders or those who really like to counsel the
> kids are on one team.

These applications and interviews had another effect as well. The practice of speaking involved in an interview comprises what linguistic anthropologists refer to as "officializing" discourse. This refers to genres of speech that encode and express "particular orders of knowledge and experience" (Bauman 2000, p. 85) in which the speech and its form serves to reaffirm or resignify social relations to reflect common cultural understandings and shared context (cf. Csordas 1997, pp. 161-63).[2] In other words, the conditions of the interview and the performance of our speech made it an important moment in the creation of our subjective experience of STM and the narratives we would employ.

These were unlike job interviews or scholarship competitions in that all of us were aware that this was less about selectivity and more about forming teams. We knew we were going in to learn about what this process entailed as much as for the interviewers to gain information. It was often difficult to find the necessary number of leaders for these trips. If individuals were seen to be utterly unsuitable for leading such a trip, they would be discouraged from applying, and it was unlikely they would reach the interview stage if they did. Yet the form of the interview varied little, in terms of practice, from what would be expected in a more competitive process. On one level this was intentional, giving the process a seriousness that was meant to leave an impression. Speaking with Charlie in the year after our trip, I asked him why they stressed both an application and an interview when most of the applicants, particularly prospective leaders, were well known by the board. He answered primarily in relation to the student applicant, but it seemed to apply to the process generally: "Well, sometimes we learn things we didn't know . . . but it does communicate the importance of this; we're not just taking

---

[2]The term *genre* is typically applied to forms of written language (e.g., the mystery genre). In linguistic anthropology, however, it has become a more widely applicable term and helpful in understanding the different contexts in which speaking about the trips planned for the GO program took on more cultural significance for those involved. As developed by Mikhail Bakhtin (1986) and others (Bauman 2000; Hanks 1987), the notion of genre includes speech engaging the "emergent elements of here-and-now contextualization" (Bauman 2000, p. 85) worked out in "particular contacts between the meanings of words and actual concrete reality under certain typical circumstances" (Bakhtin, as quoted in Hanks 1987, p. 680). In other words, it is not enough to attend to what is being said, but it is also necessary to focus on the specific context in which speech is performed and interpreted.

someone because they want to go. Someone might want to go, and be great, but they should know it's serious. We don't want to turn kids down, but they need to know this is not just a fun trip."

In a case reflecting a pattern I saw in every interview, the interviewee was invited in and directed to a chair occupying a place alone on one side of the table, or even pushed back from the table, leaving the interviewee alone somewhat exposed in the center of the room.[3] Charlie welcomed the interviewee to the meeting and introduced the other members of the committee present. In this case, the committee was talking to Rob Wilson, an adult leader applying to lead one of the GO trips. Charlie began, "Okay, Rob, this is usually where I ask, why do you want to be a part of Global Outreach?" After a few more questions more specific to the individual, the chairperson returned to the interview schedule with the question "Just give us a sense for where your skills lie or what sort of gifts you think you could bring to the leadership team. Is it making lists and checking them twice? Or is it working with a student to build an atmosphere of mentoring and discipline and making sure their hearts are in the right place? Or is it building with a team spirit and going through and working surreptitiously through the day as things are happening and creating an atmosphere of teachable moments on the trip? Or . . . ?"

Rob answered about his skills in carpentry and construction, though he felt his real gifts lay "in the relational side of things," working with the high school students. In all the interviews in which I participated, the questions followed a similar form: identify your gifts and tell us about your interests and experience.[4] The most consistent element re-

---

[3]Many social scientists have noted the relationship between interviewers, context and interviewees as structuring responses (Aledo et al. 1999; Dijkstra 1987; Proctor and Padfield 1998), but beyond that is the structuring practice of the interview setting, invoking a particular set of social relations, authority, institutional structure and power (see Martin and Elwood 2000). The linguistic genre then circumscribes the possibilities while allowing the flexibility of participation and adaptation of the options. It was the sort of "officializing" of discourse in which those in the institutional position to set the parameters of the trip did so in a way that made these moments particularly influential in shaping our eventual travel narratives.

[4]I participated in six interviews with prospective GO team leaders, not including my own. The interviews for the students, though there were more of them, were more difficult to negotiate, because I needed to get parental permission prior to my participation. I was able to participate in only five of those. For that reason, I have not made conclusions or drawn as directly from

surfacing in the interviews was the link between gifts and tasks in the short-term mission endeavor. The majority of the questions turned on the notion of the particular gifts an individual brought to the team. Sometimes this referred to personal proclivities, preferences and abilities that might contribute to the effective functioning of the group. But the language of gifts served to invoke the more specifically Christian language in evangelical Christian discourse of gifts as God-given abilities.[5] In this way, the interview genre brought together the role of leaders and their activities such as "making lists" with the spiritual call of missionary work and ministry.

Several of the interviewees answered the questions about their gifts in a manner similar to a forty-something woman who said, "I guess I'd be more comfortable helping behind the scenes, getting supplies together, that sort of thing. But I'm open to whatever God needs me to do for the team." For her, and for most prospective travelers, the most important thing was not what her preferences, desires or gifts happened to be, but her willingness to do "whatever God needs." All of us had gifts that we were to give to the teams; we were being called to abandon our own desires for the sake of the missionaries (i.e., the mission) and the team.

This process of explicitly sublimating personal desires to the needs of the team is similar to what Rebecca Allahyari (2000, p. 4) called "moral selving," or "a concern for transforming an experience of an underlying moral self, in contrast to a situated identity." Together with the interview team, the prospective leaders coming to the interview were casting their desires as necessarily less important than the needs of the group. Notably, this process of working out the nature of service and the moral self was unlike that undergone by volunteers to social service agencies studied by Allahyari, in that the prospective STM team leaders at CWC were not highlighting their desire for personal trans-

---

those data. I would argue, however, that the interviewing, as an embodied form and linguistic genre, served to shape the narratives of the high school students as strongly (if not more strongly) than those of the adults.

[5]Though the notion of "spiritual gifts" is often associated with Pentecostal emphases on glossolalia, prophecy and the like, evangelicals have used the notion in a less mystical sense for many years (McQuerry 1979).

formation; instead they were articulating a sense of calling, sacrifice and self-abnegation in line with the STM narrative.

I might not have seen this as a dynamic process or one of creating a particular sort of posture had it not been for one instance in which I sat in on an interview with a recent college graduate. She was a member of the congregation but had participated in several trips under the auspices of the college, where a somewhat different discursive process was at work (Howell and Dorr 2007). As she was asked about her gifts and how she imagined herself contributing to the team, she answered in a way distinct among those I heard interviewed:

> I think what I've come to see in these [short-term trips] is just a desire to understand the global church, how valuable it is to become aware of the ways we are part of this diverse global body. I know I can be of service, but I think I don't focus on that as much as being there and become aware of the ways we're connected, you know? I think it is so important to go as a learner.

Her answer received nods and murmurs of affirmation, but the subsequent questions came back to the script of how her skills and interests might match up with the tasks and goals of the various teams. Her interests in "learning" and "connecting" were not contrary to the goals of the GO leaders (framed as "exposure"), but at this stage of the preparation process, they were not brought into the conceptual and practical framework of activity and identity defining these trips.

As I would find, learning and connecting were explicit motivations for almost everyone going on the trip, but from the beginning, our missionary narrative pushed those aspects of experience to the margins. Central to our interviews was following the call of God, employing our gifts, serving the missionaries and sharing the gospel—all elements of "real missions." This created a relationship of each participant toward the process (a subjectivity) that made other understandings of the trip difficult or secondary. Within the structure of the interview, there was no opportunity for the interviewee to reframe the discourse into areas not opened by the interviewers themselves. The language encouraged by the interviewers, and delivered through the officializing practice of the interview, went in a particular direction. Speaking specifically to theological contexts such as ours, anthropologist Pierre Bourdieu (1991) describes this kind of embodied practice of language as the "religious field," in which social and religious practices are organized (i.e., structured) by leaders and laity working together to create a sense of the real and the possible in their religious lives. In a statement typical of French poststructuralist prose, Bourdieu argues that

> the effect of *consecration* (or legitimation) exercised by *explanation* . . . causes the system of dispositions toward the natural world and the social world inculcated by conditions of existence to undergo a *change of nature*, in particular transmuting the *ethos* of a system of implicit schemes of action and appreciation into *ethics* as a systematized and rationalized ensemble of explicit norms. (1991, p. 14)

In other words, the act of endorsing, through the interview process, a particular view of one's role and purpose for being on a team (providing relevant gifts for the task ahead) creates a particular posture toward the world (in this case, the STM trip). This posture is not necessarily clear to those who adopt it, though it is supported by a seemingly common sense or natural understanding of things.[6] I will explore possibilities of other sorts of arrangements and postures that could be adopted as I consider in chapter nine what sorts of reforms might be encouraged. Suffice it to say, this was a significant, though intro-

---

[6]My own interview was a bit different from those of prospective leaders from the congregation. In my case, the committee was asking about my role as an anthropologist and how that might affect the dynamics of the group. Even within that context, however, the group doing the interview was self-consciously aware of the ways in which they saw the interview shaping the subjectivity of the potential participants. The interview began with following:

> Okay, Brian, this is typically where we ask somebody why they want to be a part of the mission trip. And it's where people would say the Holy Spirit has really given me a vision to expose students to world missions, or I really feel called to serve our missionaries. So I'll ask you, why do you want to be part of this [Global Outreach] trip?

Thus, even as I sat explaining the ethnographic method and my interest in the topic, I had the experience of conforming my language to the expectations—or the perceived expectations—of the committee. It was not that I disagreed with these aspects of the motivations, but the embodied process of being interviewed made it more difficult to speak in ways that were not prestructured to fit into the forms I knew were already part of the format. For those beginning to create narratives for travel, it became a moment in which the "structuring structure" came into play quite strongly, pushing our personal narratives of travel toward a shared ethic of STM (cf. Bourdieu 1990, p. 49).

ductory, step in our overall orientation to how to understand ourselves as short-term missionaries.

MEETING THE TEAM

Our first meeting as a team came in early February. We gathered in a small meeting room one evening with pizza, Twizzlers and soda arrayed on one table. In one of the hazards of "nativist anthropology," it did not strike me as noteworthy that we would have such indulgent foods at an STM meeting.[7] Pizza, after all, is the culinary staple of the suburban teenager. Yet it did mark a pattern we would experience throughout our trip. While at times we focused on the hardships of our travels and the notion of "sacrifice" as a key experience of STM, there were numerous (though typically unacknowledged) ways these travels were occasions for pleasure and indulgence.[8] For this meeting, such indulgence was unremarkable and unremarked upon. The explicit purpose of this gathering was to begin forming relationships. It was my first chance to meet those with whom I would be traveling to the Dominican Republic in June.

The adult leaders were a married couple in their mid- to late forties, Paul and Ann Wright. They were first-time STM leaders, but had chosen this trip in order to travel with their high school son, Aaron. Aaron, a junior and popular athlete, had been to Linda Vista the previous summer on a trip with youth group leaders, and he was anxious to return. Paul and Ann had never been to the Dominican Republic, but Paul had been on several previous STM trips to the United Kingdom and Asia. As a highly placed executive in a major Chicago firm, he was well traveled generally, though he saw his STM trips as travel distinct from these other categories. Ann would position herself as the "mom" of the group, generally handling the preparatory details (of which there were many) and taking a genuine interest in all of us traveling.

---

[7]See Jacobs-Huey (2002) for a discussion of "nativist anthropology." See also Howell 2007.

[8]I am grateful to Jenell Williams Paris for this observation about the connection of junk food and other bodily or emotional pleasures associated with our trip. As a contrast to the language of sacrifice and mission, I do not develop this as far as I could; I have brought it out more explicitly throughout the study to illustrate further the ways our narratives often submerged personal pleasure and enjoyment as a part of our travels.

Paul and Ann were joined by Michael Daniels, the owner of a successful consulting firm, who had also traveled quite a bit, primarily for business. His son, Simon, a close friend of Aaron, would be on the trip, and Michael saw this as a good opportunity to spend time with his son before he headed into his senior year of high school. The last leader (besides me) was Ellen Meyers, a Spanish teacher at the local high school, who had decided to go in part because her niece, Elizabeth, was part of the team as well.

The kids on the team were all members of the high school youth group at CWC, a large group of more than two hundred students that met weekly for Bible studies, worship services and numerous social events throughout the year. In addition to Simon, Aaron and Elizabeth, our team included Jeremy, the youngest member of the group, a first-year student who had never traveled abroad. Amina, a witty and outgoing sophomore whose parents had come from East Africa to do missions work and training in the United States, was the only person of color on our team. Emma, a thoughtful junior who had been with Aaron on the previous summer's trip, was likewise anxious to renew her friendships with people she'd met in Linda Vista. The quietest members of our team (as I would soon discover) were Jacob, a tall freshman in high school with a mop of dark, curly hair; Mary, a small, dark-haired sophomore; and Jeanie, another slightly built sophomore with bright blue eyes and exceptionally light blond hair. Megan Goffman was a junior, a tall blonde who was similarly quiet but, perhaps because of her age, did not seem as quiet as Jacob, Mary and Jeanie. Henry Boswell, a sophomore with a notable seriousness about his faith was a tall, athletic kid with sandy blond hair and a wide smile. James Campbell, the only senior of the group, had already made plans to attend a Christian college in the fall. He was by far the most boisterous of the group, occasionally irritating but often amusing with his quips and antics. Having studied five years of Spanish, James was anxious to try out his ability to speak the language on our trip.

Most of the kids in the group were not close friends prior to joining our team. They knew each other, particularly those who were most involved in the youth group, but with a few exceptions (Aaron and Simon,

Jacob and Jeremy, Amina and Elizabeth), they were mostly acquaintances. The adults were moderately more familiar with each other, with Michael and the Wrights being friends through their sons, but they did not have deep relationships prior to our being put on the team together.

Not all the members of our team made it to the first meeting, but Charlie let us know that attendance at the preparatory events was critical. Speaking to everyone, he said, "You're going to find that if you don't have time together as a team, you're not going to be effective once you're there." At our tables, as we introduced ourselves, Paul reiterated that he felt it would be important for the team to "connect" and have "one mind" about the trip.

We met together about eight more times for the purposes of fundraising, preparing our materials and studying.[9] These were important moments for our team to internalize a common narrative, as well as an opportunity for me to learn how members of the team already understood what this missionary trip meant. At the same time, consciously forming our understanding of the trip was not only, or even primarily, undertaken through overt moments of teaching understanding and language. This understanding came powerfully through the prosaic moments of preparation, such as the need to raise money.

MISSIONS AND MONEY

I vividly recall the rummage sale my Methodist youth group held in the summer of 1985 to support our trip to Mexico. Several of us dressed in the out-of-fashion clothes as we moved among the shoppers, ginning up business to make a dent in the seemingly enormous total we needed. I'm sure we needed much less than our CWC team would need for the trip to the Dominican Republic, but it was something that required several car washes, bake sales, spaghetti dinners and rummage sales. What our Methodist church did not have was an established understanding of why and how money for such endeavors figured into the overall purpose and meaning of the trip. By contrast, CWC not only

---

[9]I say "about" eight more times, because there were events, such as a fundraising pancake breakfast, that were not specific to our team but involved all those going on STM trips that summer.

had a well-developed system of fundraising, but also a theological un-
derpinning for it.

Of the five trips going out from Wheaton, ours was not the most
expensive. Coming out to approximately 1,700 dollars per person, the
cost for each student was less than many would pay for two weeks of
summer camp. None of the families were allowed to pay out of personal
funds, because this would go against the philosophy of the whole
program. Pastor Nate explained this point to me, saying, "I know most
of these families; they could just pay. But it's important they understand this [process of raising support]—what it's like to raise support.
They get people involved and understand what missions, missionary
life, are like." Although there would be fundraisers (such as a pancake
breakfast), the most significant act of fundraising was sending out
support letters to members of the congregation as well as family and
friends outside CWC. This work was significant not merely for the
amount of money, but also for the ways writing about and representing
ourselves reinforced the missionary narrative of our trip.

We gathered one Saturday for an envelope-stuffing party. I arrived
to find the youth group room buzzing with activity as the entire group
of students on all five STM teams was given the task of sending out
form letters to approximately one thousand households. As we sat
among the mailing labels, letters, promotional materials and information from the church, Christian music played in the background and
pizza provided sustenance to the hungry crew. Even as people occasionally groaned about the piles of letters to be folded and address labels
to be affixed, there was a festive atmosphere.

In addition to the mass mailings, each student sent ten personal
letters to people they had chosen (from within or outside the church) to
solicit for financial support. Students brought copies of the letters they
had written and sent ahead of time to Ann Wright. The students had
been encouraged to personalize the letters, but also had been given a
structure to follow in terms of order and content.[10]

---

[10]In an email to our team specifically, the leader of our group gave us the details to include in the
letter:

*Dominican Republic (DR) dates: June 17 thru June 30

The immediate purpose for the letters was, of course, the raising of money, but they had a way of shaping our understanding of the trip as well. Like the interviews, the letters were a genre of linguistic practice in which the writers were encouraged to express their motivations for the trip and their understanding of its purposes within a particular narrative. Two key elements of the letters of these students concerned the relationship of this trip to the long-term missionaries currently working in the place and the calling of God on their lives to participate in this short trip. Both of these themes served to address any misgivings donors (or participants) may have to the notion of fifteen-year-olds traveling to another country for two weeks as being legitimately mission. The language also served as an expression of key missionary narratives, taken on as personal in the letter itself, to aid in the creation of the missionary identity for the team members.

In each case, the letters began by presenting the member's participation in the trip as an opportunity to be taken, rather than as a choice or desire. None of the letters I saw claimed, "I have decided to go to the Dominican Republic" or "I decided to take a short-term mission trip this summer," suggesting that these travelers did not imagine their participation as something they were doing for themselves or on their own volition, but rather as a sacrifice, calling or divine action being performed through them.[11]

---

*DR mission: to come alongside missionaries Phil and Sarah Van Sant as they minister to the children of La Casa (the orphanage) and to the children in the surrounding community AND to contribute some elbow grease in their construction projects to further their ministry there.

*What you are asking for: PRAYER for team unity, safety, that we would effectively show the love of Christ to all that we come in contact with, for our time with the children—great times of learning and love and fun—for the construction portion of our trip: safety, productivity, strength and stamina (maybe that's just necessary for us old people). FINANCIAL SUPPORT for all that's involved in financing a trip like this.

These details, provided by the GO committee, had been used for several years. Aaron and Emma had used this letter when soliciting support for their trip the prior year. Aaron's letter was sent out as a model for the others. The majority of the students ended up following the form fairly closely.

[11]I was not able to get copies of all the letters. Two of the students did not have extra letters during our time together and did not save copies—or perhaps did not want to share them. Regardless, I was able to get ten of the twelve, plus several from members of other teams (fifteen total).

Several stated simply, "I will go . . . " or "I will be going with a team to the Dominican Republic," but the majority wrote of the "opportunity" to participate in the trip as being "given," "presented" or "received" as a kind of gift, voiced in a passive tense. The sample letter proffered this example: "I have the opportunity to participate." Variations in the students' letters included phrases such as, "I have the opportunity to go to the Dominican Republic with a group from my church," "This summer I have been given an awesome opportunity to serve God by going on a missions trip" and "I have been given the opportunity to go and help serve . . . " Articulating participation in this way caused the students to think of themselves as being called to the trips, or following a path laid out for them, rather than choosing to participate, or developing expectations. In the language of these letters, the missionary narrative of service and travel were antithetical to traditional motives for foreign travel: adventure, education and encounter.

For the readers of these letters, the question "What could really be accomplished by a group of teenagers, most of whom do not speak Spanish, simply working in the Dominican Republic for two weeks?" is addressed by describing the trip as a partnership, as supporting or encouraging the long-term missionary presence. Such phrases as "Our mission is to come alongside missionaries Phil and Sarah Van Sant"; "I have been given the opportunity to go and help serve in the Dominican Republic alongside Phil and Sarah Van Sant"; and "five trips will be sent out to work side-by-side with full-time missionaries," created and communicated a meaning for the trip rooted in the historic notions of the mission work of evangelism, church planting and social transformation.[12] This served to communicate the legitimacy of the work while bringing our own subjectivity in line with the long-term missionary identity of our hosts. Through the link to missionary work, the letters make it very clear that these trips are not travel in the ordinary sense.

---

[12]There is more that could be said about the support letter as a powerful form to communicate the idea of being a missionary for the students and for those reading (and responding to) the letters. What is said is not less important, but the form of it is part of its meaning. Linguist William Hanks (1987, p. 15) notes that these sorts of linguistic practices create an "organic link between style, genre, and action," which shape the subjectivity of the producer of the language. The support letter is just such a link.

Additionally, they attach a theological significance to the travels by emphasizing the role of prayer and the work of God in the trip.

In every letter, before financial help is solicited, the author asks for prayer for the members of the team and the tasks they will undertake. One wrote, "Most importantly, I am asking for your prayer support for our trip. Prayer is an absolute necessity as we prepare for the Dominican Republic." Another clearly prioritized prayer in a bulleted list, saying,

> I would like to ask you for support. I would ask for support in two main ways: First: in prayer
>
> - I ask you to pray for unity in our team
> - To pray for the Van Sants, with whom we will be working
> - To pray for the people in the Dominican Republic who we will be ministering to. Please ask that God will be preparing their hearts for Him.
>
> Secondly, I would ask for your support financially.

In one letter, the boy writing linked the raising of support back to the missionary aspect of the trip, saying, "Finally, we need to raise financial support in much the same way that full-time missionaries do."[13]

The invocation of prayer as the primary means of support for the trip recalls a long tradition in Christian theology in which the work of the Holy Spirit (in conversion and evangelism) is carried out through the sacrifice and faithfulness of courageous individuals who step out in faith to fulfill a call of missionary service. To overly emphasize the financial needs would be to minimize the power of God to meet the needs of those he has called to particular realms of service.

On the one hand, it was personally inspiring to consider how I and

---

[13]One leader's letter listed specific areas for prayer:

> There are five main areas of concern that we would especially appreciate your prayer for. First, we will need to keep God in the front of our hearts at all time and be willing to show his love. Second, as we will be building with potentially dangerous equipment, we will need prayer for physical safety as well. Third, we need to remember that we are in the DR as servants and that like Jesus did, we must reveal a servant's heart to these people. Fourth, our team has seventeen different individuals on it and we will need to maintain team unity at all times to make this trip successful. Fifth, and possibly most importantly, we would ask for prayer that the seeds that we plant at the VBS will grow and mature in these children in the future.

The request for financial support then came as a follow-up, presented almost as an afterthought.

other members of my team could see this trip as an opportunity to experience God's provision. My own funds for the trip came from a grant given by my college in support of my research, but I certainly felt this to be a time in which I, like the others in the group, was encouraged to think about God's work in our midst. It struck me, however, that because we were going out on an STM trip, we viewed prayer and the action of the Holy Spirit as qualitatively different from what we would need or experience in our everyday lives. Framing the trip as a moment of exceptional divine action meant we created a separateness around the trip—a spiritual distinction between our lives at home and our expectations for when we were away—that was taking shape in our language. Just as the work of missionaries on the foreign field was considered distinct, so our work here was marked as spiritually distinct by its association with the coming missionary travels.

Manifesting and (re)creating the missionary ideal in the act of raising support would undoubtedly strike many evangelicals as the right thing to do. I personally believed the centrality of God guiding the trip was important to keep in mind. Similarly, the emphasis on partnerships with long-term missionaries or local believers abroad potentially prevents some short-term teams from overestimating the value of their acts or wasting resources out of ignorance of local needs. I would not disagree with any of this. But the language of mission, as expressed in these letters and throughout our preparation, also had unintended consequences.

CROSSING (OUT) CULTURES

Given that mission is imagined as a *crosscultural* trip of spiritual significance, it made sense that we would consider the nature of this cultural encounter. We were given some resources to do this, although the materials left a lot of questions unanswered. Drawing on our own context and our understanding of what it meant to engage culture as missionaries, our team often had to rely on the resources of common sense and general knowledge. Our team was certainly supplied with capable leaders and bright students, but as I have often found as a professor of anthropology teaching my relatively elite college students, understanding the nature of culture is not a straightforward proposition.

Addressing what it means to "cross cultures" in an STM encounter through a short lesson is even more difficult.

Our team's most explicit preparation for crossing cultures came during our third team meeting, in which we were going through a workbook titled *Before You Pack Your Bags, Prepare Your Heart.* The workbook provided twelve lessons in the form of inductive Bible studies on everything from goal setting and defining a purpose for the trip (lesson one) to developing the right attitude for the trip (lesson three), identifying cultural patterns of U.S. American behavior and thought (lesson five) and developing good team dynamics (lessons ten and eleven.) Our team didn't go through every lesson, although we did several, including lesson five, about identifying cultural patterns.

We met for this session at Megan's house. Megan's family lived in an upper-class neighborhood of large, newly constructed homes with brick facades and three-car garages. The back of her home faced a park, making her backyard appear to be acres of perfect lawn. Her mother welcomed us in as we arrived, and we began assembling in lawn chairs at the edge of the property. Soft drinks and chips were on the small tables between us and on a picnic table pulled over for the group. In another moment of culinary indulgence, Megan's mom prepared hot dogs and other picnic food for us while we began to talk about the lesson.[14]

Paul led our discussion, entitled "Are You an American First, or a Christian First?," by reading the opening question "What are some positive stereotypes about Americans?" Henry, a varsity athlete who did well in school, quickly called out, "Fat and lazy." The others in the group reminded him that we were supposed to be thinking about *positive* things. Henry kind of laughed, and Paul repeated the question. After thirty to forty-five seconds of silence, one of our leaders, Ann, tentatively volunteered an answer. "Um, friendly? I think people think we're friendly, don't you?"

---

[14]Hot dogs and chips are not, of course, considered "indulgent" among most North Americans. They're inexpensive, simple foods. However, as I noted about our first team meeting, throughout our time of preparation and during much of our travel (though not all), preparations tended to emphasize sacrifice in time and money but not comfort, until we got to the Dominican Republic. There, as the next chapter reveals, food became symbolic of comfort and familiarity in some cases, and sacrifice and cultural strangeness in others.

"Okay," Paul responded. "Anything else?"

Again we waited for a bit. Emma remarked, "It's a lot easier to think of the negative things."

"Well, that's the next thing," Paul said, looking back at the curriculum. "Okay, what are some negative things?"

This time the responses came rapidly. Henry again made his comment about Americans being fat and lazy. A couple of people told stories about running into media stereotypes of Americans overseas. Michael, one of the adult leaders, talked about being in Hong Kong and encountering people who knew Chicago only as a town of gangsters. Megan remarked that while in the Czech Republic the previous year, peoples' main exposure to America was through MTV. With that comment came groans around the circle. I suspected that most of these kids were not allowed to watch a great deal of MTV or that, at the very least, they would have put that into the category of things that did not reflect the Christian values they were taught in church youth group.

It struck me that, while the lesson was meant to spark our thinking about ways that American culture shaped our identity, for these students, and perhaps to some extent the adult leaders as well, "American culture" referred primarily to the negative influences that were against the church and unchristian. Assuming they did not conceive of themselves as "fat and lazy" or identify with the stereotypes of sexual promiscuity or crime they cited as standard Hollywood fare, they didn't imagine themselves as "Americans" in the sense of those people that others find offensive or irritating or unchristian. Referring to the so-called public culture of the "culture wars," in which U.S. Christians often engage (see Hunter 1992), no one seemed to think that our own understanding of the world, let alone our Christianity, was part of or significantly influenced by American culture.

The second, and far larger, part of the lesson was a theological message to encourage a willingness to give up "worldly identity" (i.e., cultural identity) for the sake of Christian identity. As Paul went on with the lesson, he read from the assigned Bible passage, Philippians

3. The chapter contains a well-known passage in which the apostle Paul renounces those "worldly" things to which he would normally point for social/religious prestige (circumcised on the eighth day, descended from the line of Abraham) as having no worth in the Christian life.

The basic thrust of the lesson was that there were "things of this world" that would have to be left behind for the sake of ministry/the gospel/heaven, including our American culture. Resonating with the sense of calling and sacrifice we had embraced and articulated through the interview process and letter writing, this notion of giving up worldly things, referred to in this lesson as the culture in which we lived, linked easily with the missionary narrative of sharing a transcultural gospel with those in a different culture, crossing a boundary to find a common Christian identity. It also framed Christian identity as something distinct from a "cultural" identity, whether Dominican, American or anything else. As I listened to the lesson, I wondered how this split between being a Christian and being a person with a culture would play out as we traveled ostensibly to meet people whose faith was shaped by their culture.

On the chilly spring day, as several of the girls huddled under a stadium blanket together and most of us kept our arms crossed close to our bodies, there was not a lot of interaction with the lesson. Thus it was not always clear how the members of the team were processing the questions of culture and Christianity being presented in the curriculum. There was not any resistance to the notion that a Christian identity was more important than an American identity, but it was not at all clear that there was much of an understanding of what it meant to be "an American" or how that affected our faith. This lesson resonated with what I had already heard about culture during our preparations. Just as American culture was framed as something opposed to Christian identity, so too was Dominican culture often conceived as distinct from Christianity.

In our support letters, though most of the students followed the template fairly closely, one went well outside the script. James was something of an iconoclast; his letter reflected a great deal more creativity than the others.[15] This particular Monday evening meeting began with logistical issues such as trip insurance, necessary vaccinations and an update on support letters. James had his done, so he read it out loud. He spent the first part of the letter describing the nature of our trip, informing his potential supporters that we would be traveling to the Dominican Republic, "a country known more for baseball players than having a culture," where we would work with "some of the poorest people the world has ever known" in a "completely undeveloped country." James's hyperbole was unusual, but his associating poverty with a lack of "Dominican culture" was not.

Throughout my pretrip interviews, I asked the team members what they knew of or anticipated in Dominican culture. Many of those who had not been to the Dominican Republic emphasized how they wanted to "see Dominican culture" (or see "another culture") for themselves. This led them to think primarily about the visual dynamic of being in another place (see Urry 2002; also Bruner 2004, p. 208). Not surprisingly, then, as they imagined this "poor country," they thought about the culture in terms of what they might see around them on a daily basis. When asked, "What do you think are the differences between U.S. and Dominican culture?" Jason ventured, "I don't know. I imagine just poverty—just poor. Like maybe kids in old clothes and in the dirt, small houses . . . " Jeremy responded similarly: "I think not as nice as here, the cars or houses. Poor." James had the most specific vision of poverty expressed as a visual encounter. At one point during our preparations, James announced to the group that for him the trip would not be complete until he saw that iconic image of Latin American poverty, "a man riding a donkey cart."

In general, asking the teens preparing to go on the trip about cultural differences was not a particularly fruitful question, given the difficulty for most in identifying what culture is. For most of the students, much more important than experiencing or learning about differences was the anticipation of overcoming whatever differences they encountered. Simon, who had traveled to Ukraine on a previous STM trip,

---

[15]I never was able to get a copy of his letter, but as he read, I wrote as quickly as I could, getting some of the more colorful phrases verbatim.

assured me, "I don't really care about how much different living is. I kind of like living wherever we are. I just kind of get scared or nervous if somehow the kids don't get along with me, or they [don't] understand me. Or they don't know [the expression] 'what's up?'"

In another interview, Paul and Ann's son, Aaron, shared his memories of the trip to Linda Vista the previous summer, saying, "I just loved working with the kids and being able to see, like, a different culture. Really, the only other time I ever left America was when I went to Japan. It was just really cool to see, like, the church in the different culture and, like, how they're far apart, but everything's still the same. People are still the same . . . "

In speaking of cultural difference and the crosscultural aspect of our trip, our STM narrative of crossing cultures made the transcendence of culture the ultimate goal. Although the narratives of our journey consistently incorporated the expectations of cultural dislocation and unfamiliarity, the triumph of these trips was in seeing how these cultural differences did *not* matter. Coming to the realization that "we are all the same" served as the high point in many of the posttrip narratives I ultimately collected (see chapter eight). Furthermore, even as we were encouraged to think about our own cultural context, I found that the language of culture available to the team members distanced our identity as Christians from our identity as U.S. Americans. Even as we intentionally worked to prepare ourselves to be sensitive to cultural difference, the operative understandings of the culture concept further supported the narrative of our journey as a moment of cultural transcendence.

Anthropologists studying travel have noted that tourists often have specific ideas of what "a culture" looks (or should look) like, framed in visual terms. In her study of British tourists in Malta, Annabel Black (1996, p. 113) noted that after commenting on the hospitality and friendliness of the people, most tourists would lament that "they don't have much of a culture here, crafts and that . . . they seem to lack imagination." In his study of Toba Batak carving in the frequently visited areas of Sumatra, Andrew Causey (2003) observed Toba Batak carvers assiduously studying Western journals and magazines for the images they thought might appeal to tourists. Instead of simply carving replicas of images traditional to their communities, they had learned that when they carved the primitive things Westerners expected of their culture, they sold a lot more carvings.

Similarly, these STM team members began with a clear idea of what Dominican culture would look like. Culture generally was something opposed to their Christian identity, through either its degradation in the United States or its relative absence and/or diminution in the Dominican Republic. That is not to say that in the experience of the trip or in the post-trip narratives culture would remain confined to these narrative themes. As we moved through the space in the Dominican Republic, and even more so as members of the team reconstructed the experience in the months after returning home, differences in culture were worked out in a variety of ways. We left with a strong expectation that we would encounter difference in some form alongside the hope, if not expectation, of overcoming the limits of cultural difference. It was in the overcoming that we could experience the sharing of the gospel.

GOING INTO THE WORLD

> Not sedentary all: there are who roam
> To scatter seeds of life on barbarous shores:
> Or quit with zealous step their knee-worn floors
> To seek the general mart of Christendom.
> —William Wordsworth, "Missions and Travels"

It seems a long way from the picture of the Victorian missionary leaving "knee-worn floors" for "barbarous shores" to the image of twelve excited high school students getting ready for a thirteen-day trip to a Caribbean island known for tropical beaches and all-inclusive resorts. Yet, in the narratives created throughout our preparation, we were becoming missionaries of a sort, or at least internalizing the emphases of sacrifice, transcending culture and the divine imprimatur on all our activities. We were coming to see our trip as a kind of missionary call. Andrew Walls (1996, 260) argues that the "self-denying life of the ideal missionary" has given way to "the missionary who no longer answers a lifetime call." While this is certainly the case, I would suggest that for these short-term missionaries, the importance of having *some* call remains and is inextricably entangled with the nineteenth-century ideal of "sacrificing country, comfort, prospects and perhaps health for the sake of the gospel," as Walls puts it.

While elements of both pilgrimage and tourist modes of travel appeared in the narrative and practice at various points, the STM trip occupies a particular space in the Christian imagination. Like tourists, we developed an emphasis on seeing other places and experiencing something *more real* in the Dominican Republic than we could "at home." We were certainly excited about coming back with new stories and experiences that would affect us beyond the trip (see MacCannell 2001). In the structure of our preparations, we overlapped with much of the structure of pilgrimage that anthropologists have described as relevant to many expressions of Christian travel (e.g., Turner and Turner 1978).[16] But through the explicit rhetoric we were given, the structures of interviews, the means of self-representation and the discourses of culture, we were encouraged to embrace and employ calling, sacrifice and Christian unity. In a word, we were headed on a mission.

---

[16]Elsewhere I have written about how this anticipatory language mirrors the themes of pilgrimage (Howell and Dorr 2007), and I saw moments of that in our travels to the Dominican Republic as well. On our trip I did not see some of the more dramatic elements of pilgrimage that I saw either in my earlier research or that I often heard from my college students about trips they had taken, particularly those with parachurch organizations that specialized in youth mission trips. The elements that did surface were not incidental, particularly those that tended to draw us together as a group and create what Victor Turner has called *communitas*, or the erasure of social distinctions and an abrogation of structure to create a sense of unity and camaraderie (Turner 1974, chap. 6). Although this was not articulated by the leaders as a primary goal of the travels, participants were certainly aware that group cohesion and the creation of bonds was a significant positive aspect of the trip. "Team building" was generally given as a means for successful service, rather than an end in itself, but the consequence was a strong emphasis on the bonding of the members of the group and the creation of community through the travels.

7

"Pour Out Your Soul"

LIVING THE NARRATIVE
OF SHORT-TERM MISSION

OUR TRIP OFFICIALLY BEGAN IN THE PARKING lot of Central Wheaton Church, where our team gathered on the morning of June 13 to load our vans and head to the airport. It was a bright day, and the high school students, their parents, members of the GO board and we adult leaders milled about excitedly, saying our good-byes and figuring out who should ride in which van. We had agreed to wear the T-shirts especially designed for our trip—dark maroon with white lettering on the front, back and sleeve. Simon did not wear his, and the other team members gave him a little grief for being a rebel. Luggage of various shapes and sizes sat in piles by the three vans lined up to take us on the first leg of our journey. We had a somewhat ritualized departure of taking group photos (for which even Simon put on the team shirt) and hugs around the group. When the last picture was taken, we moved into a circle for prayer. Charlie Gibson started us off:

> Lord, we thank you for each of these young people, these people who you've called to go out this summer. We pray for your traveling mercies as they go to the DR. Give them comfort, let everything go well. Just keep them safe, Lord, as they travel. Lord, help them to proclaim the

Word with power, to just make your Word known there and bring glory to you.

After Charlie, two of the fathers of team members prayed. The first echoed Charlie's prayer that we would "boldly proclaim the message of the gospel" and have "compassion for the lost." The second prayed more for our team, thanking God "for the resources to go on this trip" as well as giving thanks for the effect he believed this trip would have on the lives of the team members and "the way they'll affect others." Finally, Paul prayed, saying, "We know we don't go out alone and we know people here will pray. We know, Lord, your Spirit will go before us."

With the final "amen," one of the men in the sending party called out, "Git 'er done!" invoking the popular encouragement from the comedian Larry the Cable Guy and prompting a little cheer from our team. We were in good spirits for our missionary trip.

Our sendoff had some of the hallmarks of leaving for church camp or a youth retreat, with the pillows and suitcases loaded into the eleven-passenger vans, but with last-minute checks of passports and a heightened sense of purpose and importance. It was clear that we had all become familiar with the missionary narrative of our trip. Even the parents, who had received far less exposure to the preparatory discourse from the church's leadership or through our team conversations, seemed to understand the meaning of our trip. We were going to "share the gospel," "reach the lost," "serve the missionaries" and be transformed by the experience in the power of God.

This sense of common mission and meaning was relatively unremarkable in the church parking lot when compared to our feelings as we moved through the public space of the United States' second busiest airport wearing our matching maroon shirts. My own feeling surprised me. Each shirt bore the phrase "Pour out YOUR soul" under a small outline of the Dominican Republic on our sleeve. The front had a schematic of a globe and "Global Outreach 2006" across it. The back had "DR Project" (styled to resemble the Dr Pepper logo) in large white letters with a verse from Psalm 42: "My soul thirsts for God." While waiting in the airport, I wrote in my field notes:

I just got back from Manchu Wok at the food court near our gate. I was strangely uncomfortable being there without other members of the team around me. I don't know if anyone noticed my shirt, but I felt exposed with this obviously Christian-themed shirt. What were people thinking about this trip? Were there any Dominicans in the area? Were they offended to see this map of their country [on my sleeve]? I was just glad to get back to the group, where everyone is in the same situation. I wonder if this will be a feeling I have throughout this trip?

It struck me that I was experiencing the sense of separation and liminality characteristic of pilgrimages and rites of passage. Perhaps more importantly, the experience served to create the sense of community (what Turner [1974] called *communitas*) that would mark our group as being set apart from our everyday lives. When wearing the shirt, just being with the other members of the group provided a kind of safety from the perception of being stared at or judged. It also provided an opportunity to connect with fellow pilgrims on their way. At one point, a group of STMers from another large Wheaton church passed through the concourse wearing fluorescent green T-shirts, on their way to work in communities devastated by Hurricane Katrina the previous fall. Many of the members of our team knew them, and they had a few minutes to talk about their trips and share encouragement. After all, both teams—one headed to the Dominican Republic and the other the Gulf Coast of Louisiana—were going to do the same thing. In spite of this moment of *communitas*, we were anticipating something more than spiritual insight or the enhancement of our faith. We were off to do missionary work.

I thought about how our missionary narrative might play out once we reached Linda Vista. In spite of the logistics of travel, our trip definitely did not feel like tourism as we started out. At the same time, I knew the majority of our trip would be spent in the prosaic experiences of work, living together, shopping and waiting, along with our time spent in the explicitly touristic activities of visiting local waterfalls, whitewater rafting and a final day at a midlevel, all-inclusive beach resort.

Apart from the rituals of prayer or the sense of calling invoked in the parking lot, how would the missionary narrative be manifest in our experiences? Would the narrative shape the experiences, or would the realities of the Dominican Republic and our work there recast the ideas we had created of mission and identity? It was as we moved from the conversations about our trip, narrating the trip to ourselves, into the experience of the trip itself that I anticipated an opportunity to see how the realities of travel might be confronted or conformed in terms of our developing interpretation of our STM trip.

ENTERING THE FIELD

Emerging from customs with our own luggage and the dozen large duffels of supplies, we stepped into the warm tropical air and put our bags into a pile near the curb. Within a few minutes, Phil Van Sant, the long-term missionary working with Help for the Children (*Ayuda para Niños*, or AN), strode up and greeted us warmly. He pointed out the bus that would carry us to the "team house" where we would stay in Linda Vista for the next two weeks. An easygoing man with a ready smile, Phil would be our main contact over the thirteen days. He would join us on many of our excursions and visit the worksite regularly.

Phil and his wife, Sarah, had been in Linda Vista for more than ten years. They had four children and had recently moved into a lovely home just south of the city. It was actually a bit smaller than the homes immediately around it, but with a good-sized living room, three bedrooms, a nicely appointed kitchen and a large gazebo in the back. It provided a nice space for our team to meet with the family for meals and, when the water to the city was cut off in the last four days of our trip, a place for members of the team to get a shower and wash clothes.

The other long-term missionaries with whom we would have some contact were Samantha and Steve Adelstein. They were an unusual missionary couple, having become Christians while in college at the Ivy League school where they met. Steve had earned an MBA at another prestigious university while Sam had finished medical school, specializing in pediatrics at yet another Ivy League institution. He had worked for a Fortune 500 company and she in medical practice until, when faced with a long-distance move or his accepting a severance package from his executive position, they opted to take the money and move to the mission field.

They had been with AN for a shorter time than the Van Sants, but they were both proficient in Spanish and had many strong contacts among Dominican religious and civic leaders. They also had four children and had recently moved into a large home on a sizable lot near where our team would stay. As with the Van Sants, we would have one official visit to their home—for dinner and a presentation about AN's work—as well as several other visits to use water during the last four days.

The house where our group would stay was purchased by AN specifically as a site for visiting groups such as ours. Unlike some long-term mission groups, for whom STM groups would be an unwelcome burden and a distraction from the larger goals of the ministry (see A. Smith 2008, 42-43), AN had developed a program for short-term teams, utilizing them in institutionalized and regularized ways for building and maintaining infrastructure, supporting outreach programs for Dominican congregations who had joined a Protestant church network and financially supporting the ministry. Of the 1,700 dollars each of us was required to raise for our trip, approximately two hundred went to the ministry as a direct donation to operating costs and another portion paid for the building materials used on our construction project.

In the late afternoon, our bus drove us the forty-five minutes from the airport to Linda Vista up a winding but well-maintained paved road. The pink cement house we'd be staying in was constructed in a common Dominican style; a wrought-iron fence encircled the perimeter of the yard, with a large gate that could be rolled back to allow a car to pull into the covered parking area, tiled with decorative ceramic squares. The living room was spacious with a vaulted ceiling, a cool, tile floor and serviceable, if not overly comfortable, bamboo and wooden furniture outfitted with foam cushions covered in floral fabric. A kitchen with a gas range, double-basin sink and large refrigerator was just around the corner from the living room, connected to a large dining room with a sizable table, surrounded by the plastic chairs that are the staple of patios throughout the world. An electric, five-gallon water cooler, dispensing hot and cold water, sat just at the boundary of the living and dining rooms. Off the kitchen were the maid's quarters with separate toilet and shower, and room for two to sleep. On the other side of the house were three bedrooms, two smaller ones used by the girls and women, and a larger one with a separate bathroom, where we guys put our things.

As we moved our things into the house, the students expressed surprise and even a little disappointment with the quality of our accommodations. "Wow," I heard Henry exclaim at one point, "this is really nice! This is way better than I expected."

"Yeah," James responded, "it's like, why'd I come on a mission trip to live like a king?"

The ideas of sacrifice and calling were betrayed by accommodations that seemed to demand nothing from us. What I would see within the next few days, however, was how members of the team were able to find difference when they looked for it.

ENCOUNTERING DIFFERENCE

After settling in, Phil took the group out for pizza at a nearby restaurant. The team talked about the trip, asked questions about our upcoming itinerary and spent time relaxing. However, throughout the evening, there were comments about things that were "different." It certainly was not surprising that those who had not traveled outside the United States prior to this trip were keenly aware of noticeable differences—the prevalence of scooters (known locally as *pasolas*), sometimes carrying several passengers; the relatively more lush vegetation; and architectural elements common in tropical climates but unfamiliar in the United States' Midwest. There were also expressions of disappointment at things that were familiar, such as "I'm surprised how nice some of the cars are" and "I guess I thought it would be poorer." The narratives of mission and service had set some us up for some more dramatic differences, particularly related to poverty, than were immediately evident.

Throughout the week, in the evenings after our time at the work site or visiting the orphanage, La Casa, to conduct activities for the kids living there, our group often had time to stroll around the central plaza, poking into the mix of restaurants and curio shops catering to tourists, alongside the vast majority of the more prosaic shops—paper stores, supermarkets, fruit markets, hardware stores and so on—serving the needs of local residents.

One evening early in our trip, I found myself in a group including Jeremy, our youngest member. We stopped at one of the several ice cream shops around the edge of the recently renovated central plaza. It was a beautiful evening, and after a long day, Jeremy was practically overcome with the excitement of finally being in Linda Vista. "It's just so great here," Jeremy said to me as we strolled along. "I mean, it's just totally different. Like this ice cream." He indicated the small cup of Magnolia brand vanilla ice cream he had just purchased. "It's just the best ice cream. I mean, you can't get it like this in the States. It's so good and I know it's not like . . . it's still ice cream, but just totally different and amazing. Everything is just amazing." He went on for a few minutes, his excitement palpable as he remarked on the radical differences he was experiencing in this country.

I might have thought it an idiosyncratic response of a young traveler overcome with excitement on his first trip outside the United States had it not been for the response of several other team members who displayed a similar reaction to the perception and negotiation of difference. In one of the first evenings in Linda Vista, before we went to the worksite for the first time, I arrived back at the house to find several people sharing their "finds" from a shopping expedition. One of the most interesting, for a number of the members of our group, was the discovery of Diet Coke in twelve-ounce aluminum cans. It was notable that this was Diet Coke rather than Coca-Cola Light, which is the far more common name throughout Latin America and the Caribbean. When I walked into the room, several of the Diet Coke fans, particularly Ellen Meyers, one of the adult leaders of our team, were quizzing Megan, who had found the elusive product.

Apparently, someone had purchased Coke Light in a two-liter bottle, and the Coke fans were convinced it "tasted different" from the familiar Diet Coke in the silver cans. Being a Diet Coke drinker myself, I put my own taste buds to the test, but I could not detect any difference. It was not very cold, and perhaps it was a little stale, given that it may have been sitting on the shelf for a while. (Neither Diet Coke nor Coke Light seemed particularly popular among the Dominicans in Linda Vista.) Or I may simply lack a sufficiently developed palate; perhaps those asserting the inferiority of Coke Light over Diet Coke tasted something I didn't.

What was interesting to me was the vehemence with which the Diet Coke aficionados defended their perception of the difference between Diet Coke and Coke Light. It was, Ellen asserted, "Totally different."

"Oh, yeah," exclaimed one of the girls after a quick sip, "I can totally taste the difference. This [Coke Light] is disgusting!"

Unfortunately for the self-described Diet Coke addicts in our midst, Megan had bought the last few cans available at the store where she found them. The others who were concerned about having Diet Coke became, then and there, very committed to finding "real Diet Coke" as soon as possible. Later Ellen found another grocery store with Diet Coke in cans. The girls with whom she'd been speaking that first day quickly went out to purchase their own stash.

Seemingly in response to the quest for Diet Coke on the part of these team members, several others made a point of purchasing Gatorade sport drink. In those first few days, they talked about how it was like a "taste of home" and "you have to have the real American kind." Interestingly, Gatorade, and to a lesser extent Diet Coke (in cans), was not particularly difficult to find in a town the size of Linda Vista. Many restaurants served Diet Coke, and Gatorade was available at virtually all the larger grocery stores in the commercial center of town. Based on my own experience purchasing sodas of various kinds the summer before, I think it was something of a fluke that the first store where Diet Coke was found ran out of the product. It is true, however, that these things were not typically available at the local *colmado* (small corner grocery) and therefore read as "foreign" in the context of the Dominican Republic, sold as expensive specialty items alongside Pringles and Nacho Cheese Doritos. For the members of our team, seeking out such consumer goods as a kind of comfort from "home" served to exoticize the location. Even as it became clear that Diet Coke was not as rare as first perceived, it maintained a mystique as a link to home, reinforcing the strangeness of the Dominican Republic.

The fetishizing of small differences makes sense when we consider the narrative of difference with which we started. From the beginning, our trip was framed as a *crosscultural encounter*. For these travelers, who had come to view or had already viewed culture in general as the external and observable differences between "us" and "them," finding and either celebrating or coping with the differences was an important part of the experience. The disappointment many members of the team registered upon seeing our comfortable home, eating pizza and generally observing levels of material comfort similar to what we would expect to see in the United States reflected the desire to have our pretravel narratives of crossing cultures borne out in some way.[1] Finding differences, be it in ice cream or soda, became one way that we could realize our narrative of cultural difference.

The discovery of difference, and thereby culture, in such trivial things was likely not only a factor of the narrative of encountering cultural difference but also related to a widespread U.S. tendency to view culture as relatively superficial and easily ignored (Jindra 2007, 65; see also Plaut 2002). As our team demonstrated in the preparatory stage, culture was not seen as something deeply affecting us, yet we did understand the Dominican Republic to be another culture. It is not surprising, then, that the differences would be experienced in fairly superficial experiences, such as foods and landscapes.[2] But experiencing cultural difference, however conceived, was only part of the cultural crossing expected on our trip. The second element concerned the overcoming of these differences. The STM narrative was more fully realized within the perceived transcending of cultural difference, often wedded to spiritual experiences.

---

[1]This could be seen as akin to what Alma Gottlieb (1982) argued in her article "Americans' Vacations," in which she noted the class inversion that frequently occurs in travel: working-class people take on the identity of the upper class, while upper classes desire a more modest, "folk" experience. Unlike tourists seeking a temporary inversion, however, the DR team's impulses were rooted in the guiding missionary narrative of sacrifice and call.

[2]Due to the brevity of our trip, our intersection primarily with children and the lack of substantive interaction with Dominicans generally, I never observed or heard anyone encountering cultural difference in a way that created frustration (i.e., "culture shock") or even much realization regarding the significant elements of Dominican culture.

Transcending Difference

Our first workday happened on Monday, two days after arriving in Linda Vista. The days preceding work had consisted of a church service on Sunday and time to settle in and explore Linda Vista. It was a bright, cloudless summer day, and when we arrived at the worksite in the morning, it was already promising to be hot. Phil accompanied us to orient us to the site, train us in our simple construction duties and introduce us to Juste and Marcial, the Dominican staff working with us. Juste, a contractor who had been with AN for several years, would be with us each day, checking our work and helping us with the more difficult elements of laying the electrical conduits or framing windows. His assistant, Marcial, generally stuck with tasks such as mixing the cement, which was not as easy as it appeared. We were on the roof of an afterschool care center in Gato Negro, a small town near Linda Vista, to build the walls of the second story, providing additional classroom space, a computer room and a storage area.

Phil had given us a short overview of the ministry and neighborhood in which we were working. It was, he explained, "extremely violent" and "one of the poorest barrios" in the area, where single-parent homes were the norm. He described situations in which one parent had emigrated, left the family for a new romantic partner or otherwise abandoned the children and spouse. The ministry center had been able to provide nutritional and educational support to some of the most impoverished children of the community. Jane Schurmann, a North American missionary who had founded the program almost twenty years earlier, was still its director, though it had come under the umbrella of AN.

The construction project was our primary task for our time in the Dominican Republic. It was a practical form of service, and I admit I was surprised—and impressed—with the work these high school students were able to do. On several days our time was cut short by sudden afternoon thunderstorms; the heavy rains that would knock out the water to the town in our final four days kept us away from our work completely one day.[3] But in spite of these setbacks, by the end of our

---

[3]The town of Linda Vista draws municipal water from the rivers that flow from the higher ele-

time we had built most of the walls nearly to the height necessary for the roof to be installed.[4]

During the work itself, our interactions were primarily with each other. Teachers and other workers in the summer program were in the building at various points, preparing their classes. We had the opportunity to get to know several North Americans who were not career missionaries but had been with the organization for a year or more. Most significantly, in terms of our experience of transcending the cultural differences, our time working afforded several opportunities to make affective connections or discover commonality that wove into the narrative of cultural transcendence.

The personnel at our worksite consisted of our team, Juste and Marcial, occasionally Phil, and Alan, a young Minnesotan who had come to Linda Vista the summer before to spend two years working with AN. In addition, we often had a group of neighborhood kids (approximately nine to thirteen years old) come up the ramp to the second floor each morning to work with us. These local kids became an interesting presence, arriving in clothing suggesting an impoverished life, generally in flip-flops or too-large canvas tennis shoes. We had a pretty consistent group of six or seven boys who worked with us each day.

The boys seemed to enjoy the work, perhaps as a diversion from the long summer days without school and little to do in the under-resourced neighborhood. They sometimes got a little bossy as they interacted with the North Americans, who seemed to have less knowledge of construction than our twelve-year-old Dominican coworkers. It was a complex interaction, as would be expected in a situation involving dif-

---

vations around the city. Deforestation and monocropping have left the watershed vulnerable to erosion during heavy rains. The rivers become choked with mud during these downpours, forcing the city to cut off water or risk destroying the city's water processing facilities. Most middle-class homes have water storage (rooftop or cisterns) to deal with these occasional outages, but these are insufficient in the longer term, as we discovered.

[4]There was no doubt that this work would have been done more quickly and more effectively by professional construction workers such as Juste and Marcial. The materials themselves surely would have gone further had they stayed in the hands of professionals. Scores of broken cinder blocks lay around the worksite, where inexperienced hands had tried to knock out a section for the electrical conduit or split the block to the size of an awkward space. In one sense, however, this inefficiency only underscored that fact that our work was part of a larger missionary work being done in Linda Vista.

ferent languages, economic backgrounds and cultures.

The boys provided an opportunity for the team to experience transcendence in moments of unity in the face of our visual (i.e., "cultural") differences. One afternoon I had just retreated to the cool stairwell that led to the roof/second floor. Our large, orange water cooler was there, along with the many Nalgene bottles students brought along. Several team members, including Henry and James, were also there, along with Ann and three of the boys. We had learned to sing a few praise choruses in Spanish, and one of the team members began singing a simple song, "Alelu, Gloria a Dios" ("Alleluia, Glory to God"), and two of the boys joined in. Ann turned to us and exclaimed how "cool" it was that "people all over the world sing that word," referring to *alleluia*. She turned to me and asked, "Is it true that people everywhere sing that word? You know, Christians everywhere?" The singing died out, and Henry asked, "Where does that word come from?" I answered that it's a Hebrew word. James declared, "It's truly an international word."

Seeing the Dominican boys singing a Christian song with recognizable elements became a moment in which the team saw us as getting beyond culture. Since "people everywhere" use the word *alleluia* and similar Christian vocabulary, we could see ourselves as part of that global body in the stairwell in Gato Negro. This notion is a part of contemporary Christian imagination around the world, as Christians in various places imagine their connection through common language, Scriptures, rituals and theologies that create the global body of Christ in which they participate.[5] For us, this had a stronger resonance with the missionary narrative in which we were coming to discover or build relationships—"share the gospel"—crossculturally. As in the momentary (and one-sided) version of the "ethnic transcendence" Marti (2008) reports in multiethnic congregations, cultural difference becomes submerged below a spiritual identity. This came up a number of times in our interactions with children or in moments of exchange when the reactions of others could be interpreted as something of a pure faith and humanity.

---

[5]This echoes again Hancock's (2011) point about the nature of "the global" in STM language.

The missionary narrative of sharing the gospel across cultural boundaries was, if not easy to find, a natural fit with much of our work among children. Young children, when presented with an opportunity to interact with attentive teens and adults, making crafts and playing with new toys, will generally throw themselves into such tasks with abandon. The children we met in the Dominican Republic were certainly not exceptional in this regard. But the interpretations on the part of the North Americans were not simply rooted in the child-adult relationship or the opportunity to provide diversions for local kids. It was with the children that members of the team felt "real relationships" were formed, and we were able to "really connect." Henry found this particularly with the boys at our worksite. He explained it to me on an afternoon after work toward the end of our trip:

> You know, I'm going to miss those kids [we worked with] more than any of the others. I mean, I love the Casa kids and the kids from the barrios, but I really love the kids we work with. [Q: Yeah? Why is that?] Well, I just really connected with them emotionally. Especially when we gave them stuff. I mean, I just really realized how much they don't have. One kid, who I gave my shoes, he had worn a hole in the bottom of his flip-flop, all the way through. It just really hit me, you know? I mean, these kids just really have nothing, and they just really wanted to work. Especially that Juan Martin. He just had such a work ethic; he really came to work.

For other members of the team, it was a particular child at La Casa or one of the kids who came to the VBS sessions in the neighborhoods. In those cases, some of our team members didn't even learn the names of the kids, but through hugs, games of tag and smiles of kids participating in crafts, the members of our team made emotional connections that took them across the differences to experience unity and cultural transcendence.

Throughout our time, members of the team found human relationships that seemed to transcend language and culture, connecting us with those we encountered, often in ways more profound and spiritually meaningful than those shared with our teammates or people back home. As Henry expressed, this was often in the context of giving things to people living in poverty. Given that members of our team had already framed "Dominican culture" in terms of poverty, working with people perceived as poor and making social connections with them proved to be profound experiences of transcending culture.

The notion of poverty, then, was burdened with meaning. Our interpretations of who was poor and what that meant for them and us was taken to be significant, and it certainly was, although it was not always easy to know how to talk or think about what it means to be poor. In the context of our trip, I heard some team members express confusion about exactly how to make sense of what they saw, while others on my team and other STM teams had an easier time of it as they understood poverty in a more spiritual, less material sense.

INTERPRETING POVERTY

For most STM travelers, "sharing the gospel" in the context of a two-week mission has also come to mean addressing poverty and "serving the poor" (Zehner 2008; Trinitapoli and Vaisey 2009; K. Priest 2009). There was no question that the members of my team were looking forward to seeing poverty, but even before we went, it wasn't something most knew what to do with, interpretively speaking. That is, the STM narrative was about meeting needs, but no one on our team had any illusions that our trip would solve the problems of poverty in the Dominican Republic. In a pretrip interview, Emma said of STM in general,

> In short-term missions there's not a lot you can [do]. You can impact kids but you can't really [do much] . . . or they can decide to become or they can give their life to Christ while you're there, but it's the time when you're gone that the missionaries are still going to be there helping them a lot. And so, for short-term missions, it's just being there, in trying to help affect kids.

I heard many similar sentiments from my college students: "It's not like I think we'll really be changing their lives" or "I know you can't solve world hunger in two weeks," but this did not deter those students or the members of my DR team from viewing their STM travels as acts of service and sacrifice for the sake of the gospel. In fact, in being faithful with something ineffective, some could see a greater sacrifice as they were willing to undergo such travels to "do what we could."

At the same time, witnessing poverty was at times confusing, unexpected and difficult to understand, for example, when the students expressed mild disappointment that things were "so nice" when we arrived at the team house. Both students and leaders of our group also expressed some bewilderment over the juxtaposition of wealth and poverty, over the seemingly inexplicable actions of "the poor," or over how to reconcile global inequalities and the Christian virtue of generosity.

Our experience in and around Linda Vista was certainly one of seeing and interpreting poverty on a daily basis. What exactly constitutes "poverty," however, is often not self-evident or easily interpreted. We visited the home of a peri-rural farmer who sharecropped land and lived in a two-room home with a dirt floor. Did the presence of a television and CD player in his home mean he was not really poor? If families seem to have some arable land at their disposal but do not "make an effort" to grow on it, are they still poor, or just lacking initiative?[6]

In the pretrip interviews, which were mostly conducted in groups of two or three students, I asked about some of their expectations of what they would see in the Dominican Republic. Every student mentioned something about poverty, usually as the first thing.[7] In my first interview with Emma, I asked her to reflect on the expectations she had going into the trip the previous summer and how she thought about that now. She said,

> I was expecting kind of the worst, [a] completely new place to live, nothing to eat, just torn, everything is just sort of bad. . . . But then we get there and the airport's nice, and I was, like, "Oh, this is kind of a

---

[6]These were not judgments made by members of my team, though questions about the meaning of poverty—and specifically questions about why people were or were not "using their land," why they owned seemingly unnecessary goods in the face of seemingly more pressing need and why various individuals made certain choices with their time—did come up among team members at various points.

[7]One group did start with the landscape, when Amina responded, "I guess jungles and stuff. Banana trees, coconuts, you know, jungles, just a lot more green." The others in the group, as was common in these interviews, agreed and added a few more "jungle" descriptions. I followed with "Anything else?" The next response, again from Amina, was "A lot of poor people."

nice place." And then we get to [La Casa] and I am, like, "Wow!" It's not as bad as I expected, because they have these nice little houses, colored houses, eat their food. It still was not, something that you could really want, but it was okay. But then when we went out to the barrios and walked around the neighborhood, that's when I was, like, "Oh gosh," 'cause they have these little, like, half things basically, that was the part that I was, like, "Wow." It wasn't as bad as I expected 'cause I expected completely the worst, but it was still pretty bad.

Although Emma's experience informed the expectations of those team members who had not been to the worksite before the trip, their reactions during and after our trip were very similar. While we worked at our site, traveled to other communities or observed the neighborhoods around our team house, team members expressed a tension between how to feel about how "bad" it was and how to feel about the poverty not being as desperate as they had expected.

During the second week of our trip, our team split into two groups to visit "barrio churches" to work with local congregations conducting VBS sessions for children living around the church. Our group, consisting of Henry, Emma, Ann Wright, James and Simon, spent the afternoon at a small congregation just outside Linda Vista. After about twenty minutes on the paved road, our van turned onto a rutted, dirt road to drive the remaining two or three miles to the church. This was, incidentally, the only time we saw the "man with a donkey and cart" during our visit. We all exclaimed loudly when we saw the man riding a donkey pulling a small, two-wheeled cart with wooden rails and rubber tires, carrying a load of scrap lumber and metal. "Hey, James," someone exclaimed, "now your trip to the DR is complete!"

When we arrived at the small church, two other short-term teams were just finishing their work. One consisted of a Dominican doctor, some middle-class Dominican church members and several North Americans who were finishing a morning of medical work. The other was a parachurch organization that brought college students, mostly from secular universities in the United States, to "do ministry with the kids" while the medical team worked. It was something of an awkward moment for a short time, when the three overlapping North

American STM teams vastly outnumbered the Dominican children we had come to serve. As the other two teams left, leaving just our team with the Dominican church leaders, we felt a little more needed for the task ahead.

The VBS children began arriving shortly after the other teams left, with our group eventually having some fifty children between the ages of three and fifteen (most in the five- to ten-year-old range) playing on the playground, crowding around the craft tables or in the enclosed sanctuary of the church, listening to a presentation of the gospel by the church leaders. Our team was led by two older Dominican teen girls who were ministry interns part at AN for the summer.

We knew very little about the children who came to the afternoon activities. We knew they lived locally, and we could see houses around the church that certainly looked "poor." The homes were mostly one-story, wooden frame houses with galvanized iron roofs. Many had sections of deteriorated wood, broken window glass or windows equipped only with wooden shutters. Barbed-wire fencing or wooden slat fences encircled several homes, where thick bougainvillea, creeping vines or other plants partially obscured the view of the house. Like many other Dominican neighborhoods, this one contained a number of larger, cement homes, including that of one of the AN missionaries who lived nearby.

The afternoon itself was a whirl of activity: stickers were passed out; children made foam picture frames; some played soccer or other running games; and candy was given out at the end. On the ride home, I listened (and wrote) as the students talked a bit about their experience (the notes are not verbatim but reflect the content of the comments).

Henry: It was just so fun to play with the kids. They were so happy we were there.

Emma: I know. I'm sure they never get that.

Henry: I wonder if they all live there.

Emma: I'm sure they just walked over.

Simon: Did you see the houses? [presumably referring to those in the neighborhood around the church]

Emma [looking out the van window]: I know, look at these. How do you live in such a tiny house?

Henry: It's probably okay if you're used to it.

Emma [noticing a particularly large home situated on a beautiful, green hill]: That's my dream house!

From there the conversation turned to dream homes, but the exchange revealed something of an interpretation of the children and their poverty. Henry's comment that "it's probably okay if you're used to it" suggests that he did not associate "real poverty" with the kind of existence he could observe in the modest homes visible from the road or throughout Linda Vista. In fact, the perceived real needs were not so much material as they were emotional and spiritual. In this exchange, Henry and Emma saw in the encounter the emotional needs of the children. The comment that they "never get" interactions such as they had with our team was interesting, given the fact that two other teams were at the site when we arrived and that the day had been organized by the local Dominican church. Yet for the members of our team, the physical poverty of the surrounding area made it easy to imagine the children as suffering from emotional, if not spiritual, poverty as well. The enthusiasm of the children to interact with the visiting teens, their willingness to physically and figuratively embrace our team, facilitated an interpretation of the children's behavior as demonstrating poverty that flowed seamlessly from the physical, to the emotional, to the spiritual.

The conflation of multiple poverties, and the ability of wealthy people to meet those multiple needs, was a theme I consistently heard from STM participants at CWC, in my Christian college setting and in many other programs.[8] The summer prior to my trip with CWC, I

---

[8]For example, a student participating in a six-month internship with an organization in Nicaragua worked with some STM teams. Having worked on STM with me, she took notes on their interpretations of poverty. She recorded the following conversation in which two members of the team interpret the "poverty" of a community, which my student knew was suffering from a profound lack of basic resources. Here are her notes from the exchange, as she reported to me later:

took opportunities to talk with STM teams I encountered in the Dominican Republic. I wrote down a notable conversation I had with an older woman I met at a small, locally owned hotel in the coastal town of Sosua, where my family and I had gone for a weekend getaway during our summer. She had been in the Dominican Republic for a week doing urban ministry in Santiago, the country's second-largest city, in an area known as (according to her) "the Hole." She described how "heart wrenching" the experience had been for her, even while expressing some disgust with the "primitive church" with which her STM team worked. Her most poignant recollection of their week of ministry was recalling how groups of children would cluster around, "starved for attention" and seeking the affection of the visiting North Americans. "They just would come running from everywhere for a hug. I think these kids are never hugged. It's just heartbreaking."

There is no doubt that extreme poverty can debilitate parents and other caregivers, leading to situations where children are deprived of affection. However, it seems unlikely that the dozens, if not hundreds, of children running to greet the North American visitors to a poor, urban neighborhood were coming primarily for hugs and to receive needed affection. There was a strong association in her mind that the physical poverty she saw represented an emotional poverty in the children. This interpretation of the encounter allowed this woman to see her interaction as the creation of deep affective bonds in a brief encounter in which barriers of culture and language were irrelevant in light of the common human, and theologically loaded, expressions of love and of the concern she felt she was able to unambiguously convey to the nameless children of "the Hole."

"Really, I only think they're poor based on what my living standards are," S. said Wednesday morning as we prepared to leave for their last day in the community. "But I'm sure if someone from Beverly Hills saw how I live, they'd think I was poor. Actually they have everything they need. And on top of this they have such rich community and relationships. I don't even know what I have that I could give them."

"Yeah," twenty-year-old C. responded, "I was visiting one of the houses and I saw the beautiful view they have, and I thought, 'Wow, these people have so much.' But still they need us to come and show them love. They really have everything they need, but they still need our love."

"Yeah, that's true," S. said.

This is not to suggest that we did not learn about poverty in the Dominican Republic in more direct terms. Steve Adelstein presented our group with a PowerPoint presentation on the nature of poverty, educational inequality and social problems prevalent in the Dominican Republic being addressed through the work of AN. It was a well-formed, twenty- to thirty-minute overview, including contemporary statistics, a bit of history, personal stories of children brought into La Casa and an appeal for continued support. Unfortunately for our team, this presentation was postponed from the first week until the second and coincided with the water shutoff. As Steve spoke to our tired group, several people waited in line for the shower. Others seemed unable to focus after our days of hard labor.

In the follow-up interviews I did months later (presented in the next chapter), none on the team brought up this presentation as helping them interpret the context. Some could not recall it, even after I reminded them of it. It is impossible to know how this might have shaped some members' views had we heard this on the second or third night of our trip, as was originally planned, but my suspicion is that the stories of abandoned children rescued by AN or escaping abuse and neglect through their placement in La Casa would have strengthened the link of emotional/spiritual poverty and material poverty in the minds of the team members.

By minimizing our effect on the material realities of poverty and emphasizing the spiritual dimension, our trip could be more appropriately understood as mission, because our presence was working directly for the spiritual (or at least emotional) betterment of those to whom the group ministered. Moreover, it became a way for our group to feel that our modest contribution was worth something significant. Even among those acknowledging that our contributions of labor were not efficient or particularly necessary, the theological and emotional service was experienced as a key part of the mission.

The association of our mission with emotional/spiritual poverty also marked off the ministry component of our trip from everything else we did. Moving from our mission—addressing and experiencing poverty and even engaging Dominican culture (i.e., poverty)—to shopping, resting or sightseeing, we were able to demarcate and therefore disconnect aspects of the trip. This was established in the pretrip narrative in many ways, but no more dramatically than in the distinction between mission and tourism.

TOURISM IN MISSION

With its implications of pleasure and indulgence, tourism was inherently incompatible with the STM narrative. At the same time, we had several times plotted out in which to travel and do tourist activities, including a hike to local waterfalls, a whitewater rafting trip on the middle weekend and a beach day at the end of our trip. It was not always clear to me how members of the team were experiencing the moments of tourism on our trip. Much of what I would think about that time came after I reflected on my observations in light of their later reconstructions of the experiences. What I could observe during the experience itself was a kind of subjective movement the members of the team made between their times in "mission" and their times as "tourists." It was far more obvious among the high school students, who seemed less able to hold together the tensions of tourism and mission.

At several points, there was a palpable shift in the rhetorical and discursive positioning the students performed among each other as we moved from ministry activities to those of pleasure-seeking tourism. As I describe below, students would start bantering about playing in cane fields, dream about lounging on the beach or stroll through the marketplace on the hunt for souvenirs and "good deals," adopting the explicit posture (physical and rhetorical) of the tourist. These shifts were so abrupt and marked at times that the adult leaders pushed back, trying to keep the teens from fully separating their identities as tourists from their identities as missionaries. (I have notes of occasions in which one adult leader or another would gently comment, "Remember, we're guests," or "Let's calm down, guys. Remember why we're here.") At other times, the shifts were much more subtle as the practices of team members (including the adults) shifted from mission to tourism and back, often in the time it took to snap a photo, buy a trinket or gaze through a store window. As a part of the narrative from the beginning, it was not surprising that the post-trip narratives often showed the tension between tourism and mission. It was interesting to watch that tension emerge or disappear during the trip itself.

Our first full day in Linda Vista included a hike to a waterfall and swimming area popular with Dominican tourists. It was not a luxurious spot, but for a few hours it was a fun and welcome outing for a group of North Americans coming into a new setting. After walking approximately half a kilometer from a gravel parking area, where we paid an entry fee of about two dollars each, we came to a good-sized swimming area in the river. Large boulders surrounded the area, creating small rapids and eddies, while a large waterfall a few yards upstream provided a noisy natural backdrop. Some thirty or so other tourists, all apparently Dominicans of various ages, were also at the site with their towels spread out on the rocks. We swam for two hours, enjoying the water. The students generally split up into small groups of three or four to venture into various areas of the park.

What struck me at the time was the utter ordinariness of it. We didn't do anything particularly different from what I presumed other visitors to the falls had done; we did not pray together before going or leaving, or consider our time there to be an opportunity for outreach to the people there. It was simply never suggested. That evening, we didn't debrief our time at the falls as we would our workdays and VBS experiences. The students and leaders certainly enjoyed it, talked about the beauty of the scenery, the excitement of a "real tropical waterfall" and other aspects of the experience, but it was subtly cordoned off from the ministry work we had come to do.

This separation of our mission work and our tourist time was evident during our rafting trip on the middle weekend as well, but it was most on display in our final two days, when we drove from Linda Vista to the north coast to spend a day and a half at a modest, all-inclusive resort on the beach. On the way to the beach, Phil took our group to a site where AN was supporting and developing a school for children of Haitian cane workers. Unable to get *cédulas* (Dominican birth certificates or papers of citizenship), Haitians are routinely excluded from social services and legal protections, including the ability to enroll their children in school, get medical care and protest illegal working conditions.

We stopped first at a *batay*, or workers' village, outside the housing and education project of the mission. There we saw the horrific living conditions endured by many of the workers (the same village I had seen the summer prior when I observed the two mission groups described in chapter one). Phil described the difficult conditions, exploitation and oppression endured by the workers. It was a sobering moment, and everyone in the van in which I was riding listened intently to his description.

From there we went on to the mission project, where we disembarked to spend about twenty minutes touring the grounds of the small school and talking to one of the North American mission interns working at the site for the summer. Phil pointed out the medical clinic and housing that were also part of the project. It was something of a spontaneous visit that the team seemed to appreciate. With the tour concluded, we boarded the van to head to the resort.

My van contained seven high-schoolers, Ann, Ellen and me, along with Phil as the driver. As we rode through the cane field on our way back to the main road, James and several other boys began to talk animatedly about the terrain, commenting on how much fun they would have driving a four-wheeler on the rutted roads and winding paths. They joked about other adventures they might have. At one point, as the leaves of the cane plants brushed into the open windows of the van, James made a joke about how they might have feces on them, referring to something Phil told us about how the lack of facilities in the *batay* meant using the field as a toilet and the cane leaves as toilet paper.

At this point, Ann turned around and sharply rebuked James and the others joining in the joking, telling them to "just come down to reality." It was an uncharacteristic outburst for Ann, who was a pretty easygoing person with a long fuse. What struck me was the sudden change in the tone and relationship to the very countryside through which we drove. As we left the mission aspect of our trip and entered tourism, the narratives of service, cultural encounter (and transcendence) and sharing the gospel gave way to ones of pleasure, indulgence and consumerism. For Ann, it was too much as the students disengaged from ministry and mission and began to become tourists, as she was still struck by the things Phil had just shared about the poverty of the cane workers. But her words to the group had only a momentary effect of quieting the most boisterous in our van as we made our way to the beach.

While at the resort itself, I could see the transformation even more clearly. This is not to say that our group turned ugly or began acting in ways that were counter to the values and convictions that brought us to the Dominican Republic in the first place, but simply that it was clear that our relationship to the space had shifted; we did not consider these days at the beach to be part of our mission. Several of the girls, who had been conscious of modest clothing while working at La Casa or in Gato Negro, now donned bikinis. I observed those students who spoke some Spanish using English exclusively with the hotel staff (who were, for the most part, bilingual and seemed to enjoy speaking English; it was unclear whether the students considered using Spanish in the hotel context). We all spent some of our time shopping, mostly looking for souvenirs and gifts to commemorate our trip, in a pattern indistinguishable from that of the other tourists.

The souvenir has been taken up by many studying tourism. It has a long history, from the archaeological relics of the Middle Ages to the kitschy plastic mementos of today. In a classic study, Susan Stewart (1984) wrote that souvenirs, when brought from a far place and associated with experience, carry a certain magic that facilitates narrative. On the last day of our time in the Dominican Republic, several students remarked that it was important they find something to bring home. While out with Henry and several others, Jeremy remarked, "It's so great that there's a lot to buy here. I need to get something just to be like, 'See, I really did go to the DR.'"[9]

On the final night, we gathered on the beach for a "debrief" in

---

[9]This is not to imply that the only shopping we did occurred at the resort. We had a Haitian-Dominican man come to the team house with carved goods and other inexpensive items. Many students used free evenings to walk the few blocks to the center of Linda Vista to buy presents and souvenirs. One memorable outing involved Jeremy looking fervently for machetes, which he felt were most indicative of the Dominican Republic (as they would be used to cut through virgin forest or jungle overgrowth, something we never encountered). After looking in several tourist-oriented stores, he found what he was looking for in a hardware store, hanging next to the yard rakes.

which we talked about memories and impression of our time in the Dominican Republic. We went around the circle and told of relationships, how the work got accomplished, the unity of our group, the unity we felt with people in the Dominican Republic and the sense of blessing felt at having well-equipped schools and homes waiting for us in the United States (cf. K. Priest 2009). Sitting on the beach, talking about what we had done over the previous thirteen days, it very much felt like another place, far from where we had just been or where we would be the next day.

It was the beginning of a critical step in the understanding of our trip. Once we left the mission field, the next thing to do was to narrate these events, and their effect on each of us, to an audience at home.

8

"Of Course You Always Grow Close to God on a Mission Trip"

(RE)NARRATING A SHORT-TERM MISSION TRIP

◆ ◆ ◆

WHAT INITIALLY ATTRACTED ME TO THIS PROJECT were the many stories I heard from my students about their short-term mission trips. Some of these were brief accounts delivered in a one-on-one conversation or a thirty-second description in class. Others were formal presentations in chapel with music, PowerPoint slides and prepared testimonies. What stood out from all these settings were the similar themes, phrases and images that often accompanied them. "I received more than I gave," "I was changed" and "I learned that people are the same everywhere" were stock phrases in many of these personal or corporate narratives. Photos of teams, often in matching shirts, with arms slung around shoulders, a single white face surrounded by brown-faced, smiling children and photos of North Americans engaged in manual labor were the stock images. These converging narratives were my first clue that some common cultural process was in place, helping people to create meaning in the context of these trips. Needless to say, once we returned, I was looking forward to hearing how the members of our team to the Dominican Republic would narrate our trip.

I was a little disappointed to find that there were not many occasions for our team to present its travel in formal ways. I was able to witness only one such event. Most of the narratives I heard from our team were in one-on-one conversations I arranged after the trip. As with all narratives, the context of the retelling mattered a great deal.[1] It was quite different to sit with one or two of my former team members, asking questions about shared experiences and hearing them recall particular people or events, than to see a formal presentation given by a few of the team members for the youth group. At the same time, it was in listening to my teammates, others from CWC and the accounts of my college students, as well as comparing these to representations of STM in promotional websites or in the literature on STM, that I began to see more clearly how the STM narrative shaped the articulation, and even perception, of the experience.

Notably, as many of the members of our team narrated their experience of the trip to me in response to my questions, they often struggled to find ways to make sense of particular issues, such as poverty, inequality or cultural difference. Although some were able to connect the experiences in the Dominican Republic to classes at school, experiences at home or everyday Wheaton life, others found themselves without a greater sense of why the inequality existed or what to say about it. It was much easier for most of our team, and other STM travelers, to speak about the relationships they had formed, the people who had made an impression on them and the ways these experiences had affected their spiritual lives.

Themes of tourism and fun were not uncommon in the travelers' tales of STM trips, but as was true in the pretrip narratives, tourism remained distinctly separate from the mission work. Thus, even where people found themselves resisting the STM narrative, pitting it against their experiences and working to reshape it, it was clear that there was a dominant narrative shaping the cultural process of finding meaning in the reciting of STM.

---

[1]Virtually every study of narrative makes the link between narrative, narrator and context. For two discussions of the issue see Rosenwald 199, p. 267ff, and Derrida 1981.

Reciting Mission

The first formal presentation of our trip came at a youth group meeting where two of the members of our team, Henry and Emma, were asked to share briefly about their experience. Members from the Czech team also shared. On the wall, the Chicago GO team had put up a photo display of snapshots fastened to a couple of pieces of posterboard.

When it was time for our team members to talk about the trip, the members took the microphone and talked about the work we did, shared some memories and encouraged the others to consider going on a trip next time the opportunity became available. Emma said it was "really incredible to get to know these kids [at La Casa.]" She explained how she could "see God working" in the Dominican Republic, stressing to her fellow youth group members that "you can't really understand unless you go." Henry also encouraged his fellow youth group members to pray about going on a trip themselves. And he talked about the work we did. Referring to the kids in Gato Negro who would join us at the construction site, he said, "It was a great witness, great opportunity to just be with these kids, speak a little bit of Spanish and be able to communicate with them. You just know, just by the way that we were acting, they could learn from us."

It was not surprising that the narrative of the trips given by the teams to their youth group emphasized the work we did, focusing on the elements of sacrifice, spiritual growth, God's work through our actions and relationships with people, while downplaying tourist activities and educational outcomes. The setting of the presentation was designed to emphasize those very things. I was not able to find out why these particular students were asked to share, but I suspect they exhibited seriousness about the trip and their faith that made them good candidates for sharing with the rest of the group.

I learned a great deal more about how the members of our team thought about the trip when I interviewed each person individually or in pairs six to twelve months after the trip. I would have liked to have heard all the members of the team simply present their stories to the rest of the group, but our team had few opportunities to construct a formal narrative for a particular audience. Instead, they shared stories with friends and families, telling snippets of their time in particular contexts or in response to questions. My interviews with them followed a schedule, but were semi-structured, allowing me to follow various comments and allow people to narrate the trips for themselves.

When I asked them to name highlights of the trip, a common response was the acts of service, including the more physically demanding aspects of the trip, such as the construction work. Mary's response was characteristic; in response to the question "What were highlights of the trip for you?," she said, "Umm . . . playing around with the little kids. (*laughs*) I mean, I liked construction too. I really liked knowing that I'm doing something to help them out. It was hard sometimes, but it was really fun." Jeanie pointed to the construction work: "I really liked . . . um . . . I liked doing the construction work and working with those kids that came to help us. It was just fun to work hard. I thought it was really interesting trying to build something with them even though we didn't speak the same language, and the construction site and seeing how far, how the wall was building up and by the end was so tall, that was so cool."

This aspect of giving and sacrifice, the essence of "sharing the gospel," came up in every narrative the team members provided. Not everyone emphasized the construction work per se, but service and meeting needs was central.[2] For example, Henry answered the question about trip highlights by saying,

> I think, highlights for me would be—would have been building the school. That was really exciting for me to be able to [do]—and going into the neighboring towns or the area the kids were going to come from for the school, you just realize these people have nothing. And here we are, giving them education. We're making a room so that they can have computers. These people are living in huts with cement floors, if they're

---

[2]It was interesting that all but one of the girls on the trip named the construction labor as a highlight or positive aspect of the trip. Several of the boys did as well, but only three of the six. Perhaps the girls found the opportunity to do physical labor alongside the boys to be an empowering experience. One of the Dominican leaders told me that this was an important aspect of the trip from their perspective—modeling cross-gender friendship and the equality of the sexes for the Dominican teens who observe them working. None of the members of our team expressed an awareness of our trip as breaking U.S. or Dominican gender norms.

lucky. And I think that was the thing that really stood out to me, just being able to help somebody get that education.

In her study of women's STM trips, Kersten Priest reports that the dominant narrative individuals from two separate trips provided in conversations with her were ones emphasizing the service rendered and relationships built with poor people. "Women I interviewed communicated a view of their trip as primarily organized around people understood to be 'in need'" (2009, p. 164). These discourses were ones in which STM travelers (one of the teams she studied tellingly dubbed themselves "missioners") engaged in a process of defining the trip and themselves through the act of caring for people perceived as needy. Following the process by which STM travelers identify and respond to "need," Priest argues, provides a means to understand "*how* caring efforts go forward, and how meaning is achieved, established and maintained" (2009, p. 25).

For all the members of CWC's teams, exposure to need was an explicit goal of the trip. Even some of the parents of the kids on our team mentioned to me their desire for their kids to "see how it is" in other parts of the world and "appreciate what they have." As Megan's mother said, "I just want my daughter to see that it's not everyone who has this life, this kind of life with all this." But in the post-trip narratives, understanding need was not the same as understanding poverty as a social or economic phenomenon. As in K. Priest's (2009) research, need was framed first and foremost in spiritual and relational terms, rather than social or economic ones. The needs of non-Christian Dominicans (or those perceived as non-Christian) were often viewed as emotional or spiritual needs manifested in physical needs.

At the same time, among Dominicans perceived as Christians, physical poverty was understood as a means of spiritual maturity or blessing, thus "need" became a more complicated category as applied to both impoverished Dominicans and wealthy North Americans. As returned STM travelers renarrated their encounters and experiences of the trips, the North Americans gave meaning to the nature of "need" in themselves and in the world.

NARRATING NEED

Identifying who is poor and how Christians should respond to poverty is never a straightforward act of economics or Christian ethics (Elisha 2008; Bialecki 2008; Allahyari 2000; cf. Wilson 1999). For the members of our team, anticipation of seeing poverty ran high, but as the previous chapter demonstrated, it was hard to understand in experience. In the months after the trip, those on our team continued to struggle with how to understand the needs they saw as well as what the right response should be.

James met with me seven months after we returned from the Dominican Republic. I had asked him *before* we traveled if he thought he knew why the DR was poor. His answer then mostly focused on the "lack of resources" he imagined would beset a small island nation. When I asked the same question in the post-trip interview, he repeated much of what he had said earlier about the size of the country and the lack of abundant natural resources. He was a bit more reluctant to state his opinion with much authority, having had some exposure to the complexity of the problems while taking college courses. At the same time, he drew personal meaning from his experience of poverty that was not part of what he said prior to our trip.

> Howell: What would you say if somebody asked you, "So why do you think that the people in the Dominican Republic are so poor?"[3]
>
> James: Oh, I've thought about that one a lot. And I honestly don't come up with an answer that satisfies me. I don't understand why they would be so poor. I mean, I suppose less natural resources than in America. Less economic growth. I mean, when you have a smaller-sized country, you are not going to have nearly the . . . I honestly have no idea. Because every time I think of something there's always another country that is rich that has nearly the same. . . .
>
> Howell: Have you had a chance to encounter any of this in your courses

---

[3]The question in my interview schedule was more straightforward than this. It was simply, "What do you think you've learned about poverty as a result of this trip?" The reason for the wording here is that it followed a discussion in which James was telling me about poverty in the community where he was attending college. He made the statement that there was "real poverty" but that "it's not like in the DR; everybody is just so poor."

that you've done at [college]? Have you talked about global poverty, third world countries, that kind of stuff?

James: Oh yeah! I took geography one time, and we talked a ton about global poverty; unfortunately we didn't get a chance to get into the Caribbean, but we talked about it in Africa, in Asia, and I don't understand it. Like, I don't understand poverty. I don't understand it—why it exists. But all I know is that it always will exist, and all we can do is try and help the people who are impoverished, as best as we can, if we're blessed, then we need to use our blessings to help bless other people, and that's probably one of the biggest things I learned in school, too, because poverty affects everybody.

Poverty is a complex phenomenon, so it does not surprise me that a first-year college student would struggle to articulate the causes of global inequality. What is interesting about his thought process is how, in light of his efforts to link this to the STM experience, he returned to the theological language of blessing, service and transcendent relationships: "Poverty affects everybody."

Later I asked him to reflect on his faith and how this trip affected him. His answer developed his connection between the ways the poverty he identified in the Dominican Republic framed an understanding of himself and his own social and spiritual condition.

Howell: Are there certain lessons or certain thoughts that stuck with you?

James: Probably, like on the emphasis on showing all our grace to other people, and being willing to go outside of the box, and go outside your comfort zone. Probably that. A lot of it had to do with how God can work miracles without material wealth and how much God works in peoples' lives in ways that in America we wouldn't necessarily notice, but you would notice over there. So I think it was just furthering the idea of the sovereignty of God and the benevolence and graciousness of God, even though what can be seen by Americans as not being grace at all, but being—not being a blessing but a curse. And I think blessings come in different ways, and I think I learned that a lot too. So, that's probably the biggest one. And of course you always grow close to God on a missions trip.

James was not the only one to articulate this connection of spiritual growth and poverty. Virtually every student I spoke to expressed some version of the idea that the poverty of Dominicans served as a kind of spiritual blessing and a good example for us in the United States. Mary put it this way:

> It was encouraging to see how there were Christians in the DR. They don't live in the same situation [as we do]. They're poor, but they have such a strong faith in God. . . . When I think when I got right back, it was just seeing how they were happy with all they had, I was thinking about how much I had, and I was happy with what I had. I remember people in the DR just happy with what God has given them.

Imagining poverty as a spiritual blessing/physical curse emerged from the narrative that understood our trip as an exchange in which the giving of our time and sacrifice would result in our receiving spiritual insight and blessing—from those we served, but ultimately from God.[4] The meaning emerging from these narratives partly fits the narrative structure of pilgrimage, in which those traveling encountered a kind of spiritual awakening through an encounter with spiritual power "out there." Instead of traveling to a particular shrine, the "poor" become a "place" where STM pilgrims experience true community (*communitas*) with each other and receive blessing from God through their inter-action with culturally different others.[5] But unlike narratives of pil-

---

[4]Omri Elisha, in his study of evangelical Christian charity in the United States, develops this discussion of service as exchange in much more theoretical depth in his article "Moral Ambitions of Grace: The Paradox of Compassion and Accountability in Evangelical Faith-Based Activism." In particular, he argues that while the exchange analysis of these actions privileges a structuralist perspective, these views are best understood "when they help us to account for the specific *cultural* contexts in which transactional practices are situated" (2008, p. 181).

[5]As I discuss somewhat in chapter two, I am referring here to the theoretical perspective of Turner and Turner (1978), whose classic work *Image and Pilgrimage in Christian Culture* took a Durkheimian approach to pilgrimage, arguing that the pilgrimage journey took a ritualized form in which everyday structures of social life were temporarily broken down, producing a moment of *anti-structure* and *communitas* in which participants felt freed from normal social bonds, leading to heightened spiritual experiences. As I also note in chapter two that others (Eade and Sallnow 1991) have argued that pilgrimage was a more contested process in which the shrine acts as a "religious void, a ritual space capable of accommodating diverse meanings and practices . . . " (1991, p. 15). I would see STM as much more like Eade and Sallnow than Turner and Turner, although as even Eade and Sallnow admit, in the Christian context, the Turnerian perspective tends to present itself consistently. For a careful comparison of these two views of pilgrimage, as well as an explanation of how narratives of travelers structure pilgrimage, even with the recognition of "contestation," see Coleman 2002.

grimage, this spiritual experience is not thought to come from the hardship of the journey or the power of the shrine, but through the self-sacrificial giving and humble receiving that is expected to take place when wealthy North Americans give themselves to the poor and come to recognize their own bondage to wealth. Poverty, in this way, is both a curse against which God and his people align themselves and a moment in which God can reveal himself in ways hidden in the comfortable worlds of wealth.

This kind of valorization of poverty or simplicity is similar to what Renato Rosaldo (1989) noted in the colonial writings of early travelers to the Philippines, who romanticized the lives of indigenous people—the so-called primitives—as the lost past of an increasingly fragmented and often troubling modern present. For the STM traveler, the narrative similarly constructs poverty as a curse to be overcome while providing the privileged with insight into a more spiritually pure life. To the extent that the recollections of poverty diminish many of the conflicts or ambiguities experienced "in the field," the interpretation of need in STM reflects an idea of the world in which guilt can be transformed into redemption through valorizing the poor and the transcending of difference through an experience of Christian relationships.

Several scholars of U.S. evangelical Christianity have observed that through worship practices and spiritual lives, Christians seek to overcome the alienating relationships of modern life (Luhrmann 2004; Bialecki 2008). The STM narrative exhibits the same desire as we experience the transcendence of cultural and economic distance in a relatively brief, albeit intense, moment of unity. Transcending disparities of wealth produced (or made possible) "social bonds not dominated by commercial logic" and the alienating technologies of modern life (Bialecki 2009, 119). True humanity, community and ideal fellowship are glimpsed, if not experienced, in ways that are ultimately transformative.

TRANSFORMATIONAL RELATIONSHIPS
The guiding STM narrative suggests that encounters with need not

only reveal truth about the world but also transform those who engage it. For many of those promoting STM, this is an overt feature of the STM narrative. Steve Walters, an STM advocate and organizer, made this point forcefully in a presentation at an STM research conference in 2009. His talk started by asking, "How do we view those in poverty? It shakes us to the core. . . . Encountering absolute poverty forces us to rethink our identity, to rethink our concept of justice, and to rethink our theology."

His presentation moved through various existential questions of God's justice ("Why is [food] so plentiful in some places and in such short supply in others?" "Where is God in all of this?"), emphasizing the common humanity of all people ("All are created in the image of God.") and the importance of gratitude for wealth ("Seeing our blessings . . . moves us closer to God and closer to others"). In his final paragraph, Walters ended with an encouragement to those involved in short-term missions:

> This is part of what makes short-term missions (STM) so exciting. Short-term missions have the potential to change how we view others and how we view ourselves. Short-term mission is about more than doing a project or giving money, it is about making relationships that heal across the wealth divide. It is about a God-empowered love that heals those who are poor in spirit. And in that process, we ourselves are healed in areas that we did not realize were damaged. It is about soul care at the deepest level. Short-term mission is about soul care that operates on three levels: ministry to the body, ministry to the mind and ministry to the spirit.

All this occurs, according to Walters, only through personal relationships in which the STM traveler encounters poverty on a "person-to-person" basis in which he or she experiences "a new level of humility and a new level of solidarity with others." Only in personal encounters and, ideally, authentic relationship would transformation occur.

In the varied tales of my team members, every person—adult and student—pointed to personal relationships with the long-term missionaries or Dominicans as one of the most significant outcomes of the trip, a way in which they were "changed." For some this was about particular individuals they had come to know and with whom they planned to have a long-term friendship. Others talked more generally about the "the kids we worked with" or "the Dominican Christians we got to know," but, particularly for the students, these relationships were narrated through the STM encounter as a spiritual connection in which theological lessons of gratitude or contentment offered the transformative (if temporary) insight into their own spiritual condition. Although these lessons were often reflective of the "spectacle society" characteristic of these trips (Linhart 2006), it draws on a vision of the self and a moral rhetoric similar to what Allahyari (2000) calls a "personalistic" view of service.[6] For those engaging in service with those in need and giving selflessly, the narrative of STM expects personal transformation to follow.

This transformation through encounter was an enduring lesson for many of my team members. Several, like Jeremy, pointed to the example of the children we interacted with at La Casa, on the worksite or at the VBS.

Howell: So if you had to pick a highlight, what would you pick?

Jeremy: Probably that last night at La Casa, most likely. 'Cause it was just how welcoming the kids were at the beginning. And just how at first you feel a little bit overwhelmed maybe, but then, by the end you just love it. And just the connections we made with them, and how cool that last night was.

Howell: So what did you like about that?

Jeremy: They were really welcoming. And just really happy with the little that they had. Here we're not happy with the stuff we have, when we have leaps and bounds more than what they do. And they have just the necessities, and that's fine for them, you know? That's what was really cool. Just to be so thankful for what we do have, and they're thankful for what little they had. It made me think different about what I have.

---

[6]Allahyari takes this phrase from Murray (1990) to refer to one of the two cases in her research. Specifically, she portrays this personalistic view as being characteristic of Catholic social movement teaching, as compared to the "Salvationism" of the Salvation Army's Protestant, bureaucratic approach to charity and service.

Mary described her relationships with kids at La Casa as a highlight this way:

> Mary: Oh, I just [loved] all the time I spent with the kids. That was my favorite part, like at [La Casa] was really profound, and I made some close friendships.
>
> Howell: Who do you remember?
>
> Mary: I remember Isamel and a little girl named Guinevere, and Jerome the most.[7]
>
> Howell: Why was that your favorite part?
>
> Mary: Because the kids were just happy with whatever they [had] and just God. It wasn't like they wanted more. It made me feel like I should be more like that.

For Jeremy, Mary and virtually all the other members of our team, relationships with particular people or types of people were key elements in the narrative of change or growth as a consequence of the STM trip. The creation of relationships, "connections" and bonds was a constant theme among college students narrating their experience as well.

Highlighting specific relationships has become a favorite technique in presenting these trips among many of the groups at the college in the past few years. In a recent chapel presentation of a group that travels annually to Honduras to install water systems in villages without ready access to clean water, the students shared stories of their "work partners," the Hondurans who labored alongside them to dig trenches for the piping or pouring concrete in the construction of the water system. With a photo of the work partner on the screen, several students told of getting to know that person and his or her family during the week the group spent in the town.

In one of the narratives, the student began by describing a soccer game between the North Americans and the Hondurans, followed by "the most breathtaking sunset I've ever witnessed." He gave the name of his work partner and told a bit of his biography: abandoned by his father, supporting his family on meager resources. He concluded saying,

---

[7]As with all names in this book, these are pseudonyms for particular La Casa children.

"Although communication wasn't perfect, God worked through it, and now we have family in Honduras."

Another student began his narrative by describing the death of his brother in a helicopter crash two years earlier, then introduced his work partner, Antonio. Antonio, said this student, "also had reason to doubt the goodness of God" after having been deserted by his wife and struggling in the poverty of his village. After reading the biblical story of Jesus raising Lazarus, the student concluded by saying that Jesus "asks for a simple faith: 'Do you believe?' Antonio believes. I saw Antonio comforted by the same comfort." He ended his talk by saying, "We went to Honduras to help them have clean water, but the Living Water was already there."

The connections drawn between relationships, experiences and the work of God emphasized the importance of these personal relationships in how God was at work in Honduras and the success of the mission. Personally, I don't doubt that these relationships, observations and experiences were deeply significant in the lives of these students. I know from my own experience that seeing the desperate conditions in which many people live can make a profound impression, inspiring reflection, if not change, in one's life at home. I know that some members of our team made significant changes after our trip, such as those who started studying Spanish or decided to financially support a La Casa child. Several maintained Facebook relationships with some of the older Dominican children we met. A number returned at least once to work at Linda Vista again.

But what did we know, learn or accomplish through these relationships? Even among those who went back to the DR, few spent more than a few hours reconnecting with those they had met two years prior. Among the college students who had traveled to Honduras, some undoubtedly returned or made decisions regarding coursework based on their experiences there, but had they met a need in the Hondurans? Or themselves? Did the trip itself contribute to an understanding of the political and economic context producing inequalities within and between nations, or did the sense of closeness, transformation and affection inhibit some such understanding?

From the personalistic narratives favored in these recitations, it's difficult to discern how these students grew in their understanding of poverty from their time in the Dominican Republic or Honduras. One thing that might provide a more holistic interpretation of the experience would be a robust expression of how the work performed—the school built or the water system laid down—fit into a larger scheme of economic development. However, the work performed, like the relationships formed, was typically understood in personalistic terms. Among the members of our team and in several other cases, I certainly heard people talk about the work project and the accomplishments of our labor. But in the recollections of work experience, the economic or political consequences of such work become secondary to the spiritual and relational transformations at the heart of the experience.

Transformational Work

This emphasis on personal relationships as what addresses the "real" needs of poor Dominicans and wealthy North Americans allows for an understanding of the work projects that minimizes efficiency or cost-effectiveness. This was often a key element of being outside of the "comfort zone," performing work for which we were undeniably unqualified. But bumbling through the work itself became a way of making significance out of the experience. In this way, the work, along with relationships, had a transformational effect.

Many of those on our team and other GO teams were well aware that local people could do the work we were doing more quickly and effectively. This question of the best use of funds is one of the key concerns many critics of STM raise (Sheler 2006, pp. 191-92; see also Montgomery 1993; Lo 2006). At the same time, scholars and other observers of STM have noted that part of the narrative and expectation of the trip is the demonstration of God's love (i.e., sharing the gospel) through the hard work, service and often *inefficient* effort put forth by relatively wealthy North Americans in the presence of the poor. Lasting benefits or long-term solutions to structural social inequality are seen as impossible, irrelevant or impractical.

In his study of STM trips to Trinidad, Kevin Birth (2006, 506) argued that the work performed by white North Americans served as a meaningful experience of reversal in which "it is by serving and toiling that one develops the most complete sense of one's humanness." The act itself is the service; the consequence to the material poverty is not irrelevant, but it becomes secondary. Birth notes that in one short-term mission manual, the authors suggest that it is precisely in the inefficiency of the North Americans laboring in the presence of the poor that Christian service is most effectively rendered.

> This is not about efficiency or even digging up a pond. It's about other things. Like demonstrating servanthood—the Guatemalans can tell we're not doing it because we're *good* at it. If we wanted to be efficient, we would have taken the money you raised, left you behind and hired some Guatemalan workers to do in two hours what it's taken our whole group to do in two days. We're not here for efficiency, or anything else you can readily measure, we're here to demonstrate the love of Jesus. (Stiles and Stiles 2000, p. 38, as cited in Birth 2006, p. 506).

As pointed out in chapter 5, this perspective of service was at the forefront of the thinking of Barney Torrance, CWC's education director, when he began to see the entire STM program take shape at the church in the 1980s. When Torrance noted that "the work is really secondary to the purpose of the [trip]," he expressed this as an epiphany that would become a key means of interpreting the worth of these trips in Christian terms. The work, as both activity and spectacle, played a key role in the purpose of the trip.

At one point in our interview, I asked if he found any resistance among people in the congregation to the development of an STM program, and he answered,

> There was some saying we were wasting money—Why are we spending seventeen thousand dollars to send seventeen people to Ecuador?—but that's why we emphasized that our people were changing, but we're also changing the people down there because they're working with Americans and they see the way we do things.

Barry went on to share stories of how he'd seen this change and it was about service, the ways North Americans learn to serve and give in

extraordinary and sacrificial ways as a result of mission. The stories—
of adoption, financial sacrifice and humility—were profound and did
not strike me as exaggerations, but they were not about changes in the
place they visited or about the amelioration of poverty. His final an-
ecdote made the point pretty clearly.

> One of the defining moments of my time at [Central]: we took a young
> group . . . it might have been Bolivia . . . I can't remember. We had a day
> when it was kind of raining or something, so I said, "Let's go to the mis-
> sionaries' work in an orphanage." Out of that, [one of the couples on the
> trip] adopted a Bolivian child. When I dedicated that child on a Sunday
> morning, Brian, you could just hear the sobs in the congregation; it was
> such a powerful moment. I mean it was a vivid illustration of a kid who
> had no hope. I think he'd been left in a bathroom or something, and
> they adopted this kid to give him a whole new life.

The amazing thing is that the adoptive father was a trader in the
commodities exchange.

> He was the main trader of corn or barley, and he was the main trader for
> Bolivia, so in some ways he was helping setting the price, so I remember
> seeing him, here he was on top of this wall, and we had this guy we
> called *Más Agua*—more water—because he would call for "more water,
> more water," and he would just yell, and it was just a great illustration of
> a servant's attitude. I remember, here was this guy who was helping to
> set the price for the whole country of Bolivia being yelled at by this guy
> we called *Más Agua*, and he was just serving with a smile on his face and
> bringing water, and they ended up adopting this child from Bolivia. I
> think they adopted another child too.

This story captures much of what many proponents of STM would
say is most important in these experiences: demonstrating humility and
service, giving sacrificially, creating relationships and experiencing personal transformation. Spiritual and emotional connections are made,
personal growth in relatively private realms of life occur (family, personal conduct) and the needs that are met are through intimate realms
of care (such as adoption). It also demonstrates that ongoing relationships with Bolivians are not necessary for these benefits to accrue.

Of course this story is dramatic for the obvious economic element contained here as well. I didn't ask if this trader's work was affected by his experience in Bolivia. I don't know enough about commodities trading to know what sort of influence this particular man could have had, even if he had wanted to, but it struck me at the time that Barney did not seem to connect the enormous economic power this man had with the transformations in his life. The mission work was construction, for which the trader was marginally qualified. His actual occupation, which had far more substantial economic consequences in Bolivia than the house he built, was a different sort of work and not attached to his mission. The mission was successful because the work changed the man who went, not because the work (or the man) changed Bolivia.

I never heard anyone from our trip put it quite so starkly, but the same cultural logic inhered in the testimonies of our travelers as well: "success" was not in addressing poverty, but in rendering service to the poor and returning changed as a result. The members of our team could find their actions meaningful as they imagined how God would use these acts of faithfulness, small as they were, to bring about greater good. As Emma said,

> I love to go on trips in the sense that you're two weeks there, and there's a lot less distractions, and a lot less things to do, and you're there just to serve the missionaries and serve the people and to help them in any way that you can, and it's not about what you're doing, it's about the fruit of what you're doing is going to create. And if you're helping the missionaries they can reach more people for Christ. When you're building something, it's easy to see the physical, what happened, because we build something and kids are going to live there and study there. But, yet I feel like there's so many, like, seeds planted just in the kids and just revitalizing the missionaries. My sister just got back from Africa; she went on a [short-term mission] team to Africa, and she said they really didn't do a lot, but she said she felt like they helped a lot just to be there for the missionaries. They did a lot of just maintenance work, and I feel like that's kind of one the important things of short-term missions trips.

For Christians seeking to understand inequality, poverty and cultural differences, it's clear that the aspect of narrative emphasizing personal relationships and the modeling of Christian behavior in the presence of those who seem separated from us by economics, culture or nationality is problematic at best. As the narrative weaves together physical poverty with emotional/spiritual poverty, the presence of a foreign group lacking linguistic skills, cultural competence and significant time seems an inadequate, if not counterproductive, response in terms of the social problems ostensibly being addressed by the work. Of course, it should be asked if the perceptions the short-term travelers have of the needs of local people—indeed the perception of the context itself—corresponds with reality. In looking back on their trip, some of the members of my own team became aware of the ways the STM narrative and focus shaped their ability to perceive the people and places of Linda Vista.

SHORT-TERM MISSION BLINDERS

Clifford Geertz (1986, p. 373), writing the conclusion to a collection of essays on narrative and experience, noted that "we all have very much more of the stuff (of experience) than we know what to do with, and if we fail to put it into some graspable form . . . the fault must lie in a lack of means, not of substance." For the members of our team and of many who renarrate their STM travels, aspects of the experience are frequently lost, unarticulated or glossed over as we lack the narrative framework to integrate them into our missionary tales. There is a high degree of idiosyncrasy with these, because the varied experiences on an STM trip can cover an extensive range, but there were several features of the experience of our trip to the Dominican Republic in which I could see the loss or difficulty of narration. Observing how members of my team struggled to articulate, or even recall, particular aspects of the experience shed light on the relationship between narrative and experience in the STM process.

As I observed while with the team in the Dominican Republic, the times of tourism—the waterfall, the raft trip, the beach—were enjoyed by everyone. Several students on our team were quick to point out those times as prominent memories and key elements of the narrative they shared with their friends and family. But in several cases, this very fact was accompanied by some guilt or at least an apology of sorts. At one point in our conversation, I asked Jeanie about any favorite photos she had. She mentioned one in which she and some of the other girls from our team were lounging on the beach. I asked her if she saw the beach visit as a highlight. She said it was, along with the whitewater rafting trip, but added,

> It's funny because I always feel bad liking those times and talking about them, because it doesn't really fit in with our missions trip. But the resort, I definitely had a good time doing the whitewater rafting and going to the waterfalls. I thought it was fun to see the fun side of [the] Dominican [Republic]. I feel like at the same time, we get so bummed down seeing all that poverty, and I think we also have to see the other side of things where Dominicans are happy and they do have a good culture and things to do and great land. So I thought it was fun that we got to see those parts too.

Perhaps more than most of the students on our team, Jeanie was explicit in resisting some of the personalism of the STM narrative so prominent for most of the others. She mentioned that she found some of her political opinions on immigration changing as a result of the trip—a political link that came through a film she watched in her Spanish class. As a high school junior, her thoughts were not yet well elaborated, but her willingness to think beyond some of the aspects of mission may have caused her to push back on the limits of what the "proper" purposes of the trip were. She talked more about enjoying the tourism aspects of our trip and her relationships with people on the team and in the youth group generally, rather than with children at La Casa or in the towns where we worked. At the same time, she felt a tension among enjoying the natural beauty of the Dominican Republic, experiencing various aspects of Dominican life and the mission for which we had traveled there. Jeanie didn't regret these experiences or feel great angst at having had fun, but for her, it was separated from the mission aspect of the STM narrative.

Ann Wright was one of the only members of our team to voice any regret regarding the time spent in tourism. In my interview seven months after coming back to Wheaton, I met with her, Paul and Aaron at their home. At one point, Ann cautiously suggested that perhaps we should have accomplished more work in our time in Linda Vista:

> Ann: I did say to [Phil Van Sant, the long-term missionary], we should do another day of construction, and we don't need to go to the resort. But there's—
>
> Aaron: Yeah, we needed to go to the resort. (*laughter*) We definitely do.
>
> Ann: But I said that to [Phil], and I said we can—why don't we just stay another day; we'll stay another day instead [of going to] the resort. And he said no. He said, "We need to go to the resort."
>
> Aaron: I think it's a good thing, because it's just relaxing and thinking about just nothing.

Ann quickly acquiesced to Aaron's position, saying, "Just debrief a little bit. Clean up. Yeah." Aaron's (and Phil's) insistence on the time at the resort was explicitly as a break from the mission, understood as the work. Just as she had while on the trip, Ann struggled to embrace the separation of our tourism from the poverty and suffering we were there to witness and address. But in the end of this short exchange, she acceded to the narrative separation of our mission from our tourism, a good thing where we could do "just nothing."

Moreover, Ann was aware that her distance from tourism kept her from seeing and understanding what she otherwise might have. Framing the tourist as someone deliberately enjoying and taking in the context, Ann used the provocative term *blinders* to describe how she felt the STM position affected her later ability to remember things she experienced while traveling.

> You know, one thing I think about the thing [Ellen Meyers] said. I wish I would have gotten my nails done. You remember that nail place? 'Cause I'll see pictures and not even remember the place . . . if it was something that didn't have something to do with what we were doing. I felt like I had blinders on to like anything other than what we were led to do, most of the time. You know what I mean? I mean, I didn't go as a tourist.

This continuing separation of tourism and mission mirrors the distinction between learning and doing in evangelical thought generally. In his now classic *The Scandal of the Evangelical Mind*, historian Mark Noll (1994, p. 12) asserted that "the evangelical ethos is activist, pragmatist, populist, and utilitarian." It was—and I would suggest, *is*—a part of the evangelical cultural milieu that shapes the STM narrative.[8] Arguably, the pragmatism of the evangelical community is a characteristic of white, suburban America generally (Holmes and Holmes 2002). STM, like tourism, is a cultural activity that frames travel as a quest to see new things, experience difference and gain experiences for the sake of the traveler (Franklin 2003). Yet to the extent that STM is framed as the opposite of self-indulgent touring, it also creates tension with learning as a self-conscious, even self-centered, intellectual pursuit. Both tourism and STM possess narratives of personal transformation, but they move in opposite directions. Where the tourist, like the pilgrim, finds inner transformation through introspection, education and a quest for personal growth (Berger 2004, pp. 51-53; see also Fussell 1987), the STM traveler looks to be transformed through service humbly and sincerely given and through the relationships that result. At least in the narratives, learning is often secondary to, if not in tension with, the true purpose of the travel.

The personalist emphasis of travel, along with the missionary impulse and pursuit of transcendent experience, meant a number of other features of our experience were also left out of virtually everyone's post-trip narratives. When I explicitly asked members of the team to consider the causes of poverty, some gave political answers—mostly regarding the internal politics of the Dominican Republic, rather than global or international relations—but these were never linked to experiences during the trip itself. Like James's, their post-trip answers were either more unsure than those they had given before their trip or simply mirrored what they had said in the months prior to our travel.

This is not to say that the trip failed in some way, since there was no emphasis on educating the team about geopolitical economic context.

---

[8]Noll goes on in that section, as well as throughout his book, to also point out the institutional and theological dimensions of the evangelical intellectual scandal, something I also stress in the creation of STM meanings in this book.

No one had such expertise, and it was not one of the goals of the leadership putting the team together. That no one on our team thought to ask about such issues as we gazed across sugar plantations on the North Coast or questioned ways globalization and tourism factored into the inequalities of wealth and transnational connections we could see during our trip suggests that the guiding narrative of STM does not inspire such questions. The travelers in our team, relying on the "cultural tools" of individualism, antistructuralism and relationalism (Emerson 2003), did not possess a narrative frame to "see" or ask about questions in these more abstract realms of political life.

In my interviews with team members, there was an interesting exception to this. When I was interviewing Paul and Ann in the months after our trip, Paul recalled something he had learned about a situation on the North Coast in which the Dominican avocado industry had been largely decimated when U.S. avocado farmers persuaded the U.S. government to change the trade rules, excluding Dominican avocados from the market. He couldn't recall where he'd heard the story, but it was something that stuck with him as a meaningful insight into the ways international relationships, global trade and macroeconomics played into the poverty we witnessed throughout our trip. I didn't tell him then, but I had actually mentioned this to him as we toured the North Coast near the end of our trip. It was something I had learned from Phil Van Sant the previous summer as he and I discussed agriculture, poverty and land during my own trip in 2005.

It revealed to me that someone like Paul, an economically sophisticated businessman, was every bit as interested in the complexities of poverty as I was, but that apart from a random comment made by the interloping anthropologist, there were few opportunities for learning about these interlocking issues. My own background and purpose had prompted me to ask about economic issues, leading to Phil giving the account of global trade and the avocado industry. But in the context of the STM with the CWC group, there were few occasions to learn such information and, more importantly, no impetus to ask.

A bit more surprising than our lack of conversation about political economics was what seemed to be our team's blinders on more personal issues, at least insofar as those linked to structural or social dimensions. For example, although I never made it the focus of my research, I was struck by the ways we did not address the issue of race. We had one person on our team who was not white: Amina, who came to Wheaton with her family from East Africa when she was in grade school. Her physical appearance (skin tone and hair texture) was very similar to that of many of the Dominicans, and she was a source of almost constant attention wherever we went. She was an outgoing girl who was eager to engage the many Dominican children who sought her out, but not in a way that was dramatically different from many of the other students on our team. She did not speak Spanish well, so it seemed fairly clear that her most distinguishing feature, from the perspective of the Dominicans observing us, was her race. I mentioned this to her at one point— that it seemed Dominicans were particularly interested in her—and asked her if she thought it had anything to do with the fact that she was the only black person in our group. She considered it, but kind of brushed off the suggestion. "You think?" she replied. "I guess. Maybe," and then she changed the topic.

Several researchers of North American evangelicalism have noted the difficulty that white, largely suburban conservative Christians have with addressing the politics of race in the United States (Emerson and Smith 2000; Emerson 2003; see also Priest and Nieves 2007). As with the issues of international relations and geopolitical economics, it is not surprising that STM narratives, to the extent that they reflect the wider cultural context of North American evangelicalism, leave race out of the explicit purview of the STM experience. Most likely, an adult as the only person of color with an all-white STM team would have found race a more salient aspect of her experience, as members of ethnic minority groups typically have an awareness of racial dynamics that members of the white majority do not (cf. Yancey 2001). At the same time, given the emphasis on transcendent Christian unity, interpersonal connection and transcultural relationships, even among adults, race is often glossed over or denied as a significant factor of STM encounters (K. Priest 2009, p. 179).

Highlighting these dynamics of the STM narratives is not to suggest that the focus on interpersonal relationships is wholly negative or that political activism, racial awareness or structural consciousness is antithetical to the more personalistic narratives at work. The point is to expose the ways this particular emphasis on personalism impeded and shaped the understandings sought by participants. By attending to the ways the guiding STM narrative works in shaping the experience and interpretation of such travels, we gain a way to see how these travels are cultural moments, reflecting a cultural and institutional context often implicit or unrecognized in religious settings. Moreover, for those who do find themselves discontented with STM as it is often practiced, this critical analysis points toward ways in which a more self-consciously cultural approach to change might take place.

Part Four

THE FUTURE OF
THE NARRATIVE

9

"Just Bring Greetings"

CREATING A NEW NARRATIVE FOR
SHORT-TERM MISSION

I BEGAN THIS RESEARCH WITH A VISION FOR AN ethnography of short-term missions and U.S. evangelicalism that would primarily speak to my fellow anthropologists and squeeze into the emerging literature on the anthropology of Christianity (see Robbins 2003). As I shared my work with those around me, however, I found the most eager and engaged audience to be fellow Christians who wanted to know what, if anything, might be wrong with STM and what, if anything, we should do about it.

As I began to read more about STM, I found that many more experienced ministry practitioners had already written quite a bit about whether short-term missions were beneficial or not. They had likewise written a great deal about how to improve the practice and theology of STM. In the past few years, we have begun to see leaders from countries often receiving North American STM teams write their perspective on the phenomenon. I came to realize that what would be most helpful would be to think about the process by which North Americans experience these trips, providing ethnographic data of the dynamics of seeing and doing that could contribute to the ongoing efforts of critical practitioners and self-conscious travelers to (re)make these trips in order to best reflect what they can or should accomplish.

What I want to do in this final section, then, is connect the discussion of the previous chapters to the various recommendations that over the years have been made about how STM might proceed. This chapter asks where STM might be going and, based on the thoughtful analysis of my colleagues much closer to the trenches than I, where it *should* be going. I want to bring to the table what is not always explicit in the many excellent works promoting change in STM practice and theology: working from the thesis of this book—that STM is a unique *cultural* practice, not simply another form of travel or a version of mission—implies that an effort to change STM be approached through cultural change.

It is not enough simply to alter our thinking about STM, as culture is not only about cognition; it is not enough to change our language, as culture is not only rhetoric; and it is not enough to adopt new practices or behaviors within existing systems. To imagine STM as a different sort of cultural process, one that lives up to the highest ideals of STM travelers, we must imagine structural and institutional change. Theology, language and practice are not irrelevant, but narrative change must be understood within a robust theory of cultural change that takes into account the differentials of power, social networks and institutional structures that constrain and form the cultural encounters of STM.

In this chapter, I ask what it means to think and act differently about STM. I begin by considering the most basic question of whether STM is, on the whole, a good thing. Next I look at some of those who have encouraged a refashioning of STM. In particular, working from the argument of this book, I explore what it means to talk about cultural change. In the end, I argue that to the extent that STM travel is meant to create lasting change for those traveling as well as accomplish good purposes in line with an orthodox understanding of mission, those sending STM teams must consider reform in light of the larger economic, institutional and cultural context of their travel narrative.

Should Short-Term Mission Continue?

As revealed in chapter three, since the beginning of the contemporary short-term mission phenomenon there has been a contingent of missiologists and mission practitioners (to say nothing of anthropologists) who have found the idea of STM problematic. Some of these leaders have positioned themselves against the whole practice of short-term mission, particularly for youth, suggesting that it should be abandoned (Schwartz 2003). The fact that most Christian leaders in the West who have written about STM since 2000 have reconciled themselves to the reality of these trips and have focused their attention on reformation rather than refutation does not make the whole question of STM's validity irrelevant. Is the practice of STM something that is good for the church as a whole? In particular, are the dynamics of wealthy Christians traveling to poor countries irreparably fraught with pitfalls that make them something to be abandoned completely?

Dennison Nash (1989), a relatively early scholar of tourism and a strong critic, wrote a widely cited article entitled "Tourism as a Form of Imperialism." While acknowledging the many varied expressions of travel that often fall under the tourism rubric, he argues that tourism can be subsumed under a "single theoretical scheme" applicable to all (1989, p. 38). In his view, the existence of tourism owes itself to the rise of productive capacity, leisure and economic development. Spurred by the production of "metropolitan centers," tourism becomes a social and economic transaction between those from the metropole and those in "touristic areas." The existence of the touristic area, identified by travelers from the metropole, comes to be defined by the needs of the metropole. "Because a tourist system, once established, must meet the touristic needs of one or more metropolitan centers, it will inevitably reflect in its evolution the development of such needs" (Nash 1989, p. 50). While Nash ends his article with a call for more nuanced anthropological research on tourism, it is impossible to find in his theory support for touristic travel.

In critiquing or even condemning tourism, Nash and other critics (e.g., MacCannell 2001; Ness 2003), are not suggesting that all international travel should cease. Instead, they are arguing that the cultural meanings of tourism are fraught with troubling inequalities and dynamics of power that invariably pave over local identity and autonomy in favor of a homogeneous tourist culture. Critics of STM have made similar claims as they have examined the encounters of North American STM travelers with the developing world through the guiding STM narrative. Some, such as Linhart (2006), Livermore (2006) and Birth (2006), have found that STM travelers project or imagine the lives and relationships of those to whom they minister, often coming away with romantic or unsubstantiated impressions of poverty and of the faith of the non-Western other. Even more critical voices, such as David Maclure (2001) and Richard Slimbach (2008), argue that these trips invariably reproduce the power inequalities, negative stereotypes and romantic illusions with which travelers began.

This effect is known enough among evangelical Christians that the satirical Christian news site LarkNews.com mocks these cultural dynamics in two fictional "stories." One comes under the facetious headline "Inner-City Mission Trip Confirms Youths' Worst Impressions," detailing how members of an imaginary suburban St. Louis youth group were disgusted by the conditions in the inner-city, causing them to vow never to return "except to show their own children how bad life could get if they make poor choices" (LarkNews.com, May 2008). In another of these satires, "Short-Term Missions Team Returns in Righteous Anger," a team returned from Guatemala to declare their fellow Indiana Christians "backslidden, fat and lazy," while praising the faith of poor Guatemalans.

> "All we hear since they got back is, 'You should see those Guatemalans. They're really committed to God,'" says one spouse who did not go on the trip. She, like many others, says her spouse and friends have become intolerable scolds since coming home (LarkNews.com, August 2005).

Of course, Christian satirists are not the only ones questioning the effects of short exposure to unfamiliar cultural context through STM. As noted in chapter one, a number of scholars have questioned the more empirical claims of STM. Some have tested the assertion that STM produces stronger support for long-term missions (Manitsas

2000; Priest, Dischinger and Rasmussen 2006; cf. Ver Beek 2008, pp. 486-87), while others have looked at the notion that participation in STM increases giving to development work generally (Ver Beek 2006) or works against ethnocentrism (Park 2008). In most cases, where results were based on data other than self-reporting, the researchers found that the claims of STM fell short. The findings are not unequivocal, but they raise many questions as to whether STM is a legitimate practice in the context of Christian theological and ethical commitments to missions and responsible stewardship.[1]

Yet even among the researchers cited above, the calls to abolish STM are relatively few. Much more common is the view that, while it is true that STM can be done poorly, with proper training the benefits for both hosts and travelers outweigh the costs. With some important caveats, I put myself in this camp. As one who has researched and read about STM for many years, I do not think the abolition of STM is either possible or desirable. Travel is a privilege and potentially a gift to the church. Theologically, the opportunity for Christians to learn from and interact with Christians in other parts of the world is a new and valuable theological resource that should be nourished, not extinguished.[2]

At the same time, travel is never simply travel. The question facing STM is *how* we travel. What sort of cultural interaction do we create? What sort of experience do we seek and why? How can we reshape STM into the kind of encounter that leads to the engagement and long-term personal changes most STM proponents seek?

For the reformers of STM, there is a consensus that by properly preparing travelers, negative outcomes and unwanted cultural dynamics can be avoided or at least lessened. Some of these are practitioners who

---

[1]One of the most comprehensive statistical studies to date, demonstrates a positive connection (if not causation) between going on an STM trip and increased levels of "civic participation" (Beyerlein, Adler and Trinitapoli 2011). Many of the claims, such as STM service causing an increase in the number of long-term missionary candidates, have not been quantitatively demonstrated, and the relatively stable (or even declining) numbers of long-term missionaries generally (with the massive increase in short-termers) would suggest the opposite.

[2]Many Christian scholars who write about global Christianity from a theological or historical perspective make the case that the opportunity for Christians of various cultural contexts to interact is a profoundly important resource for theological innovation and faithfulness that is now more available to the church than ever. See, for example, Walls 1996, chap. 4.

have sought to develop programs that can be implemented in every STM trip to produce a "maximum impact in . . . mission outreach" (Peterson, Aeschliman and Sneed 2004, p. 194). Others are scholars who have applied various educational theories and methods to consider how these trips might be better structured. Within these growing resources is much help for any STM traveler wishing to engage the process more thoughtfully. Underlying many of these more sophisticated efforts, however, may be an inadequate view of cultural change that leaves reform efforts limited in scope and effectiveness.

REFORMING SHORT-TERM MISSION

As the evangelical language and practice of short-term missions developed in the early 1980s, various leaders in the movement began coordinating to develop common standards of what a well-done STM trip would look like. One of the most well known is the Fellowship of Short-Term Mission Leaders (FSTML), formed in 1981 as a loosely affiliated group of STM leaders. Some of the core members of that group would later create Standards of Excellence, a kind of STM accreditation organization. Joining the organization and receiving endorsement required that any STM sending body, whether church, college or parachurch ministry, would affirm seven guidelines ranging from "God-centered" and "Empowering Partnerships" to "Appropriate Training" and "Thorough Follow-up." An application process and standardized review of STM sending bodies provided assurance to prospective STM travelers that the problems often attributed to STM travels (cultural insensitivity, ineffective work, negative experiences by the travelers) would be ameliorated or eliminated.[3] One reviewer of the standards wrote, "A coalition of short-term mission leaders concluded that the benefits of short-term missions outweigh their weaknesses—weaknesses which can be minimized with careful preparation and planning" (Collins 2006).

Scholars studying and writing on STM have similarly concluded that the beneficial or detrimental dynamics of these trips is largely, if

---

[3]It's not clear how widespread these standards have been disseminated or adopted. I'm aware that the organization holds a yearly conference drawing several hundred STM leaders from around the country.

not wholly, dependent on the training of the participants and administration of the event. Robert Priest, one of the most insightful and
critical evangelical scholars to study STM, has compared unprepared
STM travelers to "dogs in an art museum; they see everything and
understand nothing" (Priest and Priest 2008). In analyzing the problem
of insufficient preparation, Priest and Priest modify their metaphor
to say "dogs—and children—running through art museums see everything and understand nothing. But while dogs do not belong in art
museums and will never be able to understand what they see, children—
within an appropriate pedagogical framework—do belong in an art
museum in order that they will come to see and understand" (2008,
pp. 70-71).

David Livermore, professor of mission at Grand Rapids Theological
Seminary and director of its Global Learning Center, has been writing
and speaking on STM for many years. Having published several widely
read articles and a book, and having served as a lead consultant on a
Christianity Today International training program DVD to help participants prepare for "effective, life-changing short-term missions,"
Livermore is a staunch advocate for changing the expectations and experiences of STM travelers, largely through an increase in "cultural
intelligence," the "ability to interact effectively when we cross cultures"
(2006, p. 110). In his STM preparation book, as well as in the DVD
preparation guide, he gives considerable anecdotal evidence of the sort
of interpretive processes on the part of North American evangelical
STM travelers described here, along with fascinating comparisons to
the sorts of interpretations occurring among the leaders of receiving
communities. Livermore's and the Priests's works are critical reading
for anyone interested in understanding and reforming STM toward the
sorts of experiences many travelers seek. At the same time, there is a
question as to whether reforming the training process is sufficient for
changing the cultural dynamics of STM.

In 2007, Naomi Haynes reviewed Livermore's book, *Serving with
Eyes Wide Open*, in a special issue of the *Journal of Latin American Theology* devoted to short-term missions. At the time, Haynes was a
graduate student studying Zambian Pentecostalism in a top anthro-

pology program. In her review she attributes her scholarly career track to early experiences on STM trips in Latin America as a high school and college student. She also notes her experiences witnessing STM teams among Pentecostals she came to know in Zambia, where the experiences for the receiving communities were decidedly mixed. Although she praises Livermore's critical tone and ample examples, she ultimately asks if he and other such reformers do enough to change STM. After citing a quote in Livermore's book in which an African church leader remarked that a group of STM travelers had "just enough preparation to make them dangerous," she suggests, "I am not sure it is enough to keep [Livermore's] book from simply adding to just such a 'dangerous' amount of preparation" (Haynes 2007, pp. 262-63).

> Much of the book carries a sense that, while STM participants must slow down and widen their perspective, the direction in which they are going and the institutions of which they are a part can and will work effectively, provided these certain steps are taken. . . . However, I am unconvinced that the kind of thoughtful, sensitive encounters among believers that he advocates can be achieved within the existing structures of STM. (2007, p. 263)

Haynes (and I) is not saying that STM is an inherently unreformable cultural practice. Yet there are facets of change beyond the training of individual participants or the theological commitments of travelers that need to be considered. The guiding narrative of STM is not created merely through verbal acquisition or mental assent; it is an embodied culture produced in the institutions and wider practices surrounding STM. While we should not neglect the important insights of curricular and educational theorists who have advocated for the reform of STM, it is important to note that change is dependent on more than just better training and follow-up.

SHORT-TERM NARRATIVE CHANGE AS CULTURAL CHANGE

From the Fellowship of Short-Term Mission Leaders to the most ardent critics of STM, the one point of agreement every Christian writing about the phenomenon shares is a desire to make each trip "meaningful." I don't take this to mean that some trips are without meaning, but that each trip should have the *right* meanings emerge. These right meanings include an increased passion for mission and evangelism, a desire to give more money to missions and development, and increased Christian faithfulness. Most importantly, these increases must be permanent (Cook and Van Hoogen 2007, pp. 57-58; cf. Ver Beek 2008). The question this raises is, how? How does an STM trip become something other than an encounter in which the guiding narrative of personalism, transcendent equality and individualism are reproduced to the exclusion of structural insights and long-term commitments? How can these trips become opportunities to create long-lasting and significant links between Christian communities, while helping those who travel to interpret the encounter in a transformative way? Working from the argument of this book means that imagining reform of STM is to consider how culture generally changes.

Changing culture to reflect the priorities of Scripture has been a significant focus of Christians for centuries but has had a particular place among evangelicals, partly defining us as a distinct tradition within Western Christianity (see Bebbington 1989). In recent years, several North American evangelical leaders have notably taken up the question of how to produce cultural change within the church and the wider society. In 2010, sociologist James Davison Hunter addressed several views of how culture "actually changes," to confront the inadequacies he saw in various perspectives. His argument elaborates the point Haynes raised in regard to Livermore and other STM reformers who did not address the institutional context in which STM exists. It is worth briefly summarizing Hunter's work to explore how it applies to STM.

Hunter's main concern with contemporary approaches to cultural change is that they are too simplistic, theoretically and theologically. He writes that "the dominant ways of thinking about culture and cultural change are flawed, for they are based on both specious social science and problematic theology. In brief, the model on which various strategies are based not only does not work, but it cannot work" (2010,

p. 5). Beginning with two views of Christianity and culture popular among Christians today, Hunter argues that Christians routinely ignore or underplay the role of history, institutions and power when considering how culture changes.

Hunter begins with a discussion of the worldview approach to culture, in which culture is conceived primarily as the values individuals hold. He frames his discussion largely in relation to the writings of Charles Colson, a well-known evangelical author who has produced and championed an entire worldview training program administered through the Chuck Colson Center for Christian Worldview. The underlying assertion of Colson's worldview approach to cultural change is that "transformed people transform cultures" (Colson and Pearcey 2004, p. 295, as cited in Hunter 2010, p. 16). This is a widely held view, in Christianity and beyond: culture is changed one heart at a time, and most social problems can be solved through cognitive and affective commitments at the individual level.

What Hunter points out is that this view can't account for the discrepancy between what the majority of the people in the United States say they believe and the sorts of laws, systems and practices that prevail in the public sphere.[4] The neo-idealism of the worldview theory of cultural change reflects the individualism and pietism that are characteristic of U.S. evangelicalism,[5] but it does not provide an adequate explanation of how cultural forms become dominant or persist even in the face of explicitly divergent values and beliefs by the majority. Asserting that changing one's value orientation or enlightening the mind changes how symbolic systems and institutions op-

---

[4]Hunter draws several examples from the cases that frustrate many conservative Christians the most. For example, he cites Colson posing the question "Why is Darwinism still the official creed in our public schools?" Colson argues that the answer is the number of people who believe (erroneously in his view) that Darwinism is true. Yet according to survey data, most U.S. Americans either did not believe that Darwin's theory is supported by scientific evidence or felt they did not know enough to have an opinion. Only 13 percent believed God had no part in evolution. If the values and beliefs of individuals lead to cultural change, Hunter argues, the majority would have more influence than the minority; Darwinian evolution should have a very small hearing in schools or the wider society.

[5]The individualism of historic and contemporary Protestant Christianity in the majority Euro-American traditions has been well documented by scholars. See, for example, Marsden 1984; Noll 1994; Smith and Lindquist 2005; Emerson and Smith 2000.

erate underestimates the strength of these systems and vastly overestimates the ability of ideas—even good ideas—to effect change apart from a host of other conditions.

Similarly, Hunter attacks the view that culture is largely the accumulated results of creative individuals working to get their ideas, products or cultural practices accepted in the wider culture. In what he calls the "market populism" perspective, culture changes when individuals create new culture that wins out in the marketplace, such that it is eventually taken up by others. Hunter attributes this view to Andy Crouch, the author of the influential book *Culture Making*, who coincidentally was one of the authors of what is arguably the most comprehensive and sophisticated STM preparation curriculum available (Blumhofer and Crouch 2008). Whether Hunter gets Crouch quite right or not,[6] he argues that this view also fails to make sufficient room for an understanding of the way history, institutions and power influence the formation and potential *trans*formation of culture. "In the end," Hunter writes, "this view of culture and cultural changes shares many of the basic problematic assumptions of the dominant [i.e., worldview] view. This perspective is individualistic—cultures are constituted by and changed through the actions of aggregated individuals" (2010, p. 31).

Hunter's critique of culture change suggests why the many important and thoughtful efforts to reform STM have so far failed to make a profound impact on the experiences of the bulk of STM travelers, at least as viewed through the empirical measures and guiding narrative prevalent today.[7] Short-term mission, like other cultural forms, comes with a history and an embodied practice that is not easily changed on the individual level. Merely attending to the ideas or commitments of individual travelers risks continuing to reproduce the narratives generated

---

[6]Crouch reviewed Hunter's book in the book review journal *Books and Culture* in May/June 2010 (Crouch 2010). In an overall positive review, Crouch questions whether the conclusions Hunter reaches are ultimately vastly distinct from his own.

[7]"Empirical measures" refers to those that examine behavior, such as are cited earlier in the chapter. There are several studies that survey participants of STM and find strong agreement with such questions as "This trip changed my life" (e.g., Tuttle 2000; Horton et al. 2011), but I would argue that this sort of self-reporting would be expected, given the guiding narrative surrounding these trips. See also Ver Beek 2008.

in the wealthier "sending" countries. This is Haynes's concern in her response to Livermore.

> As Livermore points out in the final chapter of *Serving with Eyes Wide Open*, short-term missions should be about listening, so much so that those who go must be willing to surrender their ability to plan and do and instead humbly seek to understand how God is working in a particular place. If the existing infrastructure and ideology of STM can make this kind of qualitative shift, which Livermore believes they can, then let us continue on the same path with a widened perspective. But if, as I suspect, the existing institutions of STM are inherently colored by the need to *do* something (which the world "mission" certainly connotes), then perhaps it is time to abandon them in favor of some other model, a model that would preserve the spirit of *Serving with Eyes Wide Open* while altering the structure of short-term missions. (2007, p. 263)

ALTERING THE STRUCTURE

For all the variation in STM, there is a very common structure to the experience, a tripartite narrative arc moving from pretrip, through the trip, to the post-trip stage. This arc is recognized by everyone from staunch advocates to secular anthropologists, and STM reformers have suggested thoughtful and important interventions at each of these stages.[8] Many of those suggesting reform come from educational backgrounds. They have generally encouraged a more robust preparation, emphasizing education about the country to be visited, preparation in cultural understanding and greater theological background in mission. In particular, a number of scholars have pointed to the literature on service learning as providing a model or method to transform the STM experience and, subsequently, the STM traveler (e.g., Radecke 2006; Weber 2011).

Terence Linhart (2005, 2006), a professor of Christian education and a particularly insightful researcher of STM notes that one of the goals of STM trips is the transformation of travelers through an implicit curriculum of preparation and training "centered on what the stu-

---

[8]"Staunch advocates" would include the Fellowship of Short-Term Mission Leaders.

dents were to *become* because of the experiences" (2005, p. 267). The emphasis on *becoming* lacks clarity, he argues, since it assumes that the experience itself is sufficient for the *becoming*. It is not enough to encourage *becoming* without sufficient attention to the content that guides the nature of that becoming. "If the curricular nature is one of becoming," Linhart asks, "what is it, or who is it, that we want a student to become from these trips? Is it our place or the students' place to determine that? What educational structures will best assist in answering these questions?" (2005, p. 268).

Like other educational reformers, Linhart emphasizes the post-field stage in which travelers are encouraged to reflect on the experience in a more extensive manner than is typically afforded in the gatherings where photos are shared or testimonies are given to donors or church members.[9] More importantly, Linhart acknowledges that we must pay attention to the structures—the systems and institutions—in which these educational practices take place. Who are the teachers? How is the curriculum established? What determines the agenda for an STM trip? These are questions that bring us to the heart of power and control in the practice and experience of STM.

The most radical suggestions typically come from those who recognize the cultural structures built into the STM travel experience and seek to encourage ways to disrupt or reimagine the structure of the trip. As a doctoral student in the United Kingdom, Nicholas Shepherd (2005) found himself serving as a receiving member of an STM experience known as Soul in the City (SITC). In a fascinating case study in which dozens of urban London congregations partnered with a suburban megachurch to put on a massive service event of "[sending] young 'missionary delegates' for the purpose of 'impacting the capital for Christ,'" Shepherd reflects on the cultural and social dynamics of the event (2005, p. 258). As he participated in the preparation and examined the rhetoric being supplied by the suburban congregation, Shepherd saw the cultural implications in the structure of the SITC event: it necessarily drew on the culturally preexisting narratives and

---

[9]See also Johnstone 2006; Blomberg 2008, pp. 606-7; Tuttle 2000; Swartzentruber 2008.

practices of tourism, creating "inevitable" dynamics for those participating. "What we have in effect is the emergence, and recognition, of
the *tourist-missionary*," he writes. "This is an inevitable consequence of
both the role of tourism as a structural facet of our culture and the or-
ganizational management of SITC using touristic principle and practices" (2005, p. 259).

As is the case in this book, Shepherd does not argue that STM is a
type of tourism, and his case was significantly distinct in a number of
ways from the Central Wheaton Church program, but his observation
that cultural structures already in place inevitably shape the experience
of the event makes the point. In his case, after a great deal of conflict
between the suburban megachurch leaders and the coalition of urban
congregations with whom they sought to partner, the event produced a
number of positive, longer-term effects that the organizers (particularly
the local urban organizers) sought.

But, according to Shepherd, the positive experience of both "sending"
and "receiving" churches took place only as the urban churches receiving the suburban megachurch teams were able to push back during
the planning stages, refiguring and recasting many of the events to fit
what the urban congregations were already doing. It was a difficult
process of negotiation, Shepherd writes, but one that ultimately caused
the experience to be one that he, personally, found more rewarding
than he anticipated. Of course, this all occurred between congregations
within a common cultural and economic context, in which divisions of
race, culture and language were minimal. Even the differentials in economics were far less than what is experienced between a congregation
such as CWC and the typical Protestant church of Kenya, Peru or the
Dominican Republic.

In the current configuration of international STM projects as they
flow out from North American colleges, congregations and communities, it is difficult to imagine such negotiations taking place.[10] In spite

---

[10]Bonk (1991) discusses the dynamics of wealth inequality in missions in his classic work *Missions and Money*. He, along subsequent mission scholars writing on STM (e.g., Schwartz
2003), argue that the control and distribution of resources creates dynamics of dependence and
inhibits the very relationships STM travelers believe they have experienced or created.

of the 4.5 million-plus dollars provided by the suburban church in Shepherd's study, the urban London congregations were able to push back on what they felt to be the "arrogance and insensitivity in 'forcing' this [SITC] event upon us in what I considered at the time to demonstrate a lack of appreciation for ongoing work in the capital" (2005, p. 256). The differences in wealth and power between many of the small congregations receiving STM travelers around the world and the North American travelers themselves make this sort of relationship difficult, if not impossible.

Changing the cultural structure of STM will require attention to the power imbalances created through the inequalities of wealth present in these encounters. More specifically, it will require those with more resources to intentionally subvert the inequalities as they exist. In their STM preparation curriculum, Blumhofer and Crouch (2008) included several interviews with significant African church leaders. Dr. David Zac Niringiye, assistant bishop of the Kampala Diocese of the Anglican Church in Uganda, affirmed the call of many STM reformers to reorient these trips around listening, as opposed to projects or activities. In response to the question of how STM travelers can best engage Ugandan Christians, Bishop Niringiye answered,

> It is very simple. Come and be with us, with no agenda other than to be with us. One friend of mine by the name of Mark, a pastor of a large church, amazed me when he came to visit. He came for three weeks and he said, "All I want is to come and be with you." At first, I didn't believe him. . . . We went to northern Uganda, where the civil war is causing such suffering. And Mark didn't ask, "Is it safe for me?" That amazed me. If it was safe for me, then it would be safe for him. He was not unaware of his power, as a *mzungu* [foreigner, and more specifically, white person], and that people would think he had a lot of money. He asked me, 'What should I say? What would be appropriate?'
>
> "Just bring greetings," I said. (Niringiye, as quoted in Blumhofer and Crouch 2008, p. 88)

This kind of humility and openness may strike many as romantic but impractical: how, exactly, could one pitch a trip to bring greetings as a "short-term *mission*"? The history and cultural context of mission makes such an association difficult, to say the least. The guiding STM narrative can do little with a trip where the primary activity is greeting. For this reason, some church leaders have continued to call for the word *mission* to be dropped. Oscar Muriu, a pastor at Kenya's Nairobi Chapel, spoke to the Urbana missions conference in 2009, where he suggested that the structure of U.S. missions is a largely one-directional activity. Addressing the North American crowd, he aligned himself with his listeners saying,

> And so we jet into the hard places of this world, especially among the poor and the powerless. We get into our air conditioned limousines and short-term mission buses. We drive into the inner city communities, into the slums and the *favelas* of the world while the poor stand by the roadside and they wave us by. We get out; we address them; we paint a clinic or two; we take a few pictures. We make a few promises about building them schools or sending them scholarships, and then we get back into our limos and we go off to debrief on some safari. Mission accomplished. Quick, clinical, easy. But nothing changes through these helicopter missions.[11]

It is not the material conditions that Muriu is referring to when he says, "nothing changes." Rather, like the STM travelers and organizers, he hopes to see greater faithfulness to the gospel as the result of these trips.[12] As a middle-class Kenyan, he is personally aware of the problems with wealthier people becoming only momentarily aware of poverty, developing appreciation for their own wealth and making relatively few significant changes as a result. For this reason, Muriu joins the chorus of reformers who want the primary activity of STM to be listening.

> We don't call them "short-term missions" any more. We call them "short-term learning opportunities." The problem with calling it a

---

[11]Oscar Muriu speaking at Urbana 2009, December 29, 2009.

[12]Stephen Offutt, in his study of the effect of STM interactions on congregations in El Salvador and South Africa, notes that many of these church leaders see a number of positive spiritual effects when their congregations receive STM teams from foreign countries. For example, one pastor reported his congregants as developing a vision for service and development work in other parts of the country as a result of following the example of an STM team. A South African mission administrator noted that one large congregation in El Salvador grew in its desire to "minister beyond the boundaries of their neighborhood" (2011, p. 804).

mission is that it implies an agenda. There's something I need to come and do for you, or to you, to better your life. In reality that doesn't happen in two weeks. Life is far too complex for that. (Muriu, as quoted in Blumhofer and Crouch 2008, p. 102)

Craig Stephen Smith, a Native American (Chippewa/Ojibwe) church leader, refers to these trips not as mission but as "plight-based ministry" in which the purposes of the travel are defined by the perceived needs of the community to be visited and the resources of those visiting. "Plight-based ministry," he writes, "is the easiest one to present to the supporters of that mission work" (C. S. Smith 1997, p. 68).

> Plight-based ministry meets a tremendous need for the supporting churches, because it provides a means by which they can help those who are less fortunate, which is a biblical command, but in doing so often perpetuates the stereotypical view that those from the dominant society churches have of native Americans. . . . They actually hinder and impede the very people their ministry is intended to help. (1997, pp. 68-69)

What Smith, Muriu and Niringiye are proposing is more than simply a change in nomenclature or better preparation, although these are not irrelevant. They are pointing out the fundamental institutional arrangements of these trips: they are initiated by North Americans (either located in North America or connected to North American missionaries in receiving countries); the funding is controlled by the North Americans; and in response to these funding needs and cultural context, the trips are conceptualized in accordance with a missionary model of action and exchange. Without changing these structures of STM, changing the cultural dynamics and the narratives of STM may become an exercise in futility.

Recognizing some of the problems in STM has led many congregations to consider how to mitigate these issues. Some innovative congregations have long-term relationships with particular denominations or developed exchange programs (cf. C. Brown 2008). This is a response suggested by a number of thoughtful short-term mission advocates (e.g., Rickett 2009). In a special 2007 issue of the *Journal of Latin American Theology* (*JLAT*) dedicated to the topic of short-term missions, a number of Latin American pastors, theologians and church leaders wrote about their experiences receiving and sending STM teams. All encouraged the continuation of STM (and defended it as something good for their own church members to do), but all called for greater partnership and collaboration. Paraguayan seminary professor and pastor Martin Eitzen concluded his essay, saying,

> On the basis of relationship, we, as Latin American Christians, would like STM groups to keep coming. Not to teach us how to evangelize, or how to work correctly and efficiently in the church, but to live with us, get to know us, have fellowship together and thus, living together, to learn from one another and teach one another. (Eitzen 2007, p. 47)

Seminary dean and international church leader Francisco Cerron was somewhat more critical of STM overall, but likewise concluded with a call for reform. Writing to his own church, he said,

> It is in our hands as Latin Americans to raise our voice and, if necessary, to say, "Stop!" The time has come for us to sit at the negotiating table and establish an agenda together, with foreigners and locals, sending and receiving churches on equal footing, because in the end, we shall all stand before Christ's throne to glorify his name together. (Cerron 2007, p. 32)

Though a number of the contributors to the special issue of *JLAT* called for greater "contextualization" or cultural sensitivity on the part of visiting North American STM teams, what they ultimately advocated was the reorganization of power in STM relationships.

MISSIONS AND POWER

The missionary narrative, and the North American notion of "mission," is a key contributor to the inability of STM participants to see the power relationships inherent in their encounters. Miguel Ángel Palomino, a Peruvian pastor with a Ph.D. from the University of Edinburgh and the director of an international Spanish-language graduate program, was one of the more critical authors in the papers gathered in the *JLAT* volume. Noting that "STM may be seen as an expression of a postmodern type of U.S. American missionary colonialism" (2007, p.

220), Palomino returned to the argument of the 1990s that the word *mission* no longer be applied to short-term trips. But in contrast to those who have made theologically based arguments, Palomino ultimately argued that the mission narrative works against mutuality.

> Here we should ask if the proliferation of the so-called STM will not be an obstacle to strengthening the partnerships that have already been formed. Would US American and European churches accept "short-term Latin American missionaries" coming to help them with ministry? . . . In the United States, someone said to me, "I can't imagine having Latinos coming over to help us evangelize people when they don't even speak English." I thought, "How interesting. US American short-termers speak neither Spanish nor Portuguese, yet they come to Latin American anyway, trusting churches will receive them warmly and make the effort to find interpreters." Why do we not see the same attitude in northern countries? (2007, p. 222)

I observed a similar blindness in CWC during a GO board meeting some months after our DR trip. One of the other summer teams had gone to Costa Rica to work with a private Christian school. The middle- and upper-class Costa Rican students had visited Wheaton the previous year in a kind of exchange. In that previous visit, they had shadowed North American peers in the high school, an activity they apparently found less than interesting. What they had enjoyed was the day they spent helping with the childcare in a refugee tutoring program CWC hosted during the week. As the Costa Rican group looked ahead to a return visit, they requested more time doing "ministry," such as working in a soup kitchen, tutoring and doing childcare.

For nearly twenty minutes, the board debated whether they felt this was a good idea. A number of comments suggested a discomfort with the idea of the Costa Rican teens spending their time working in various ministries of the church. "I don't know if I feel good about asking them to work while they're here," said one member. "They're guests. I feel like we should be hosting more."

Another said, "I don't think we really need them to do these things. They're covered, right? Would it be just duplication?"

As the idea of honoring their request to work in a soup kitchen was discussed, one woman said, seemingly unself-consciously, "I don't really want to send them to the ugly things. . . . I mean, it's not like we're a poor town. I want them to see the nice side of Wheaton."

This discussion went unimpeded for twenty minutes before I heard a person say, "I wonder if this is how they feel when we come down to do work down there."

It surprised me a bit that the conversation had gone on as long as it did before someone saw the evident parallel of the Costa Rican teens' desire to serve "the poor" in Wheaton, with CWC's own program of STM. But in retrospect, I could see that even this modest insight was possible because CWC was interacting with the experiences and perspectives of the Costa Rican group directly. Through their request, the Costa Rican church had entered the narrative, forcing a reframing, at least potentially. What virtually all Latin Americans writing about STM sought was a way to bring their perspectives into the conversation, such that their experiences could be more directly available to North American STM teams.

MISSIONARY MEDIATION

Many congregations and other STM organizations are aware of the problems frequently encountered when powerful North American teams arrive to deploy a missionary agenda among a host community. One strategy a number of congregations have developed to mitigate these effects is to have STM groups work under the auspices of long-term missionaries who are presumably familiar with the local culture, context and needs. At CWC, the structure allows some, like the Mission Board member quoted in chapter one, to see STM as "real missions" when short-term projects support the ongoing work of career missionaries.

No doubt, this provides a way to insulate the local population from having to interact directly with North Americans unaccustomed to the cultural or economic context. It provides a way to deploy resources more strategically to longer-term development projects by those who have far greater knowledge of local conditions than an STM team could get working on its own. It provides accountability to those receiving resources through the normal checks and balances the congregation has developed for supporting the career missionaries. [13] What it also can do, however, is facilitate a cultural encounter in which the experiences of STM travelers are further mediated through the narratives of North American culture and context, placing greater control in the hands of foreign or expatriate Christians and often inhibiting interaction with local leadership.

In his concept of "tourist culture" described in chapter 2, Dean MacCannell (2001) argues that by providing the experience tourists come to expect when they travel anywhere, local people reproduce a uniform "tourist culture," differentiated by only superficial local distinctions. The local people providing the tourist experience, known as "tourates," serve as the mediators between the local culture and the expectations of the tourists. These tourates, argues MacCannell, are motivated to make the experience predictable, comfortable, and meaningful by keeping stress, surprise, and real differences to a minimum.

It's not difficult to see the corollary in STM, particularly in a context such as Linda Vista, where career missionaries have developed a consistent STM experience for visiting teams. This is not to say that there is no variation to the activities or experiences of the teams. Emma and Aaron, who had been to the same place in the previous year, remarked on a number of differences between the trips, primarily rooted in the goals of the team leaders (the first trip was specifically for "leadership development") and the group dynamics. What did not seem to change was their experience of the Dominican Republic. In our interview nine months after our trip, Emma told me about what she felt she'd learned. I was not sure whether she was referring primarily to the first trip or

---

[13]It is worth mentioning that the AN missionaries with whom I spoke generally welcomed the STM teams as an important resource for their ministry and an enjoyable aspect of their work. The visits from the teams became opportunities for the missionaries to see those from supporting congregations, some of whom they knew personally. It also allowed them, along with their children, to accompany the teams on recreational activities. However, it could not be said that our presence significantly "freed up" the career missionaries to do other work, because during the "STM season" from May to September, the missionaries spent a great deal of their time organizing and hosting the STM teams. As would be the case with the construction work, there is no doubt that were we to send the funds, the missionaries could hire local people to perform tasks that would provide them more time for ministry-related work.

the second, so I asked her to clarify. She answered,

> I think they were the same. I think the first trip, I definitely I learned I
> needed to be more patient and more reliant on God. I think the second
> time around, it was just kind of like, wow, I need to revisit that lesson
> that I learned a year ago. . . . Maybe the first time I came, we were more
> sheltered—we only worked with [La Casa], so we saw most of the kids
> who had either changed their lives because of Christ or have had a lot of
> interaction with people who had believed and shown God's love, as op-
> posed to the people who still have yet to really comprehend or under-
> stand that. The first time I went, I realized that people in the Do-
> minican were poor and physically and monetarily needy. But I feel like
> the second time around it was more of a "wow," especially when Phil
> took us around [Gato Negro] and was telling us how it was. . . . I think
> I just kind of glazed over that the first time and [didn't] comprehend it.

Our group received most of its explicit exposure to poverty through
the missionaries who were with us throughout the trip. Like tour guides
with package tours, our missionary docents provided commentary on
what we saw, what it meant and, for most of the members of the group,
literal and figurative translation of what people were saying and what
we were seeing.

At one point in our experience, a missionary (Jane Schurmann) served
as a literal tour guide as we walked through the neighborhood around the
afterschool center. As she took us into the homes of an impoverished
farmer, the mother of a student and a local family, we were introduced
and familiarized with the local economic conditions through her narrative. Although it was one of the few opportunities that we had to hear
from Dominican community members, it felt like being led on a tour of
important sites. Like tourists viewing the ruins of Athens or the art of
Rome, we were seeing things we were "supposed" to see. At one point,
five members of our group stood in front of the farmer's house with their
arms around each other, while an adult leader took their photo. I never
saw the photo itself, but as I watched the members of my team placing
themselves for the photo, I could see that it had the same staging as
photos taken in front of landmarks, overlooks and other touristic scenes.

Scholars of tourism have argued that it is these local mediators of travel who have the most influence on the construction of knowledge in crosscultural encounters (Cheong and Miller 2004). This could be particularly true in the case of long-term missionaries, in whom the STM visitors are conditioned to place a great deal of trust. This is not to suggest that the missionaries were not gracious, well-informed and thoughtful interpreters of our experience. But because most of our team members interacted primarily with Dominican children and North American adults, the ability of local leaders or other community members to shape our interpretations, along with our exposure to the more complex or locally particular dynamics of the community, was limited.[14]

Moreover, in primarily interacting with North American missionaries, STM teams inadvertently withhold "linking social capital" that some scholars of STM believe to be the most important consequence of STM travel (Priest 2010b, pp. 95-99; K. Priest 2009, p. 35ff). Social networks between North Americans are reinforced, while new networks involving national leaders and other members of the communities visited are left undeveloped or underdeveloped. Hunter (2010) argues that it is through well-established social networks, in which elites (e.g., relatively wealthy North American STM travelers) become linked to non-elites or those outside their network, that new voices and ideas can become influential in cultural processes.[15] When the links created by STM travel are made primarily with North American missionaries, it precludes non-North Americans from gaining access to the networks by which they might influence the experiences, to say nothing of the actual practices, of STM travel.

Carl Brown (2008) argues that mediation of "bicultural or transcultural people" in the context of STM is important for both sides to gain

---

[14]Such opportunities were not absent, as we did have some interaction with Juste and Marcial at the worksite, our cook, Carmela, and our driver, Esteban. In addition, several older teen girls who worked as ministry interns with the organization accompanied us on our VBS trips to neighborhood churches. I recall Ann Wright being moved by the teaching of one of these interns, in which she described heaven as "a place where you are never hungry." Ann noted how this was something "you would never hear from a North American." While such exposure to Dominican leaders was often meaningful to our team, it was quite limited.

[15]Among his eleven propositions about how cultures change, Hunter (2010, p. 38) argues that "the key actor in history is not the individual genius but rather the network and the new institutions that are created out of those networks." Likewise, cultural change is inhibited or precluded when those with revolutionary ideas are excluded from networks.

an understanding of the other and develop partnerships. In some cases, he notes, this may be an expatriate missionary with extensive linguistic and cultural experience in the community that a team hopes to visit. In three specific cases he cites, however, it was the formation of bridging or linking capital between local and North American congregation members that led to successful—and mutual—partnerships. In cases where the North American congregation linked primarily with a North American missionary or where the power differences between the North American and (in his case) the Ukranian "partner" was not recognized, there were misunderstandings, serious conflicts between the congregations and, in one case, ruptured relationships and failure.

Such challenges should push us to ask about the purpose of STM travel generally. The CWC leadership in charge of the GO program felt the four purposes they outlined for the trips—exposure to missionary life, recruitment of long-term missionaries, personal spiritual growth, service to others—were being accomplished. But is that enough? For the Christian, it is not enough to define what those traveling want to accomplish or even what the local hosts want a visiting team to accomplish. For us, the question should always be, what is God's purpose for STM?

Embracing the Missio Dei in Practice

Mission is first and foremost a theological enterprise. While some point to the mission moniker as a problem in STM travel, theologically speaking, the life of a Christian is a missionary life (Bosch 1991, p. 8). We are called to engage the world in both extraordinary and ordinary ways, sharing our hope through travel and through staying put. At the same time, the cultural category of "missions" has taken on a much more specific and historically particular meaning than the everyday life of a believer. While changing our theological understanding of missions to fit with a more theologically robust understanding is not enough to alter the historical and cultural meanings of the term, it is an important element in reshaping the guiding narrative. Specifically, by making the STM experience one in which mission conflicts with tourism or even education, STM travel demands the kind of frenzied activity that leads to the STM blinders Ann Wright experienced and Christian leaders such as Smith, Muriu, Palomino and Niringiye warn against.

Mission theologians give the same caution when they stress that missionary activity must be defined by the *missio Dei*, or the mission of God. Theologian Kevin Vanhoozer (2005) uses missio Dei as the linking concept for all of theology and Christian life. Explaining that the nature of the triune God is in sending, he declares that the life of the entire church should be oriented around this larger notion of God's mission: "The Father sends the Son in order to share his truth with others; the Father sends the Spirit in order to share the love he bears for the Son with others. *The purpose of the two missions, then is communion, and community: a sharing in the truth and love—the very life—of God"* (2005, p. 70; italics in original).

This expansive notion of the mission of God works against the dichotomy of education and mission, listening and doing, and even personal enjoyment and sacrificial service. If God's mission is the reunification of all things to himself, including the restoration of fellowship within the church and among people everywhere, then any time spent listening to local leaders or visiting with villagers is as legitimately a part of STM as is building a house, performing a mime or leading a VBS. Moreover, activities such as visiting a beach, touring a museum or even shopping should be incorporated into the entire mission of the trip and performed with the same posture of service and care brought to the VBS program or construction site. These can no longer be time off from the "real" work of mission—a break from the actual purpose of the trip; they too become sacred encounters with God's world and his people. Mission theologian David Bosch (1991, pp. 10-11) writes,

> The missionary task is as coherent, broad and deep as the need and exigencies of human life. . . . People live in a series of integrated relationships; it is therefore indicative of a false anthropology and sociology to divorce the spiritual or the personal sphere from the material and the social. . . . Therefore, neither a secularized church (that is, a church which concerns itself only with this-worldly activities and interests) nor a separatist church (that is, a church which involves itself only in soul-saving and preparation of converts for the hereafter) can faithfully articulate the *missio Dei*.

In addition to introducing a robust theological framework, the preparation stage of STM frames the cultural context and produces the guiding narrative that will inform the trip. The example of CWC demonstrates the many ways the narrative framing of the trip occurs through the words *and* actions in this phase. Relatively speaking, CWC has a substantial and thoughtful preparation process for STM teams, but when those teams are led by laypeople with no more expertise in crosscultural training than those going, they rely on the structures of American evangelical culture to inform the narrative preparation and are likely to reproduce narratives drawn from their own culturally particular narratives and theologies. There is no doubt that employing substantive preparatory curricula, such as those from Livermore (2006) or Blumhofer and Crouch (2008), empowers STM travelers to become more aware of, and potentially resistant to, the interpretive context from which they travel, but the more significant change seems to be in refashioning the embodiment of the trip in all three phases.

One particularly strong resource for rethinking the STM narrative, *Mission Trips That Matter*, has the subtitle *Embodied Faith for the Sake of the World* (D. Richter 2008). Among a number of good suggestions its author makes for how the individuals participating in STM travel might be more sensitive, open and engaged, he suggests some radical structural changes. In particular, he cites Joanne van Engen (2000), who together with her husband, sociologist Kurt Ver Beek, runs Calvin College's Honduras semester program. In her article "The Cost of Short-Term Missions" (2000), she suggests that every STM team

> spend at least as much money supporting the projects you visit as you spend on your trip and then turn this money over to locally based (and presumably indigenously staffed) organizations engaged in the sorts of programs and projects the STM team wants to support.
>
> Invest your money in people and organizations working on long-term solutions. If you are interested in evangelism, support nationals who want to share the gospel. If you are concerned about health issues, support programs that are seeking to address those problems. Better yet, find programs that minister to people wholistically [*sic*] by meeting their spiritual, physical, social, emotional and economic needs. (2000, p. 23)

Like Muriu and Niringiye, she encourages visiting teams to spend their time listening to national development workers and to visit with local leaders already engaged in the work of sharing Christ's love. If foreign teams want to work, she encourages them to work on the buildings of the development agencies, who may be working in poor areas but often locate their offices in the middle-class business districts of urban centers. Van Engen (2000, p. 22) argues that going into under-resourced communities to do the work among unemployed people who would be happy to do the work themselves simply adds to the humiliation of chronic poverty: "Third world people do not need more rich Christians coming to paint their church and make them feel inadequate. They *do* need more humble people willing to come share their lives."

Without structural and narrative change, however, all this can lead to a great deal of agreement—and relatively little reform. I have no doubt that virtually everyone involved in STM would agree with the idea that those traveling should be "humble people willing to come share their lives,"[16] but until the agendas of STM are structurally reoriented around the missio Dei, with education and community as the *primary* goals, or at least equally *missional* as the activities and projects of visiting groups, then the narratives of these trips will continue to be created primarily by the cultural context and historical trajectory from which travelers come. Lasting transformation of travelers and local communities will best be brought about by relocating control of the trip itinerary from the hands of North Americans (whether church leaders or long-term missionaries) into the hand of local Christian leadership.

If North Americans are willing to risk giving a great deal more control of these travels to members of communities being visited, developing networks through which ongoing relationships with the

---

[16]The second and third standards of the Standards of Excellence are "empowering partnerships" and "mutual design." The organization issuing the standards is not opposed to or unaware of the need for STM travels to be structured in ways that are focused on "intended receptors." However, the more significant restructuring of control is not something highlighted in much of the STM literature. For example, the Standards of Excellence are designed to "establish (formally or informally) trusting and accountable partnerships with each other as the overarching design of our short-term mission efforts." Without acknowledging the unequal dynamics of control in such a partnership through the control of resources, such mutuality becomes rhetoric without substance.

leaders of Christian communities in receiving countries can have substantive and meaningful interaction with those planning and participating in STM travels, the cultural dynamics of STM could begin to
shift in significant ways. By recognizing the cultural dynamics of STM
and then reshaping them through an understanding of how culture
changes, these travels may begin to have more lasting and substantive
effects on everyone involved.

10

"And What Does the Lord Require of You?"

SUGGESTIONS AND AN
ENCOURAGING POSTSCRIPT

♦ ♦ ♦

It has never been my intention to be negative in presenting this research, and I hope that in spite of my recommendations for change in the previous chapter, I will not be interpreted as primarily a detractor of STM. I do think that the case presented here, and the writings of many others who have engaged STM far more deeply than I, demonstrate the need for structural and cultural change in order for these trips to affect travelers in more theologically and socially significant ways. At the same time, I believe God is capable of using *any* occasion to glorify himself.

I do not think that, even as they exist now, these trips are overwhelmingly negative. Though in many cases they may be less effective in producing long-term changes in the material, social or spiritual lives of any of those involved, there is little doubt that some good things come from this work. First, most tourists traveling to the Dominican Republic leave behind a few tips, not the second floor of an afterschool center. Second, as privileged North Americans are exposed to conditions of inequality and injustice outside their day-to-day lives, the opportunity for personal and social change is enhanced. Our challenge now is to bring the best resources and most careful consideration we can to STM travels.

In talking with the members of my team and with many who have traveled on STM trips over the years, there is no doubt that for a number of people the exposure has prompted further investigations, travels and sincere desires for a deeper and more faithful Christian witness. A number of those on my team and many of my students and colleagues have voiced frustration that the insights and emotional impetus for change faded over time. Though none of the members of my team went so far as to question the legitimacy of our trip, I have heard a number of the students in my classes question whether their trips were worth the time and money. Though some of these students hoped I would position myself against STM in general, while others hoped I would be a staunch advocate, all wanted some concrete suggestions of both long- and short-term reforms they could make or suggest in their own contexts to push STM travels toward more holistic and potentially inclusive narratives. In the spirit of giving the people what they want, I offer a few ideas of both sorts.

SUGGESTIONS TOWARD RESTRUCTURING STM NARRATIVES

1. Read (and do) the research on short-term missions. I remain hopeful that STM will move in positive directions in the future. First, as I have read and researched STM, I have been impressed by the quality of thinking available for those who would seek it out. Robert Priest (2008, pp. 68-69), who has thought as deeply about STM as anyone working in North America and who teaches in a seminary setting, has suggested six changes to seminary education that might empower future youth leaders and pastors to begin making structural changes that can bring about new cultural dynamics in STM.[1] Ulrike Sallandt (2007), a

---

[1]Priest and Priest (2008, pp. 68-69) provide extensive discussion of the six points, but in brief they include changes in standard seminary coursework, the support of STM research, the inclusion of experiential learning components in seminary education (for *all* seminarians) and the connection of this STM education to other areas of life and ministry, such as multiculturalism in the United States, immigration policy and race relations.

German theologian and pastor living and teaching in Peru, has offered a succinct mission theology for STM, a preparation guide and even guidelines for STM activities that she believes could reshape STM encounters. Anthropologist Laura Montgomery was one of the first to publish research-based scholarship on STM and has offered a list of six specific actions for short-term medical missions to avoid some of the problems she identified when studying such trips to Mexico. She calls for more robust assessments of health outcomes, coordination with local health practitioners, an emphasis on equipment transfers and training rather than direct patient care and the development of a clearer understanding of health as a factor of economic, political and social conditions (Montgomery 1993, p. 341). While much of this research remains unread by many who would benefit from its findings—as research so often does—the fact that it exists and that more is being produced is a reason to be hopeful.

Of course, the existence of such research should not suggest that enough such work has been done. Research should always beget research. I'm hopeful about the future of STM as anthropologists and sociologists in secular and Christian institutions have begun to publish a wide variety of research.[2] In particular, we have yet to build a substantial body of research exploring the cultural and social effects of these trips on receiving communities (for a notable exception, see Offutt 2011). In my own work, I found many Dominicans who were enthusiastic supporters of these trips, but this represented only those closest to the trip, those who benefitted most materially and in terms of "linking capital" (Priest 2010b).

What about those on the margins of STM visits? I wondered how the families of the boys who came to work on the roof with us in Gato Negro thought about the time their children were spending working

---

[2]By "secular" I do not necessarily mean the scholars themselves, but the venues in which they publish. Some of my own work has been "secular" in this way (see Howell and Dorr 2007). For recent examples, see Wuthnow 2009; Trinitapoli and Vaisey 2009; Beyerlein, Adler and Trinitapoli 2011; and Offutt 2011. There is promise of more research to come, as panels of papers have recently been presented on the STM phenomenon at the American Anthropological Association, Latin American Studies Association and the Society for the Scientific Study of Religion (see Offutt 2011, p. 797).

for no wage with a group of North Americans. I wondered how the families around the building, seeing this bunch of foreigners working in their community, thought about our presence. I would have liked to have spoken with the leaders of the community—the mayor, local Catholic priests, university presidents and government service providers—to understand their thoughts about our visit, if they were aware of us at all. This sort of deep research on local communities would take time and expertise but would be the next step in understanding the complex encounters in STM travel.

Likewise, we should continue to pursue various kinds of research on those who make these trips. Kurt Ver Beek's review of quantitative research on STM found only thirteen studies that employed "basic research procedures for measuring change in a population" (2008, p. 480). This was out of only forty-four quantitative studies available. There have been studies since he wrote, but as a movement involving well over one million participants per year, there is no question that it is understudied.[3]

Qualitative research, such as this book, brings other dimensions to the table, but this is often done by advocates rather than by friendly critics or those seeking the naked truth regardless of how it might look. To think about how short-term missions shape the experiences and remembrances of participants is to delve into the question of subjectivity, specifically Christian subjectivity. We should continue to ask how these experiences and the telling of them shapes, or is shaped by, the ideas these Christians have of themselves. This requires some discussion of the process of creating ideas of the self (i.e., one's "subject position") in order to connect those processes to the specific events and ideas of these Christians as they experience STM for themselves.

At the same time that these travels influence perceptions and understandings of the self, they also reflect the conscious engagement of global flows—cultural, material and spiritual. For many of the proponents of STM, the rhetoric of globalization is central to their under-

---

[3]Just prior to the submission of this book, the most extensive statistical study of STM participants yet published appeared in the *Journal for the Scientific Study of Religion* (see Beyerlein, Adler and Trinitapoli 2011).

standing of why and how these trips serve Christian purposes. For the travelers on our team, awareness of the world and expectations of travel were certainly linked to globalizing phenomenon. There are interesting ways in which STM works against some of the typical understandings of global process, drawing on nostalgic or anachronistic Christian language of travel and mission, even while the reality of these trips is only made possible by the globalized industries of travel and tourism. Scholars have begun to think about how STM intersects with religion and globalization generally, but there is much to be done in order to understand the many denominations, practices and influences involved.

Of course, all the necessary research will mean little if it is not read by those involved in the trips themselves. I have no illusions that the average high school junior (or busy adult volunteer, for that matter) is going to go through a course packet of readings prior to setting out on an STM trip. I do hope, however, that such reading would become part of seminary curricula for those who become youth workers, mission pastors, lead pastors and priests in the congregations, parishes and youth groups in which these trips are most practiced.

For Christians, this research and increased understanding should prompt greater faithfulness. As with all knowledge, this can provide ways for us to understand ourselves and our purposes in God's kingdom more clearly. Thus, in addition to providing good social scientific reflection, STM should continue to elicit strong theological reflection.

2. Develop a theology of short-term mission. Given that STM is not exactly tourism, pilgrimage or mission but a hybrid of all three and a thing unto itself, theologies around any one of these are inadequate for shaping our thought and practice. Most STM theology comes directly from mission theology, but given the particular dynamics of STM, this seems a poor fit. In chapter two I referred to Matthew 28 as a kind of guiding missional Scripture for evangelicals. This passage, which has animated the evangelical impulse of generations of missionaries, often provides an explicit framework for STM, in spite of the fact that so little of the overall STM movement is devoted to evangelism or even goes to communities in which Christianity is not already present. Perhaps a better verse would be one so often used in Christian development work from the Old Testament prophet Micah.

Addressing the nation of Israel before their exile to Babylon, Micah spoke to encourage the people of God to live up to the standards of community and compassion God had called them to. In the verses immediately prior to 6:8, Micah mocks the use of sacrifice and ritual to appease God's sense of justice. He then gives the nation a clear statement of God's commands: "He has shown you, O mortal, what is good. And what does the LORD require of you? To act justly and to love mercy and to walk humbly with your God" (Mic 6:8 NIV).

I would not suggest that theology can be built on a single Bible verse, nor do I want to diminish the considerable theological reflection on mission that speaks to the STM traveler. At the same time, we may find in this powerful Scripture the motivation to pursue STM in terms of the wider understanding of the missio Dei. There is no question that traveling to poor communities for the sake of delivering material aid, as well as building beneficial relationships (i.e., "linking capital"), can be understood in terms of mercy and justice. However, these commands should also force consideration of how we engage recreation, tourism and education in the contexts of these travels. They should motivate us to consider the political, social and economic dimensions of our relationships and actions (or inactions) in the context of these trips.

On the basis of this command, it would be impossible to argue that all forms of STM should end or that acting justly, loving mercy and walking humbly with God can't be brought into the experience of STM. In many cases it already is. Yet if we consider this verse as relevant to every aspect of STM travel, it may open a wider theological and social vista on how and why these trips are done. Our guiding narrative should be one of humility and fellowship even more than service and sacrifice.

Scholars of tourism note that travelers should consider the ecological and economic impact of the choices of where they stay, what they eat and from whom they choose to buy their souvenirs (e.g., McLaren 2010). If secular travel scholars can ask this of the average tourist, how much more should the Christian seek to consider his or her actions on the whole of creation—physical, social and spiritual. For example, development experts note that it is always more constructive to a local economy to stay in a smaller, locally owned hotel than in a larger, foreign-owned, all-inclusive resort (Richter 2001). Who owns the hotel where the STM team spends the beach day? How much do they pay their workers (in relative terms)? Are there options for our "tourist" excursions that are more beneficial to local people, the environment and the overall economy? These are questions STM travelers should learn to ask their local partners.

Of course, this assumes the STM team has local partners. Increasingly, many do (Priest 2010a), but this is of little value if we do not recognize the complexities of culture and inequalities of power frequently involved. In her book, *Cross-Cultural Partnerships: Navigating the Complexities of Money and Mission*, Mary Lederleitner (2010, pp. 122-23) tells of an Anglican bishop in Tanzania who told John Watters, a Wycliffe area director, "You are too powerful to be good partners." By way of explanation, she quotes from Watters's book: "He was not saying we could *not* be partners; just that it would take a lot of work for us to be *good* partners. . . . With our strengths we could pursue almost anything we wanted without regard for others. But would such an attitude or unilateral action achieve what we really wanted to achieve? It was highly unlikely."

Lederleitner, along with others writing on money in Christian work (e.g., Bonk 1991; J. Rowell 2007), emphasizes that the term *partnership* (like *mission* or *poverty*) is a culturally embedded term with a history and nuances that must be understood on both sides before it can be lived out. This is part of unpacking the creation of the narratives; by changing the process by which narratives are produced and who is involved in the production of those narratives, new ideas can be brought into the mix. Our theology, like our trips, must be a collaborative event.

WHAT ABOUT NOW? QUICK INTERVENTIONS

For many reading this book, possibilities for redesigning the financial or administrative structure of a short-term mission are limited at best. Even addressing the theological framework may be outside the purview of an STM leader who works in a large congregation in which others set the theological agenda. At the same time, there are ways a typical STM member or lay leader can push the preparation process to shift the conversation and potentially change the narrative structure of the travel.

In the preparation phase, a team could consider the following:

Spend as much time studying the history, economics, politics and spiritual context of the community as is spent preparing for the activities. With our DR team, much of our preparation time was spent practicing our skits and bagging Popsicle sticks and cotton balls. While this was fun and enabled us to be more efficient while in Linda Vista, it inhibited our ability to understand more about the country and community to which we were traveling. It would have been worth the sacrifice in efficiency to develop a more robust ability to see and understand the context in which we worked.

Invite people from the country or community to which the team is traveling to address the group. In some communities, this may not be possible, but certainly in a community like Wheaton there are numerous Christian Dominicans (and Mexicans, Czechs, Spaniards) who would be available to come and talk about their country with the group preparing to go. This person (who would likely speak English) would not serve as a representative of the Dominican Republic, but could bring an adult perspective on the country, history and culture. If the group could do a bit of reading and prepare questions, that would help engage a visitor, but at the very least it would open up ways of speaking about what is happening in the country (politically, spiritually, economically) in ways that are both personal and relevant.

While "in the field," the STM team might consider a few of these suggestions:

Spend time talking to leaders of the community—Christian and non-Christian—about the problems, solutions and initiatives already at work. Many STM groups, such as ours, spend the vast majority of their time with children. Children are more available, less threatening and generally more willing to hang out for a few hours with strangers who can't speak their language. The risk is that interactions with children fail to challenge the narratives travelers bring. Children are less likely to point out the ways a traveler is misunderstanding a situation. Talking with adults, particularly leaders and those of a social position less in-timidated by (often) relatively more wealthy visitors, may apply some constructive pressure on the narratives STM members employ.

Present visits to a museum, educational institution, monument or natural site as part of the mission, rather than "just tourism." Taking time to learn about the country, in the light of a theology emphasizing the missio Dei, should be seen as every bit as *mission* as the time spent leading a VBS, building a wall or painting a house. All aspects of learning and exposure that lead to the healing and creation of com-munity honor God and his purposes in the world. As a secondary con-sideration, making all these outings reflective of the missio Dei would imply that whatever standards of behavior, dress or conduct are ap-propriate to interactions in mission would be appropriate in these times as well.

Once a team returns, the members become critical agents in the on-going creation of the STM narrative. Yet this may be a point when the team is least involved in the intentional shaping of how people think about the trip. In the months after the trip, a team could do the following:

Plan several mandatory follow-up meetings to review what people have learned, how it has affected them and what changes they have made or should make in their thinking or behavior. Often the returned team meets once to exchange photos and perhaps gives a presentation of the trip, but has little time to speak about the travels. Particularly for high school students, it struck me that what churches typically call "follow-up" is a weak part of the overall experience. That is, there is little time dedicated for it. Some of my team members said that talking with me seven months after our trip was first time they had really spoken about their experience since coming back. In the absence of guidance, the narrative formed strongly around the preconceived notions and un-guided observations that the travelers either took into or brought out of our trip. The months *after* the trip would be the time to shape the nar-rative of what "really" happened.

Prepare a presentation of the trip, focusing on resources in the country and the work going on there, rather than a portrayal of the needs and how the team met them. Presentations of STM travels are an important aspect of the generation of narratives, and they deserve a whole study of their own. What I have often encouraged my college students to consider as they put together these photo displays is how the photos represent the people in them. Who is at the center? Who is shown as having power? As being competent? As being in control? Do the photos make some people appear "exotic" while others seem "normal"? These are questions with many layers, but even a superficial attention to the photos being selected with these questions in mind yields a different portrayal than what is seen in the usual STM PowerPoint presentation.

HOPE AND A FUTURE

I have no doubt that STM will continue, and as an anthropologist, I am quite glad. I want to see people travel, encountering cultural diversity and seeking the good of others when they do. Of course, I would not have written this book if I didn't have questions about this particular mode of travel, and my research has confirmed some of my misgivings about the processes involved. However, as both my relatively simple as well as more complex suggestions demonstrate, I don't think narratives are immutable artifacts of history and power. We have the ability to intervene and reshape them in ways that can lead to better outcomes in the experiences and understandings STM trips provide.

As a believer in Christ, I also think the ultimate success of ministry is beyond the scope of ethnographic analysis. God's mission—missio Dei—is not thwarted or achieved through our efforts, whether guided by social science or not. I bring my abilities to the table, believing God would have me use this opportunity to advance his work in the world toward what I believe his Word promotes. Everything we do is part of this calling, and thus we are the beneficiaries of coming alongside his work with our best understanding not only of what *is*, but also of what *can be*.

Notes on Transcription

♦ ♦ ♦

Throughout my research, I recorded interviews and transcribed passages spoken by various people involved in the trip I studied. When written out, our spoken language often has a quality that makes it appear more vapid, or less thoughtful, than it sounds in person. In cases where I had exact quotations, I have tried to preserve the voice of the speaker by *not* always rendering their language exactly as it came out of their mouths. In the end, I think the written language comes closer to how it sounded in the moment.

This is particularly true for the teenagers in the group with whom I spent the most time. Speaking as teenagers, the transcripts of their language contain all the stops and starts, filler words (e.g., "like") and pauses ("um . . .") that are typical of most speakers, but perhaps more pronounced in young people being asked to respond to an adult's queries. In writing down their words I have edited to avoid making them appear less articulate or confident than I think most people would suggest they are, as well as making it easier for the reader to follow.

Here is an example of what I mean: The following quotation was spoken by Emma, who was a smart, articulate 16-year-old at the time.

> Like in short-term missions there's not like a lot you can, like you can impact kids but you can't really . . . or like they can decide to become or

they can give their life to Christ while you're there, but it's the time when you're gone that . . . that the missionaries are still going to be there helping them a lot. And so, for short-term missions it's kind of just, being there, in like affecting, trying to help affect, help the kids.

In the book, where this quotation appears, I render it as:

In short-term missions there's not a lot you can [do]. You can impact kids but you can't really [do much] . . . or they can decide to become or they can give their life to Christ while you're there, but it's the time when you're gone that the missionaries are still going to be there helping them a lot. And so, for short-term missions it's just being there, in trying to help affect the kids.

The majority of my quotations, where they are noted as direct quotations, are relatively less edited than this, but the intent in every case is to be as faithful to the sense of how an individual spoke, along with accurately conveying what he or she said in a more reader-friendly way. This is an anthropological convention not uncommon in contemporary ethnography, and I trust it will serve both the subject and the reader well (cf. Luhrmann 2012, p. ix).

References

Adams, Velma. 1964. *The Peace Corps in Action*. Chicago: Follett Publishing.

Adeney, Miriam. 2006. "Shalom Tourist: Loving Your Neighbor While Using Her." *Missiology* 34 (4): 463.

Adkins, Andrew. 1991. "'Work Teams'?: No, 'Taste and See' Teams." *Evangelical Missions Quarterly* 24 (4): 356-78.

Aeschliman, G. 1992. *Short-Term Mission Handbook: A Comprehensive Guide for Participants and Leaders*. Evanston, Ill.: Berry Publishing Services.

Allahyari, Rebecca Anne. 2000. *Visions of Charity: Volunteer Workers and Moral Community*. Berkeley: University of California Press.

Ammerman, Nancy Tatom. 2005. *Pillars of Faith: American Congregations and Their Partners*. Berkeley: University of California Press.

Ammerman, Nancy Tatom, and Farnsley Arthur Emery. 1997. *Congregation and Community*. New Brunswick: Rutgers University Press.

Anthony, Michael. 1994. *The Short Term Missions Boom: A Guide to International and Domestic Involvement*. Grand Rapids: Baker.

Armstrong, Roger D. 1965. *The Peace Corps and Christian Missions*. New York: Friendship Press.

Asad, Talal. 1993. *Genealogies of Religion: Discipline and Reasons of Power in Christianity and Islam*. Baltimore: Johns Hopkins University Press.

Ashabranner, Brent. 1971. *A Moment in History: The First Ten Years of the Peace Corps*. New York: Doubleday.

Atienza Aledo, Julian. 1999. "La Encuesta Interacción Social: un Approximación Empírica." *Empíria* 2: 73-92.

Badone, Ellen, and Sharon R. Roseman. 2004. *Intersecting Journeys: The Anthropology of Pilgrimage and Tourism*. Urbana: University of Illinois Press.

Bahktin, M. M. 1986. *Speech Genres and Other Late Essays*. Trans. V. McGee. Austin: University of Texas Press.

Barnes, Seth. 1992. "The Changing Face of the Missionary Force." *Evangelical Missions Quarterly* 28, no. 4 (October): 376-81.

Barr, Judy. 1969. *Overseas Short-Term Service.* Wheaton: Short Terms Abroad.

Barthes, Roland, and Lionel Duisit. 1977. "Introduction to the Structural Analysis of Narratives." *New Literary History* 6 (2): 37-272.

Bauman, Richard. 2000. "Genre." *Journal of Linguistic Anthropology* 9 (1-2): 84-87.

Bebbington, D. W. 1989. *Evangelicalism in Modern Britain: A History from the 1730s to the 1980s.* Boston: Unwin Hyman.

Beckwith, Ivy. 1991. *Youth Summer Mission Trips: A Case Study.* Ph.D. diss., Trinity Evangelical Divinity School.

Berger, Arthur Asa. 1997. *Narratives in Popular Culture, Media and Everyday Life.* Thousand Oaks, Calif.: Sage.

————. 2004. *Deconstructing Travel: Cultural Perspectives on Tourism.* Walnut Creek, Calif.: AltaMira.

Beyerlein, Kraig, Gary Adler and Jenny Trinitapoli. 2011. "The Effect of Religious Short-Term Mission Trips on Youth Civic Engagement." *Journal for the Scientific Study of Religion* 50 (4): 780-95.

Beyerlein, Susan. 1976. "What I Did Over Summer Vacation." *HIS* 36 (March): 12.

Bialecki, Jon. 2008. "Between Stewardship and Sacrifice: Agency and Economy in a Southern California Charismatic Church." *Journal of the Royal Anthropological Institute* 14 (2): 372-90.

————. 2009. "Disjuncture, Continental Philosophy's New 'Political Paul,' and the Question of Progressive Christianity in a Southern California Third Wave Church." *American Ethnologist* 36 (1): 110-23.

Bidwell, Kevin. 2000. "Mission-Trip Prep." *Group* 26 (4): 32-36.

Bielo, James. 2011. "'How Much of This Is Promise?': God as Sincere Speaker in Evangelical Bible Study." *Anthropological Quarterly* 84 (3): 631-53.

Birth, Kevin. 2006. "What Is Your Mission Here? A Trinidadian Perspective on Visits from the 'Church of Disneyworld.'" *Missiology* 34 (4): 497-508.

Black, Annabel. 1996. "Negotiating the Tourist Gaze: The Example of Malta." In *Coping with Tourists: European Reactions to Mass Tourism*, edited by J. Boissevain, pp. 112-43. Oxford: Berghahn.

Blomberg, Fran. 2008. "From 'Whatever' to Wherever: Enhancing Faith Formation in Young Adults through Short-Term Missions." In *Effective Engagement in Short-Term Missions: Doing It Right!*, edited by R. Priest, pp.

591-613. Evangelical Missiological Society Series 16. Pasadena, Calif.: William Carey Library Press.

Blumhofer, Chris, and Andy Crouch. 2008. *Round Trip Missions*. Carol Stream, Ill.: Christianity Today International.

Boers, Arthur. 2007. "Walking Lessons: the Practice of Pilgrimage." *Christian Century* 124 (26): 22-26.

Bohn, Lauren. 2009. *Spring Break*. In *Time*, vol. 173. New York: Time Warner.

Boissevain, Jeremy, ed. 1996. *Coping with Tourists: European Reactions to Mass Tourism*. London: Berghahn Books.

Bonk, Jonathan. 1991. *Missions and Money: Affluence as a Missionary Problem*. Maryknoll, N.Y.: Orbis.

Borthwick, Paul. 1981. *How to Plan, Develop and Lead a Youth Missionary Trip*. Lexington, Mass.: Grace Chapel Super Summer Programs.

———. 1988. *Youth and Missions: Expanding Your Students' Worldview*. Wheaton.: Victor.

———. 1991. *How to Be a World Class Christian: You Can Be Part of God's Global Action*. Wheaton: Victor.

———. 2003. "Mobilizing the Next Generation." *Evangelical Missions Quarterly* 39 (4): 434-42.

Bosch, David. 1991. *Transforming Mission: Paradigm Shifts in Theology of Mission*. Maryknoll, N.Y.: Orbis.

Bourdieu, Pierre. 1984. *Distinction: A Social Critique of the Judgement of Taste*. London: Routledge and Kegan Paul.

———. 1990. *The Logic of Practice*. Stanford: Stanford University Press.

———. 1991. "Genesis and Structure of the Religious Field." *Comparative Social Research* 13: 3-45.

Bowman, Glenn. 1991. "Christian Ideology and the Image of a Holy Land: the Place of Jerusalem Pilgrimage in the Various Christianities." In *Contesting the Sacred: The Anthropology of Christian Pilgrimage*, edited by John Eade and Michael Sallnow, pp. 98-121. Urbana and Chicago: University of Illinois Press.

Brown, C. M. 2005. Field Statement on the Short-Term Mission Phenomenon: Contributing Factors and Current Debate. Unpublished paper. Trinity International University, Deerfield, Ill.

———. 2008. "Friendship is Forever: Congregation-to-Congregation Relationships." In *Effective Engagement in Short-Term Missions: Doing It Right!*, edited by Robert Priest, pp. 209-38. Pasadena, Calif.: William Carey Library.

Brown, Sally A. 2005. "Voluntourism—Traveling with a Purpose: Understanding the Motives and Benefits." Ph.D. diss., Purdue University, West Lafayette, Ind.

Bruner, Edward M. 2004. "The Maasai and the Lion King: Authenticity, Nationalism, and Globalization in African Tourism." In *Tourists and Tourism: A Reader*, edited by S. Gmelch, pp. 208-236. Long Grove, Ill.: Waveland Press.

————. 2005. *Culture on Tour: Ethnographies of Travel*. Chicago: University of Chicago Press.

Bruner, F. Dale. 1960. "New Strategy: Statesmanship in Christian Mission." *Christianity Today* 4 (22): 3.

Bruner, Jerome. 2003. *Making Stories: Law, Literature, Life*. Cambridge, Mass.: Harvard University Press.

Burns, Ridge, and Noel Bechetti. 1990. *The Complete Student Missions Handbook: A Complete Step-by-Step Guide to Leading Your Group Out of the Classroom and into the Field*. Grand Rapids: Zondervan.

Bush, Luis. 2000. "The Long and Short of Mission Terms." *Mission Frontiers* 22 (1): 16-19.

Causey, Andrew. 2003. *Hard Bargaining in Sumatra*. Honolulu: University of Hawaii Press.

Cerrón, Francisco. "Short-Term Missions: An Initial Assessment from Experience." *Journal of Latin American Theology* 2 (2): 21-33.

Cerwonka, Allaine, and Liisa H. Malkki. 2007. *Improvising Theory: Process and Temporality in Ethnographic Fieldwork*. Chicago: University of Chicago Press.

Cheong, So-Min, and Marc L. Miller. 2004. "Power Dynamics in Tourism: A Foucauldian Approach." In *Tourists and Tourism: A Reader*, edited by S. Gmelch, pp. 239-66. Long Grove, Ill.: Waveland Press.

Coggins, Wade. 1967. "Whither the Short-Termer?" *Evangelical Missions Quarterly* 3 (3):156-60.

Coleman, Simon. 2006. "Materializing the Self: Words and Gifts in the Construction of Charismatic Protestant Identity." In *The Anthropology of Christianity*, edited by F. Cannell, pp. 163-185. Durham, N.C.: Duke University Press.

Coleman, Simon, and Mike Crang. 2002. *Tourism: Between Place and Performance*. New York: Bergham Books.

Collins, Jenny. 2006. "Standards of Excellence in Short-Term Missions." *Common Ground Journal* 4 (1): 10-16.

Collins, Randall. 2004. *Interaction Ritual Chains*. Princeton, N.J.: Princeton University Press.

Colombijn, Freek. 2007. "The Search for an Extinct Volcano in the Dutch Polder: Pilgrimage to Memorial Sites of Pim Fortuyn." *Anthropos* 102 (1): 71-90.

Colson, Charles, and Nancy Pearcey. 2004. *How Now Shall We Live?* Carol Stream, Ill.: Tyndale House.

Cook, Charles, and Joel Van Hoogen. 2007. "Towards a Missiologically and Morally Responsible Short-Term Ministry: Lesson Learned in the Development of Church Partnership Evangelism." *Journal of Latin American Theology* 2 (2): 48-69.

Coote, Robert. 1995. "Good News, Bad News: North American Protestant Overseas Personnel Statistics in Twenty-Five-Year Perspective." *International Bulletin of Missionary Research* 19 (1): 6.

Corwin, Gary. 2000. "The Message of Short-Term Missions." *Evangelical Missions Quarterly* 36 (4): 422-23.

Cox, Jeffrey. 2005. "Master Narratives of Imperial Missions." In *Mixed Messages: Materiality, Textuality, Missions*, edited by J. Scott and G. Griffiths, pp. 3-18. New York: Palgrave.

Cozzarelli, Catherine, Anna Wilkinson, and Michael Tagler. 2001. "Attitudes Toward the Poor and Attributions for Poverty." *Journal of Social Issues* 57 (2): 207-227.

Crick, Malcolm. 1995. "The Anthropologist as Tourist: An Identity in Question." In *International Tourism*, edited by M. F. Allfont, J. Allcock and E. M. Bruner, pp. 205-23. London: Sage.

Crouch, Andy. 2010. "How Not to Change the World." *Books and Culture* (May/June). Carol Stream: Christianity Today International.

Csordas, Thomas J. 1997. *Language, Charisma, and Creativity: The Ritual Life of a Religious Movement*. Berkeley: University of California Press.

Cunningham, Loren. 1984. *Is That Really You God?* Grand Rapids: Chosen Books.

Davis, Raymond J. 1965. "A New Dimension in Missions." *Evangelical Missions Quarterly* 1, no. 4 (Summer): 25-28.

de Certeau, Michel. 1984. *The Practice of Everyday Life*. Translated by S. Rendell. Berkeley and Los Angeles: University of California Press.

Demko, David. 2009. University California Research Expedition Vacation Market Trand AgeVenture Vol. 2009: AgeVenture. <www.demko.com/cb000127.htm>. Accessed Feb 28, 2009.

Derrida, Jacques. 1981. "The Law of Genre." In *On Narrative*, edited by W. J. T. Mitchell, pp. 51-78. Chicago: University of Chicago Press.

Dijkstra, Wil. 1987. "Interviewing Style and Respondent Behavior." *Sociological Methods and Research* 16 (2): 309-334.

Douglas, Bronwen. 2001. "From Invisible Christians to Gothic Theatre: The Romance of the Millennial in Melanesian Anthropology." *Current Anthropology* 42 (5): 615-50.

Eade, John. 2000. "Introduction to the Illinois Paperback." In *Contesting the Sacred: The Anthropology of Christian Pilgrimage*, edited by John Eade and Michael Sallnow, pp. ix-xxiix. Urbana and Chicago: University of Illinois Press.

Eitzen, Martín Hartwig. 2007. "Short-Term Missions: A Latin American Perspective." *Journal of Latin American Theology* 2 (2): 33-48.

Elisha, Omri. 2008. "Moral Ambitions of Grace: The Paradox of Compassion and Accountability in Evangelical Faith-Based Activism." *Cultural Anthropology* 23 (1): 154-89.

———. 2011. *Moral Ambition: Mobilization and Social Outreach in Evangelical Churches*. Berkeley: University of California Press.

Ellis, Carolyn Sue, and Michael Flaherty, eds. 1993. *Investigating Subjectivity: Research on Lived Experience*. Thousand Oaks, Calif.: Sage.

Emerson, Michael. 2003. "Faith that Separates: Evangelicals and Black-White Race Relations." In *A Public Faith: Evangelicals and Civic Engagement*, edited by M. Cromartie, p. 187-204. Lanham, Md.: Rowman and Littlefield.

Emerson, Michael, and Christian Smith. 2000. *Divided by Faith: Evangelical Religion and the Problem of Race in America*. London: Oxford University Press.

Engelke, Matthew Eric. 2007. *A Problem of Presence: Beyond Scripture in an African Church*. Berkeley: University of California Press.

Engelke, Matthew Eric, and Matt Tomlinson. 2006. *The Limits of Meaning: Case Studies in the Anthropology of Christianity*. New York: Berghahn Books.

Fenton, Horace L. 1964. "Hand Wringing or Hard Questions?: An Approach to the Candidate Shortage." *Evangelical Missions Quarterly* 1 (1): 24-31.

Fernando, Ajith. 1999. "Some Thoughts on Missionary Burnout." *Evangelical Missions Quarterly* 35 (4): 440-43.

"First Journeymen Enter Training." *The Commission* 28: 28.

Foucault, Michael, and Paul Rabinow. 1984. "Truth and Power." In *The Foucault Reader*, ed. Paul Rabinow. New York: Pantheon.

Franklin, Adrian. 2003. *Tourism: An Introduction.* Thousand Oaks, Calif.: Sage.

Fussell, Paul, ed. 1987. *The Norton Book of Travel.* New York: W. W. Norton.

Geertz, Clifford. 1973. *The Interpretation of Cultures: Selected Essays.* New York: Basic Books.

———. 1986. "Making Experiences, Authoring Selves." In *The Anthropology of Experience,* edited by V. Turner and E. M. Bruner, pp. 373-380. Urbana, Ill.: University of Illinois Press.

Gilbert, Kellen, and William T. Hamilton. 2009. "Short-Term Mission Trips and the Enhancement of Cultural Awareness." *The Applied Anthropologist* 29 (2): 33-41.

Glasser, Arthur F., and Eric Fife. 1961. *Missions in Crisis: Rethinking Missionary Strategy.* Chicago: InterVarsity Press.

Gmelch, George. 2003. *Behind the Smile: The Working Lives of Caribbean Tourism.* Bloomington, Ind: Indiana University Press.

Gmelch, Sharon. 2004. "Why Tourism Matters." In *Tourists and Tourism: A Reader,* edited by S. Gmelch, pp. 1-41. Long Grove, Ill.: Waveland.

Gottleib, Alma. 1982. "Americans' Vacations." *Annals of Tourism Research* 9 (2): 165-87.

Graburn, Nelson. 1977. "Tourism: The Sacred Journey." In *Hosts and Guests,* edited by Valene Smith, pp. 17-31. Philadelphia: University of Pennsylvania.

Gration, John. 1964. "a.i.m.'s First Short-Termer." In *A.I.M.* Bulletin, edited by A.I.M. Missions, pp. 10. Wheaton: A.I.M.

Guthrie, S. 2003. *Missions in the Third Millenium: 21 Key Trends in the 21st Century.* London: Paternoster Press.

Hancock, Mary. 2011. "Practicing Globality/Practicing Christianity: The Geospatial Imaginary of Christian Youth Missions." Paper presented at Society for the Anthropology of Religion, Santa Fe, N.M., April 14-16.

Hanks, W. 1987. "Discourse Genres in a Theory of Practice." *American Ethnologist* 14 (4): 668-92.

Hardaway, Gary. 1974. "Teen Missions: Get Dirty for God." *Christian Life* 36 (June): 18-19.

Harding, Susan F. 1987. "Convicted by the Holy Spirit: The Rhetoric of Fundamental Baptist Conversion." *American Ethnologist* 14 (1): 167-81.

———. 1991. "Representing Fundamentalism: The Problem of the Repugnant Cultural Other." *Social Research* 58 (2): 373-93.

———. 2001. *The Book of Jerry Falwell: Fundamentalist Language and Politics.* Princeton, N.J.: Princeton University Press.

Harris, Paula. 2002. "Calling Young People to Missionary Vocations in a 'Yahoo' World." *Missiology* 30 (1): 33-50.

Hart, W. R. 1965. "The Missionary Journeymen." *The Commission* 28 (9) 4-9.

Hartford, Paul F. 2000. "Not an End in Itself." *Mission Frontiers* 22 (1): 20-22.

Haynes, Naomi. 2007. "Review of *Serving with Eyes Wide Open: Doing Short-Term Missions with Cultural Intelligence.*" *Journal of Latin American Theology* 2 (2): 260-63.

Hefferan, Tara, Julie Adkins and Laurie Occhipinti. 2009. *Bridging the Gaps: Faith-Based Organizations, Neoliberalism, and Development in Latin America and the Caribbean.* Latham, Md.: Lexington Books.

Heppenheimer, T. A. 1995. *Turbulent Skies: The History of Commercial Aviation.* New York: Wiley and Sons.

Hill, Jane. 2008. *The Everyday Language of White Racism.* London: Blackwell.

Hofmeyr, Isabel. 2005. "Inventing the World: Transnationalism, Transmission and Christian Textualities." In *Mixed Messages: Materiality, Textuality, Missions,* edited by Jamie Scott and Gareth Griffiths, pp. 19-36. New York: Palgrave.

Holmes, Lowell D., and Ellen Rhoads Holmes. 2002. "The American Cultural Configuration." In *Distant Mirrors: America as a Foreign Culture,* edited by D. P. R. and J. D. Armstrong, pp. 4-27. Belmont, Calif.: Wadworth/Thompson Learning.

Holmes-Rodman, Paula Elizabeth. 2004. "'They Told What Happened on the Road': Narrative and the Construction of Experiential Knowledge on the Pigrimage to Chimayo, New Mexico." In *Intersecting Journeys: The Anthropology of Tourism and Pilgrimage,* edited by E. Badone and S. Roseman, pp. 24-52. Urbana: University of Illinois.

Horton, Dennis, et al. 2011. "The Effects of Short-Term Missions on Mission Team Members." Paper presented at Association for the Scientific Study of Religion—Southwest, Dallas, Texas, 2011.

Howard, David M. 1970. *Student Power in World Evangelism.* Downers Grove: InterVarsity Press.

———. 2001. *From Wheaton to the Nations: The Story of Cross-Cultural Missionary Outreach from Wheaton College.* Wheaton, Ill.: Wheaton College.

Howell, Brian M. 2007. "The Repugnant Cultural Other Speaks Back:

Christian Identity as Ethnographic 'Standpoint.'" *Anthropological Theory* 7 (4): 371-91.

———. 2009. "Missions to Nowhere: Putting Short-Term Missions into Context." *International Bulletin of Missionary Research* 33 (4): 206-11.

Howell, Brian, and Rachel Dorr. 2007. "Evangelical Pilgrimage: The Rhetoric of Short-Term Missions." *Journal of Communication and Religion* 30 (2): 236-65.

Hudson, Kenneth, and Julian Pettifer. 1979. *Diamonds in the Sky: A Social History of Air Travel.* London: British Broadcasting Corp.

Hunter, James Davidson. 1992. *Culture Wars: The Struggle to Control the Family, Law, Education, Art, and Politics in America.* New York: Basic Books.

———. 2010. *To Change the World: The Irony, Tragedy, and Possibility of Christianity in the Late Modern World.* London: Oxford University Press.

Hurst, Kim, and Chris Eaton. 1991. *Vacations with a Purpose: A Handbook for Your Short Term Missions Experience.* Colorado Springs, Colo.: NavPress.

Hutchinson, William R. 1987. *Errand to the World: American Protestant Thought and Foreign Missions.* Chicago: University of Chicago Press.

———. 1989. "Americans in World Mission: Revision and Realignment." In *Altered Landscapes: Christianity in America, 1935-1985*, edited by D. W. Lotz, D. W. Shriver and J. F. Wilson, pp. 155-71. Grand Rapids: Eerdmans.

Hutnyk, Josh. 1996. *The Rumor of Calcutta: Tourism, Charity and the Poverty of Representation.* London and New Jersey: Zed Books.

InterCristo. 2009. "Our History." Unpublished newsletter.

Jindra, Michael. 2007. "Culture Matters: Diversity in the United States and its Implications." In *This Side of Heaven: Race, Ethnicity, and Christian Faith*, edited by R. Priest and A. Nieves, pp. 63-81. London: Oxford University Press.

Johnstone, David M. 2006. "Closing the Loop: Debriefing the Short-Term College Missions Team." *Missiology* 34 (4): 523-33.

Kane, J. Herbert. 1973. *Winds of Change in the Christian Mission.* Chicago: Moody.

Keane, Webb. 2007. *Christian Moderns: Freedom and Fetish in the Mission Encounter.* Berkeley: University of California Press.

Knowles, Melody. "Pilgrimage to Jerusalem in the Persian Period." In *Approaching Yehud: New Approaches to the Study of the Persian Period*, ed.

Jon Berquist, pp. 7-24. Ithaca, N.Y., and Atlanta: Snow Lion Publications Society of Biblical Literature.

Kristof, Nicholas. 2002. "Following God Abroad." *New York Times*. May 21.

LarkNews.com. 2005. "Short-Term Missions Team Returns with Righteous Anger." In *Lark News*. Vol. 3. Denver: LarkNews.com. <http://www.larknews.com/archives/446>.

———. 2008. "Inner-City Ministry Trip Confirms Youths' Worst Impressions." In *Lark News*, Vol. 6. Denver: LarkNews.com. <http://www.larknews.com/archives/763>.

Lederleitner, Mary. 2010. *Cross-Cultural Partnerships: Navigating the Complexities of Money and Mission*. Downers Grove, Ill.: InterVarsity Press.

Linhart, Terry. 2005. "Planting Seeds: The Curricular Hope of Short Term Missions Experiences in Youth Ministry." *Christian Education Journal* 2 (2): 256-72.

———. 2006. "'They Were So Alive!': The Spectacle of Self and Youth Group Short-Term Mission Trips." *Missiology* 34 (4): 451-62.

Livermore, David. 2004. "AmeriCAN or AmeriCAN'T? A Critical Analysis of Western Training to the World." *Evangelical Missions Quarterly* 40 (4): 458-68.

———. 2006. *Serving with Eyes Wide Open: Doing Short-Term Missions with Cultural Intelligence*. Grand Rapids: Baker.

Lo, Jim Umfundisi. 2006. *Concerns Regarding Short-Term Missions*. Marion, Ind.: Indiana Wesleyan University.

Loobie, Susan. 2000. "Short-Term Missions: Is It Worth It?" *Latin America Evangelist* (January/March).

Löfgren, Orvar. 1999. *On Holiday: A History of Vacationing*. Berkely: University of California Press.

Luhrmann, Tanya M. 2004. "Metakinesis: How God Becomes Intimate in Contemporary U.S. Christianity." *American Anthropologist* 106 (3): 518-28.

Lupton, Robert. 2011. *Toxic Charity: How Churches and Charities Hurt Those They Help (And How to Reverse It)*. New York: HarperOne.

MacCannell, Dean. 1976. *The Tourist: A New Theory of the Leisure Class*. Berkeley: University of California Press.

———. 2001. "Remarks on the Commodification of Cultures." In *Hosts and Guests Revisited: Tourism Issues of the 21st Century*, edited by V. L. Smith and M. Brent, pp. 380-90. New York: Cognizant Communication Corp.

MacDonald, Jeffrey G. "On a Mission—A Short-Term Mission: Americans

Love to Help Others, but Good Intentions Can Go Bad." *USA Today*, June 18, 2006. <http://www.usatoday.com/news/religion/2006-06-18-mission-vacations_x.htm>.

Maclure, David. 2001. "Wholly Available? Missionary Motivation Where Consumer Choice Reigns." *Evangel* 20 (3): 134-37.

Manitsas, David. 2000. *Short Term Missions Trips: A Vehicle for Developing Personal and Spiritual Well Being*, PhD diss., George Fox University.

Marsden, George M. 1984. *Evangelicalism and Modern America*. Grand Rapids: Eerdmans.

Marti, Gerardo. 2008. "Fluid Ethnicity and Ethnic Transcendence in Multiracial Churches." *Journal for the Scientific Study of Religion* 47 (1): 11-16.

Mattingly, Cheryl, Mary Lawlor, and Lanita Jacobs-Huey. 2002. "Narrating September 11: Race, Gender, and the Play of Cultural Identities." *American Anthropologist* 104 (3): 743-53.

McAdoo, Jennifer, and Anne Principe. 2010. *Journeys of the Spirit: Planning and Leading Mission Trips with Youth*. Boston: Unitarian Universalist Association.

McLaren, Deborah. 2010. "Rethinking Tourism." In *Tourists and Tourism*, edited by S. Gmelch, pp. 465-78. Long Grove, Ill.: Waveland Press.

McMillon, Bill, Doug Cutchins, and Anne Geissinger. 2012. *Volunteer Vacations: Short-Term Adventures That Will Benefit You and Others*. Chicago: Chicago Review Press.

McQuerry, Maureen Doyle. 1979. "Some Terms in Evangelical Christianity." *American Speech* 54 (2): 148-51.

Meier, Scott. 2009. "Missionary, Minister to Thyself." *Youth Specialties: All About Youth Ministry*. October 5, 2009. <http://www.youthspecialties.com/articles/missionary-minister-to-thyself>.

Miles, John. 2000. *An Assessment of Short-Term Missions*. M.A. diss., Birmingham Bible Institute.

Mitchell, W. J. T., ed. 1980. *On Narrative*. Chicago: University of Chicago Press.

Moffitt, Robert. 1969. "What Missions Can Learn from the Peace Corps." *Evangelical Missions Quarterly* 5 (4): 234-38.

Montgomery, Laura. 1993. "Short-Term Medical Missions: Enhancing or Eroding Health?" *Missiology* 21 (3): 333-41.

Moore, Don. 1982. *Youth Try the Impossible!* Duluth, Minn.: Mission Outreach.

Moreau, A. Scott. 2008. "Short-Term Missions in the Context of Missions, Inc." In *Effective Engagement in Short-Term Missions: Doing It Right!*, edited by R. Priest, pp. 1-34. Evangelical Missiological Society Series 16. Pasadena, Calif.: William Carey Library Press.

Morgan, Garry, and John Easterling. 2008. "The Potential Value of Short-Term Missions and Preparation for Long-Term Cross-Cultural Ministry and Service: A Case Study of the Internship Program of Northwestern College." *Global Missiology* 1 (6) <http://ojs.globalmissiology.org/index.php/english/article/viewFile/33/91>.

Morinis, Alan. "Introduction." In *Sacred Journeys: The Anthropology of Pilgrimage*, ed. Alan Morinis, pp. 1-30. Westport, Conn.: Greenwood Press.

Muriu, Oscar. 2009. *Money and Power.* St. Louis: Urbana Missions Conference.

Murray, Harry. 1990. *Do Not Neglect Hospitality: The Catholic Workers and the Homeless.* Philadelphia: Temple University Press.

Nash, Dennison. 1989. "Tourism as a Form of Imperialism." In *Hosts and Guests: the Anthropology of Tourism*, edited by V. L. Smith, pp. 37-55. Philadelphia: University of Pennsylvania Press.

Neill, Stephen. 1964. *A History of Christian Missions.* Baltimore: Penguin.

Ness, Sally A. 2003. *Where Asia Smiles: An Ethnography of Philippine Tourism.* Philadelphia: University of Pennsylvania Press.

Neumann, Mark. 2002. "Making the Scene: The Poetics and Performances of Discplacement at the Grand Canyon." In *Tourism: Between Place and Performance*, edited by Simon Coleman and Mike Crang, pp. 38-53. New York: Berghahn Books.

Noll, Mark A. 1994. *The Scandal of the Evangelical Mind.* Grand Rapids: Eerdmans.

Noy, Chaim. 2004. "This Trip Really Changed Me: Backpackers' Narratives of Self-Change." *Annals of Tourism Research* 31 (1): 78-102.

Ockenga, Harold John. 1959. "Rising to the Missionary Task." *Christianity Today* 3 (15): 7-9.

Offutt, Stephen. 2011. "The Role of Short-Term Mission Teams in the New Centers of Global Christianity." *Journal for the Scientific Study of Religion* 50 (4): 796-811.

Oliver, Kay. 1974. "You Can Beat That Summer Slump." *Moody Monthly* 70 (June): 80-83.

Ortner, Sherry B. 2006. *Anthropology and Social Theory: Culture, Power, and the Acting Subject.* Durham: Duke University Press.

Ott, Craig, Stephen J. Strauss, and Timothy Tennent. 2010. *Encountering the Theology of Mission: Biblical Foundations, Historical Developments, and Contemporary Issues*. Encountering Mission series vol. 5. Grand Rapids: Baker.

Palomino, Miguel Ángel. 2007. "'If Everything Is Mission, Nothing Is Mission': Reflections on Short-Term Missions." *Journal of Latin American Theology* 2 (2): 208-26.

Park, Kyeong Sook. 2008. "Researching Short-Term Missions and Paternalism." In *Effective Engagement in Short-Term Missions: Doing It Right!*, edited by R. Priest, pp. 505-30. Evangelical Missiological Society Series 16. Pasadena, Calif.: William Carey Library.

Pelt, Leslie. 1989. "Wanted: Black Missionaries, but How?" *Evangelical Missions Quarterly* 25 (1): 28-37.

———. 1992. "What's Behind the Wave of Short-Termers?" *Evangelical Missions Quarterly* 28 (4): 384-88.

Peterson, R., G. Aeschliman, and W. R. Sneed. 2003. *Maximum Impact Short-Term Mission: The God-Commanded, Repetitive Deployment of Swift, Temporary, Non-Professional Missionaries*. Minneapolis: STEM Press.

Plaut, Victoria. 2002. "Cultural Models of Diversity in America: The Psychology of Difference and Inclusion." In *Engaging Cultural Differences*, edited by R. Schweder, M. Minow and H. R. Marcus, pp. 365-95. New York: Russell Sage Foundation.

Priest, Kersten. 2009. "'Caring for the Least of These': Christian Women's Short-Term Mission Travel." Ph.D. diss., Loyola University, Chicago.

Priest, Robert, ed. 2008a. *Effective Engagement in Short-Term Missions: Doing It Right!* Evangelical Missiological Society Series 16. Pasadena, Calif.: William Carey Library.

———. 2008b. "Introduction." In *Effective Engagement in Short-Term Missions: Doing It Right!*, edited by R. Priest, pp. i-xi. Evangelical Missiological Society Series 16. Pasadena, Calif.: William Carey Library.

———. 2010. "Short-Term Missions as a New Paradigm." In *Missions After Christendom: Emergent Themes in Contemporary Mission*, edited by O. Kalu, P. Vethanayagamony and E. K.-F. Chia, pp. 84-100. Louisville, Ky.: Westminister John Knox Press.

———. 2011. "Short-Term Missions and the Reconfiguring of North American Global Missions Involvement." Paper presented at Saving the World? The Changing Terrain of American Protestant Missions, 1910 to the Present. Durham, N.C.

Priest, Robert J., T. Dischinger and S. B. Rasmussen. 2006. "Researching the Short-Term Mission Movement." *Missiology* 34 (4): 431-51.

Priest, Robert J., and Alvaro Nieves, eds. 2007. *This Side of Heaven: Race, Ethnicity, and the Christian Faith.* London: Oxford University Press.

Priest, Robert, and David Priest. 2008. "'They See Everything, and Understand Nothing': Short Term Mission and Service Learning." *Missiology* 36 (1): 53-75.

Priest, Robert, Douglas Wilson and Adelle Johnson. 2010. "U.S. Megachurches and New Patterns of Global Mission." *International Bulletin of Missionary Research* 34 (2): 97-104.

Prigodich, Raymond. 1969. "Wanted: Missionaries, Two Weeks to Five Years." *Eternity* (March 1969): 15-16.

Procter, Ian, and Maureen Padfield. "The Effect of the Interview on the Interviewee." *Social Research Methodology* 1 (2): 123-36.

Pulleyn, Simon. 2007. "Pilgrimage in Graeco-Roman and Early Christian Antiquity: Seeing the Gods." *Journal of Theological Studies* 58 (1): 268-70.

Putnam, Robert. 2000. *Bowling Alone: The Collapse and Revival of American Community.* New York: Simon & Schuster.

Radecke, Mark W. 2006. "Service-Learning and the Spiritual Formation of College Students." *Word and World* 26 (3): 289-98.

Randall, Ian. 2008. *Spiritual Revolution: The Story of OM.* Oxford: Authentic Books.

Richter, Don C. 2008. *Mission Trips That Matter: Embodied Faith for the Sake of the World.* Nashville: Upper Room.

Richter, Linda. 2001. "Where Asia Wore a Smile: Lessons of Philippine Tourism Development." In *Hosts and Guests Revisited*, edited by V. L. Smith and M. Brent, pp. 283-97. Elmsford, N.Y.: Cognizant Communications Corporation.

Rickett, Daniel. 2009. "Narrative, Communion, and Development: Transformational Short-Term Missions." *Mission Maker Magazine.*

Robbins, Joel. 2003. "What is a Christian? Notes Toward an Anthropology of Christianity." *Religion* 33 (3): 191.

———. 2006. "Anthropology and Theology: An Awkward Relationship?" *Anthropological Quarterly* 79 (2): 285-94.

Rodriguez de Gante, Jorge, 1998. "International Testimonials on Short-Term Service." *Missions Focus* 6: 154-57.

Rosaldo, Renato. 1989. *Culture and Truth: The Remaking of Social Analysis.* Boston: Beacon Press.

Rosenwald, George C. 1992. "Conclusion." In *Storied Lives: The Cultural Politics of Self-Understanding,* edited by G. C. Rosenwald and R. L. Ochberg, pp. 265-90. New Haven: Yale University Press.

Roth, Amy Fischer. 2005. "Have Faith, Will Travel: Part-Time Missionaries Reap Rewards." *Chicago Tribune,* May 13, 2005.

Rowell, Pamela. 2009. "Vacations with a Purpose." North American Mission Board.

Sallandt, Ulrike. 2007. "Short Term Mission: A Great Opportunity." *Journal of Latin American Theology* 2 (2): 190-208.

Sarkela, Sandra, and Patrick Mazzeo. 2006. "Rev. James H. Robinson and American Support for African Democracy and Nation Building 1950s-1970s." In *Freedom's Distant Shores: American Protestantism and Post-colonial Alliances with Africa,* edited by D. R. Smith, pp. 37-53. Waco, Tex.: Baylor University Press.

Schiffrin, Deborah. 1996. "Narrative as Self-Portrait: Sociolinguistic Constructions of Identity." *Language in Society* 25 (2): 167-203.

Schwartz, Glenn. 2003. "How Short-Term Missions Can Go Wrong." *International Journal of Frontier Missions* 20 (4): 27-34.

Shepherd, Gary, and Gordon Shepherd. 1998. *Mormon Passage: A Missionary Chronicle.* Urbana: University of Illinois Press.

———. 2001. "Sustaining a Lay Religion in Modern Society: The Mormon Missionary Experience." In *Contemporary Mormonism: A Social Science Perspective,* edited by M. Cornwall, T. Heaton and L. Young, pp. 161-181. Urbana: University of Illinois Press.

Shepherd, Nicholas. 2005. "Soul in the City—Mission as Package Holiday: The Potential Implications of a 'Tourist' Paradigm in Youth Mission." *Anvil* 22 (4): 255-68.

Short Terms Abroad. 1968. *Short Terms Abroad Newsletter,* p. 6.

Sinclair, M. Thea. 1998. "Tourism and Economic Development: A Survey." *Journal of Development Studies* 34 (5): 1-51.

Slate, Philip. "Short-Term vs. Long-Term and the Stewardship of Western Missions Money." Missions Resource Network. <http://mrnet.org/system/files/library/short_term_vs_long_term_and_the_stewardship_of_western_missions_money.pdf>.

Slimbach, Richard. 2000. "First, Do No Harm: Short-Term Missions at the

Dawn of a New Millennium." *Evangelical Missions Quarterly* 36 (4): 428-41.
———. 2008. "The Mindful Missioner." In *Effective Engagement in Short-Term Missions: Doing It Right!*, edited by R. Priest, pp. 153-84. Evangelical Missiological Society Series 16. Pasadena, Calif.: William Carey Library.

Smith, Alex. 2008. "Evaluating Short-Term Missions: Missiological Questions from a Long-Term Missionary." In *Effective Engagement in Short-Term Missions: Doing It Right!*, edited by R. Priest, pp. 35-63. Evangelical Missiological Society Series 16. Pasadena, Calif.: William Carey Library.

Smith, Christian. 1998. *American Evangelicalism: Embattled and Thriving.* Chicago: University of Chicago Press.

Smith, Christian, and Melinda Lunquist Denton. 2005. *Soul Searching: The Religious and Spiritual Lives of American Teenagers.* New York: Oxford University Press.

Smith, Craig Stephen. 1997. *Whiteman's Gospel.* Winnipeg, Man.: Indian Life Books.

"SOE." 2003. *History of the SOE,* Vol. 2011: US Standards of Excellence in Short-Term Missions.

Sparks, Evan. 2008. "The 'Great Commission' or Glorified Sightseeing?" *Wall Street Journal,* October 10, 2008.

Stewart, Susan. 1984. *On Longing: Narratives of the Miniature, the Gigantic, the Souvenir, the Collection.* Baltimore, Md.: Johns Hopkins University Press.

Stiles, Mack, and Leanne Stiles. 2000. *Mack and Leanne's Guide to Short-Term Missions.* Downers Grove, Ill.: InterVarsity Press.

Stromberg, Peter G. 1993. *Language and Self-Transformation: A Study of the Christian Conversion Narrative.* Cambridge and New York: Cambridge University Press.

Swartzentruber, Conrad. 2008. *The Effect of International Short-Term Mission Trips on Intercultural Sensitivity in Secondary Christian School Students.* Ph.D. diss., Duquesne University, Pittsburgh, Penn.

Swatos, William, ed. 2006. *On the road to Being There: Studies in Tourism and Pilgrimage in Late Modernity.* London: Brill.

Timothy, Dallen J., and Daniel H. Olsen, eds. 2006. *Tourism, Religion and Spiritual Journeys.* vol. 4. London and New York: Routledge.

Travlou, Penny. 2002. "Go Athens: Journey to the Center of the City." In *Tourism: Between Place and Performance*, edited by S. Coleman and M. Crang, pp. 108-27. New York: Berghahn Books.

Trinitapoli, Jenny, and Stephan Vaisey. 2009. "The Transformative Role of

Religious Experience: The Case of Short-Term Missions." *Social Forces* 88 (1): 121-46.

Turner, V. 1974. *Dramas, Fields and Metaphors: Symbolic Action in Human Society.* Ithaca, N.Y.: Cornell University Press.

Turner, V., and E. Turner. 1978. *Image and Pilgrimage in Christian Culture: Anthropological Perspectives.* New York: Columbia University Press.

Tutttle, Kathryn. 2000. "The Effects of Short-Term Mission Experiences on College Students' Spiritual Growth and Maturity." *Christian Education Journal* 4 (3): 123-40.

Urry, John. 1995. *Consuming Places.* London and New York: Routledge.

———. 2002. *The Tourist Gaze.* Thousand Oaks, Calif.: Sage Publications.

van Engen, Joanne. 2000. "The Cost of Short Term Missions." *The Other Side* 36 (1): 20-23.

Vanhoozer, Kevin J. 2005. *The Drama of Doctrine: A Canonical Linguistic Approach to Christian Theology.* Louisville, Ky.: Westminster John Knox Press.

Ver Beek, Kurt. 2006. "The Impact of Short-Term Missions: A Case Study of House Construction in Honduras after Hurricane Mitch." *Missiology* 34 (4): 477-97.

———. 2008. "Lessons from the Sapling: Review of Quantitative Research on Short-Term Missions." In *Effective Engagement in Short-Term Missions: Doing It Right!*, edited by R. Priest, pp. 475-505. Evangelical Missiological Society 16. Pasadena: William Carey Library.

Volck, Brian. 2007. "Short Trip to the Edge: Where Earth Meets Heaven—A Pilgrimage." *Christian Century* 124 (21): 60-62.

Wallace, A. F. C. 1970. *Culture and Personality.* New York: Random House.

Walls, Andrew F. 1996. *The Missionary Movement in Christian History: Studies in the Transmission of Faith.* Maryknoll, N.Y.: Orbis.

Wan, Enoch, and Geoffrey Hartt. 2008. "Complementary Aspects of Short-Term Missions and Long-Term Missions: Case Studies for a Win-Win Situation." In *Effective Engagement in Short-Term Missions: Doing It Right!*, edited by Robert Priest, pp. 35-62. Pasadena, Calif.: William Carey Library.

Weber, Donovan. 2011. *Evangelical University Students in a Cross-Cultural Context: An Examination of Short-Term Missions through the Lens of Critical Service-Learning.* Ph.D. diss., Miami University of Ohio.

Weber, Linda, and Dotsey Welliver, eds. 2007. *Mission Handbook: U.S. and Canadian Protestant Ministries Overseas 2007-2009.* Wheaton: EMIS.

Weber, Max. 1956. *The Protestant Ethic and Spirit of Capitalism*. London: MacMillan.

Wertsch, James. 2000. "Narratives as Cultural Tools in Sociocultural Analysis: Official History in Soviet and Post-Soviet Russia." *Ethos* 28 (4): 511-33.

Wetzel, Charles. 1966. "The Peace Corps in our Past." *The Annals of the American Academy of Political and Social Sciences* 365 (1): 1-11.

Wilson, Matthew J. 1999. "'Blessed are the Poor': American Protestantism and Attitudes Toward Poverty and Welfare." *Southeastern Political Review* 27 (3): 421-37.

Winter, Ralph D. 1970. *The Twenty-Five Unbelievable Years: 1945 to 1969*. Pasadena, Calif.: William Carey Library.

———. 1996. "Editorial." *Mission Frontiers*.

Wright, Christopher J. H. 2010. *The Mission of God's People: A Biblical Theology of the Church's Mission*. Grand Rapids: Zondervan.

Wuthnow, Robert. 2009. *Boundless Faith: The Global Outreach of American Churches*. Berkeley: University of California Press.

Wuthnow, Robert, and Steve Offut. 2008. "Transnational Religious Connections." *Sociology of Religion* 69 (2): 209-32.

Yamane, David. 2000. "Narrative and Religious Experience." *Sociology of Religion* 61 (2): 171-189.

Yancey, George. 2001. "Racial Attitudes: Differences in Racial Attitudes among People Attending Multiracial and Uniracial Congregations." In *Research in the Social Scientific Study of Religion* 12, edited by D. O. Moberg and R. L. Piedmont, pp. 185-207. London: Brill.

Zehner, Edwin. 2008. "On the Rhetoric of Short-Term Missions Appeals, with Suggestions for Team Leaders." In *Effective Engagement in Short-Term Missions: Doing It Right!*, edited by R. Priest, pp. 185-208. Evangelical Missiological Society Series 16. Pasadena, Calif.: William Carey Library.

Index